KANTIAN ETHICS
ALMOST
WITHOUT
APOLOGY

KANTIAN ETHICS
ALMOST
WITHOUT
APOLOGY

Marcia W. Baron

CORNELL UNIVERSITY PRESS

ITHACA AND LONDON

First published 1995 by Cornell University Press
First printing, Cornell Paperbacks, 1999

Library of Congress Cataloging-in-Publication Data
Baron, Marcia.
Kantian ethics almost without apology / Marcia W. Baron.
p.   cm.
Includes bibliographical references and index.
ISBN 0-8014-2829-7 (cloth : alk. paper)
ISBN 0-8014-8604-1 (pbk. : alk. paper)
1. Kant, Immanuel, 1724-1804-Ethics.   2. Ethics.   I. Title.
B2799.E8B28   1995
170´.92—dc20   95-9555

Printed in the United States of America

Cornell University Press strives to use environmentally responsible
suppliers and materials to the fullest extent possible in the publishing of
its books. Such materials include vegetable-based, low-VOC inks and acid-
free papers that are recycled, totally chlorine-free, or partly composed of
nonwood fibers.

1 3 5 7 9   Cloth printing   10 8 6 4 2

1 3 5 7 9   Paperback printing   10 8 6 4 2

Contents

Acknowledgments

◆◆◆

In the ten years during which this work has slowly developed I have accumulated many institutional and personal debts. I began it in 1984–85, while holding a fellowship from the American Council of Learned Societies and enjoying the hospitality of Stanford University. Its increasingly Kantian turn was due in part to the outstanding National Endowment for the Humanities Summer Institute on Kantian Ethics directed by Jerome Schneewind and David Hoy in 1983. Course reductions and sabbaticals from the University of Illinois Research Board and fellowships from the Center for Advanced Study and the Program in Cultural Values and Ethics, both of the University of Illinois at Urbana-Champaign, provided crucial research time.

I am deeply grateful to audiences at conferences and departmental colloquiums for their incisive questions. These forums have played a major role in stimulating and sharpening my thinking. Special thanks to the Randall Harris family; an early version of Chapter 2 was presented as the 1988 Randall Harris Memorial Lecture at Harvard University. My book was greatly improved by astute comments from the following people: Henry Allison, Karl Ameriks, Chris Blakey, Stephen L. Darwall, Alan Donagan, William Frankena, Richard Henson, Barbara Herman, David Heyd, Thomas E. Hill Jr., Craig Ihara, Steven L. Johnson, Scott Kim, Christine Korsgaard, Richard McCarty, Laura Melim, Susan Mendus, Onora O'Neill, Nelson Potter, Thomas Pogge, Henry Richardson, Mario von der Ruhr, Walter Schaller, Nancy Sherman, Peter Simonson, Michael Slote, Steven J. Wagner, and Nicholas White. Special thanks to my research assistants, Steven L. Johnson and Mario von der

Ruhr, and to the members of the graduate seminar that I taught at the University of Chicago in spring 1990. My greatest debt is to my husband, Fred Schmitt, for his steady support, helpful discussion, and gentle prodding to quit reading travel books and otherwise plotting escapes from the Midwest and instead reimmerse myself in my work. I thank my son, Nathaniel Baron-Schmitt, for making life so delightful, and my parents and sisters, for providing the familial support that one takes for granted until one sees the suffering of those who lack it. I am grateful to the editors at Cornell University Press for their patience, to a formerly anonymous referee—who I have just learned is Stephen Engstrom—for excellent criticisms and suggestions, and to Cheri Beck, Judith Short, Glenna Cilento, and Patricia McDonald for fine secretarial assistance.

Material from two of my previously published papers is used here with the permission of the *Journal of Philosophy*. Much of Chapter 1 was published as "Kantian Ethics and Supererogation," *Journal of Philosophy* 84 (1987): 237–262. Parts of Chapter 4 appeared in "The Alleged Moral Repugnance of Acting from Duty," *Journal of Philosophy* 81 (1984): 197–220.

M. W. B.

Abbreviations, Sources, and Translations

❖❖❖

WORKS BY KANT CITED BY ABBREVIATION

A   *Anthropologie in pragmatischer Hinsicht* (*Kants gesammelte Schriften*, vol. 7).
       Anthropology from a Pragmatic Point of View. Trans. Mary J. Gregor. The Hague: Nijhoff, 1974.

CJ   *Kritik der Urteilskraft* (*KGS*, vol. 5).
       The Critique of Judgement. Trans. James Creed Meredith. Oxford: Oxford University Press, 1952.

E   *Pedagogie* (*KGS*, vol. 9).
       Education. Trans. Annette Churton. Ann Arbor: University of Michigan Press, 1960.

G   *Grundlegung zur Metaphysik der Sitten* (*KGS*, vol. 4).
       Groundwork of the Metaphysics of Morals. Trans. H. J. Paton. New York: Harper and Row, 1964.

L   *Logik* (*KGS*, vol. 9).
       Logic. Trans. Robert Hartman and Wolfgang Schwarz. Indianapolis: Bobbs-Merrill, 1974.

LE   *Eine Vorlesung über Ethik*. Hrg. Paul Menzer. Berlin: Rolf Heise, 1924.
       Lectures on Ethics. Trans. Louis Infield. Indianapolis: Hackett, 1981.

MM   *Die Metaphysik der Sitten* (*KGS*, vol. 6).
       The Metaphysics of Morals. Trans. Mary J. Gregor. Cambridge: Cambridge University Press, 1991. I also utilize *The Doctrine of Virtue: Part II of "The Metaphysics of Morals."* Trans. Mary J. Gregor. New York: Harper and Row, 1964. Reprint, Philadelphia: University of Pennsylvania Press.

PrR   *Kritik der praktischen Vernunft* (*KGS*, vol. 5).
         Critique of Practical Reason. Trans. Lewis White Beck. Indianapolis:
         Bobbs-Merrill, 1956.

R   *Die Religion innerhalb der Grenzen der blossen Vernunft* (*KGS*, vol. 6).
         Religion within the Limits of Reason Alone. Trans. Theodore M. Greene
         and Hoyt H. Hudson. New York: Harper and Row, 1960.

V   *Metaphysik der Sitten Vigilantius. Vorlesungen,* vol. 4. *Vorlesungen über*
         Moralphilosophie, zweite Hälfte, erster Teil (*KGS*, vol. 27).

OTHER WORKS BY KANT CITED IN THE TEXT

Beobachtungen über das Gefühl des Schönen und Erhabenen (*KGS*, vol. 2).
Observations on the Feeling of the Beautiful and Sublime. Trans. John T.
Goldthwait. Berkeley: University of California Press, 1960.

"Das Ende Aller Dinge" (*KGS*, vol. 8).
"The End of All Things." In *Perpetual Peace and Other Essays on Politics,*
History, and Morals, trans. Ted Humphrey. Indianapolis: Hackett, 1983.

"Mutmasslicher Anfang der Menschengeschichte" (*KGS*, vol. 8).
"Speculative Beginning of Human History." Trans. Ted Humphrey. In *Perpetual*
Peace and Other Essays on Politics, History, and Morals, trans. Humphrey.
Indianapolis: Hackett, 1983.

"On Philosophers' Medicine of the Body." Trans. Mary J. Gregor. In *Kant's*
Latin Writings: Translations, Commentaries, and Notes, ed. Lewis White Beck in
collaboration with Mary J. Gregor, Ralf Meerbote, and John A. Reuscher. New
York: Peter Lang, 1986.

Praktische Philosophie Powalski. Vorlesungen, vol. 4. *Vorlesungen über*
Moralphilosophie, erste Hälfte (*KGS*, vol. 27).

Vorlesungen über die philosophische Religionslehre. Hrg. Karl Heinrich Ludwig
Pölitz. Leipzig, 1830.
Lectures on Philosophical Theology. Trans. Allen W. Wood and Gertrude M.
Clark. Ithaca: Cornell University Press, 1978.

"Was Ist Erklärung?" (*KGS*, vol. 8).
"An Answer to the Question: What Is Enlightenment?" Trans. Ted Humphrey. In
Perpetual Peace and Other Essays on Politics, History, and Morals, trans.
Humphrey. Indianapolis: Hackett, 1983.

Apart from the *Lectures on Ethics, Lectures on Philosophical Theol-*
ogy, and "On Philosophers' Medicine of the Body," all references to
Kant are to *Kants gesammelte Schriften* (*KGS*), *herausgegeben von der*

Deutschen (formerly *Königlichen Preussischen*) *Akademie der Wissenschaften*, 29 volumes (Berlin: Walter de Gruyter [and predecessors], 1902). References to the *Lectures on Ethics* are to the translation indicated of *Eine Vorlesung über Ethik*, edited by Paul Menzer (Berlin: Rolf Heise, 1924). I have also cited some sets of notes taken by Kant's students on his ethics lectures which are not included in Menzer's compilation: *Praktische Philosophie Powalski* and *Metaphysik der Sitten Vigilantius*. Both are in volume 4 of *KGS*.

References to "On Philosophers' Medicine of the Body" are to *Kant's Latin Writings*. "On Philosophers' Medicine of the Body" was published in 1881 by Johannas Reicke, who found the manuscript among the papers of his father, Rudolf Reicke, archivist of Kant's *Nachlass*.

My citations of all works in *KGS* give the page number of the German text, and where the translations used do not provide the page number of the German text, I also provide the page number of the translation. I have in some instances altered the translations; in those instances, I indicate the alteration in a footnote. With some reluctance, I decided against substituting 'people' for 'men' as a translation of *Menschen*, even though 'people' is certainly more accurate. *Mensch* and *Menschen*, unlike 'man' and 'men', are clearly gender-neutral. To correct for this error was, I decided, too large an undertaking, for although *Menschen* translates more accurately as 'people' or 'humans' than as 'men', it would be misleading to suggest that Kant has both males and females in mind whenever he speaks of *Menschen* (where the context doesn't indicate otherwise). Sometimes he (apparently) does—and so I recoil when I quote the translation of "ich bin ein Mensch; alles, was Menschen widerfährt, das trifft auch mich" (*MM* 460) as "I am a man; whatever befalls man concerns me too." (I do alter one such translation in Chap. 6; see n. 44.) But often he does not, and so it does not seem right to replace all translations of *Mensch* and *Menschen* with gender-neutral terms. Unsure how to resolve the problem, I generally deferred to the standard translations.

KANTIAN ETHICS
ALMOST
WITHOUT
APOLOGY

Introduction

◆◆◆

Many who ally themselves with Kant's ethics quietly dissent on one key matter: his emphasis on duty. Here, they suggest, he goes too far: he tries to subsume too much under duty and places too much value on acting from duty.

This work evaluates Kant's ethics in light of the criticism that duty (to put it vaguely for now) looms too large in it. This is a criticism, or a set of criticisms, with a venerable history. But although the criticisms are not new, they have been refined and buttressed, no doubt partly in response to the resurgence of interest in Kant's ethics and the new wave of Kantian scholarship. The criticisms have, moreover, taken an interesting turn, highlighting the clash between the demands of impartial morality, on the one hand, and, on the other, the claims of love, friendship, and other partial ties.[1] The objections that concern partiality take as their target both utilitarianism and Kantian ethics, but my concern is with the latter.[2]

---

1. Partial ties also include ties to community and nation. See Alasdair MacIntyre, "Is Patriotism a Virtue?" (Lawrence: University of Kansas Philosophy Department, 1984); and Andrew Oldenquist, "Loyalties," *Journal of Philosophy* 79 (1982): 173–193.

2. Peter Railton defends consequentialism against objections that concern the claims of love and friendship in "Alienation, Consequentialism, and the Demands of Morality," *Philosophy and Public Affairs* 13 (1984): 134–171. William Wilcox replies in "Egoists, Consequentialists, and Their Friends," *Philosophy and Public Affairs* 16 (1987): 73–84. Sarah Conly discusses the problem in her "The Objectivity of Morals and the Subjectivity of Agents," *American Philosophical Quarterly* 22 (1985): 275–286, and argues in her "Utilitarianism and Integrity" (*Monist* 66 [1983]: 298–311) that utilitarianism is not vulnerable to Bernard Williams's claim that impartial moral theory is in conflict with the value of integrity.

The criticisms are of enormous interest in their own right, and this work is almost as much about them as about Kant's ethics. As the title indicates, for the most part I defend Kant's ethics, but I am drawn to the criticisms and find them philosophically intriguing. Indeed, it was my fascination with the criticisms as much as my interest in Kant's ethics that led me to write this book. Accordingly, I write not only for those with a strong interest in Kantian ethics but for all who are interested in issues concerning impartiality and partiality in ethics; conflicts between acting from friendship or love for another person and acting from duty (or on principle, or from a conception of the good); issues concerning the alleged supremacy of morality; the danger that morality alienates us from others and perhaps from ourselves—in short, a host of issues that have been raised recently by Julia Annas, Lawrence Blum, Alasdair MacIntyre, Michael Stocker, Bernard Williams, and Susan Wolf, among others.[3]

The charge that Kant puts too much emphasis on duty needs to be developed and refined. We can start by dividing it into two criticisms. The first faults Kant for giving duty a scope so broad that it precludes recognizing the category of supererogatory actions. The second (and more familiar) criticism is that Kant sees too much value in acting from duty and too little value in acting from love, fellow feeling, sympathy, loyalty, and the like. In short, the first concerns the scope of duty and the second concerns duty as a motive or an incentive.

When I began this project, my focus was on the latter objection. Surely something is wrong if I view a friend, a spouse, or a lover as a sort of placeholder, as someone who meets certain conditions rather than as the particular person he or she is. Many of us have had the unsettling experience of seeing an old friend who has remarried and appears to treat his new wife exactly as he treated the first wife: the same expressions of

---

3. Julia Annas, "Personal Love and Kantian Ethics in *Effi Briest*," *Philosophy and Literature* 8 (1984): 15–31; Lawrence Blum, *Friendship, Altruism, and Morality* (London: Routledge and Kegan Paul, 1980), and "Iris Murdoch and the Domain of the Moral," *Philosophical Studies* 50 (1986): 343–367; MacIntyre, "Is Patriotism a Virtue?"; Michael Stocker, "The Schizophrenia of Modern Ethical Theories," *Journal of Philosophy* 73 (1976): 453–466; Bernard Williams, *Problems of the Self* (Cambridge: Cambridge University Press, 1973), *Moral Luck: Philosophical Papers 1973–1980* (Cambridge: Cambridge University Press, 1981), and *Ethics and the Limits of Philosophy* (Cambridge: Harvard University Press, 1985); and Susan Wolf, "Morality and Partiality," *Philosophical Perspectives 6: Ethics* (1992): 243–259. See also Oldenquist, "Loyalties"; Hugh LaFollette and George Graham, eds., *Person to Person* (Philadelphia: Temple University Press, 1989); and *Ethics* 101 (July 1991), special issue on impartiality and ethical theory.

endearment, the same style of interacting. Does he, we wonder, see her (and did he see his first wife) as a particular person, or simply as his wife? Or again, we observe someone who seems—judging from the presents she buys her, the topics she brings up in talking with her—to view her seven-year-old granddaughter (or, worse, daughter) simply as a seven-year-old girl, not as a particular person with particular interests. She seems not to pay attention to who this child is, but to define her as she thinks seven-year-old girls usually are (or perhaps as they should be).

All this is familiar and a cause of unease; but how much does it have to do with morality, with being committed to acting morally, with acting on principle? Is it part of acting from duty that one sees others as mere placeholders? Does acting from duty somehow alienate one from others, and preclude or impede genuine sentiment for that person (and genuine recognition of that person as a particular person)? Just what is it, anyway, that is supposed to be so objectionable about acting from duty?

Among the worries about acting from duty that I wanted to develop and examine was the suspicion that to act from duty is to act just minimally morally. Dissatisfied with the treatment I had given that objection in my essay "The Alleged Moral Repugnance of Acting from Duty,"[4] I probed further and found that a thorough examination of the criticism required addressing another question: To what extent does Kant's ethics leave room for supererogatory actions (actions that are beyond duty)? An answer gradually emerged: it does not leave room for the category of supererogatory actions but at the same time does not encourage minimal morality. It is often assumed that a theory that cannot leave room for the supererogatory is ipso facto defective. In examining why Kant did not recognize the category of supererogatory actions, I found that his approach not only is a plausible alternative to the usual "supererogationist" approach, an alternative that contemporary theorists should take seriously, but is arguably superior to it.[5]

The two objections—that the scope of duty is too broad in Kant's

---

4. Marcia Baron, "The Alleged Moral Repugnance of Acting from Duty," *Journal of Philosophy* 81 (1984): 197–220. The relevant section is sec. 2.

5. I use 'supererogationist' to refer to those who hold that there are acts that are beyond duty and are morally good and praiseworthy; for more details, see Sec. 2 of Chap. 1. I apologize for that abomination of a term, but I need some such term; this one is already in use (in David Heyd, *Supererogation: Its Status in Ethical Theory* [Cambridge: Cambridge University Press, 1982]), and it is easier to pronounce than 'supererogatorian' (listed as obsolete in the *Oxford English Dictionary*).

ethics, leaving no room for the supererogatory, and that Kant places too much value on acting from duty—provide the book's structure. Part I addresses the first objection; Part II addresses the second.

Part I consists of three chapters. A revised version of my "Kantian Ethics and Supererogation,"[6] Chapter 1 takes up the claim that Kant's ethics is inadequate in that it lacks, and has no room for, a category of the supererogatory. Unlike others who defend Kant, I agree that he has no room for that category. I argue, however, that this is not a shortcoming. Kant's ethics provides an excellent alternative to what are usually seen as the only options in moral theory. It neither accepts the division between the morally required and what is "above and beyond the line of duty" nor requires that we do all the good that we possibly can. An examination of the reasons why Kant would be loathe to incorporate a category of supererogatory actions into his theory suggests why it might be preferable not to draw a line between what is morally required and what is beyond duty. In sum, Chapter 1 argues against the supererogationist thesis that any ethical theory that does not leave room for the supererogatory is ipso facto flawed and suggests that Kant's classification of imperfect duties offers a promising approach to the moral phenomena that are usually thought to require the category of the supererogatory.

Why is it so often held that any adequate ethical theory will leave room for the supererogatory? The arguments typically are based on the assumption that any theory that does not include a category of supererogatory acts will be extremely demanding, asking of agents that they promote as much good as they possibly can. (Or, if it does not do that, it will, many critics assume, equate morality with fulfilling some minimal duties—not to murder, torture, steal, etc.—and thus fail to capture much of morality.) The assumption may hold for consequentialist theories that take as their starting point that the good is to be maximized, but it does not hold for theories in which maximizing plays no major role. It does not hold for Kant's ethics, since (as I argue in Chap. 3) the fact that some ends are obligatory for us—specifically, the happiness of others and our own perfection—does not entail that we are morally required to promote them maximally. Indeed, it is not even apparent that the more we promote them, the better (or the more we promote them, the better we are).

---

6. Baron, "Kantian Ethics and Supererogation," *Journal of Philosophy* 84 (1987): 237–262.

As will emerge toward the end of Chapter 1, to the extent that the arguments for the supererogationist thesis are compelling, they tend to support Kant's approach as much as they support supererogationism. Whatever force they have applies only with respect to theories that require moral agents to do as much as they possibly can to promote the good. Because the arguments support Kant's approach as much as the conclusion they purport to establish, it is difficult to determine just what disagreements, if any, supererogationists have to Kant's approach. One might think that the problem is simply that they have not considered the Kantian approach and, once they grasped it, would "convert," or at least regard that approach as not inferior to their own. Chapter 2 argues otherwise. From remarks in the writings of those championing supererogationism, I piece together positions implicit in their arguments which reveal sharply differing views of the nature of moral constraint, character, and moral excellence than those in Kant's ethics. My claim is not that supererogationists are, as such, logically committed to the views that I tease out of their writings. The point of articulating the views, rather, is to uncover a basis for rejecting the Kantian approach and to see more fully what is at issue. In Chapter 2 I try to locate the underlying disagreements between supererogationists and Kantians as well as to highlight the Kantian picture of character and moral excellence by contrasting it with views implicit in the writings of supererogationists. In addition, the chapter serves to uncover subtle assumptions about morality, duty, and moral excellence which may be a basis for rejecting Kant's ethics—or, viewed another way, which distort and hinder appreciation of Kant's ethics.

The first interlude lists various stands one might take concerning moral excellence and duty, and the duties we have with respect to character and moral excellence. This serves to situate the views discussed in Chapter 2 in a broader perspective and to bring their differences into relief.

Chapter 3 addresses an interpretive question. How much latitude do Kant's imperfect duties—the duties to promote the happiness of others and one's own perfection—allow? In Chapters 1 and 2, I follow for the most part the account of imperfect duties put forth by Thomas Hill Jr. in an article discussed in Chapter 1.[7] In Chapter 3, I consider some sharply opposing views concerning the degree of latitude that they allow. I reject the opposing views, but in assessing them I reach the conclusion that

7. Thomas E. Hill Jr., "Kant on Imperfect Duty and Supererogation," in his *Dignity and Practical Reason in Kant's Moral Theory* (Ithaca: Cornell University Press, 1992).

although Hill's interpretation is roughly right, the duty to perfect oneself involves slightly less latitude than does the duty to help others. That is, the former duty is slightly more rigorous than the latter. In addition, all of the wide imperfect duties have a bit less latitude than Hill seems to allow. These conclusions do not require a revision in the claims of Chapters 1 and 2; in fact, they strengthen my argument against Hill's attempt to locate in Kant's ethics room for the category of super-erogatory actions since they show that the imperfect duties require con-siderably more than that we sometimes perform acts that fall under the principles of imperfect duties. They also add to our understanding of Kant's imperfect duties and the implications that these duties have for moral excellence and responsibility for one's character.

Part II, comprising Chapters 4–6, addresses the other objection: the objection not to the scope of duty but to duty as a motive or an incentive. Chapter 4, based on (but quite different from) my "Alleged Moral Repugnance of Acting from Duty," seeks to determine just what is supposed to be objectionable about acting from duty. My point of departure is a well-known example of Michael Stocker's. The example is of someone who visits a hospitalized friend not essentially because of his friend but because he thought it his duty. I argue that what is disturbing about the example turns out, on inspection, not to be the fact that the friend acted from duty. There are various ways in which we may be filling out the picture sketched by the example, and in each case what is disturbing is something other than the fact that the agent acts from duty. For instance, it may be that the visit reveals that whereas the hospitalized person expects her friend to view her as a friend, in fact he views her merely as a member of a group to which they both belong (a church or political action group, perhaps). What is alienating is that he views her in this way, not that he acts from duty. This is evident from the fact that his conduct would be equally alienating if he visited her from an *inclination* to visit someone from his church.

Still, it might be argued that the problems are more deeply rooted. Perhaps the problems that seemed to be the source of our unease about the conduct that Stocker describes are themselves mere symptoms. They are symptoms of a deeper problem, it might be said, and the deeper problem is that acting from duty gets in the way of acting from friendlier, warmer motives. The balance of the chapter pursues this possibility. I divide it into two objections. First, insofar as one acts from duty, this shows something awry in one's "natural affections." Second, whatever affection for one's friends one does have is undermined insofar as one acts from duty. In the course of evaluating these objections I uncover common assumptions about what it is to act from duty which may explain some of the animosity to Kant's emphasis on acting from duty, and I suggest a different way of thinking about acting from duty. I do not argue in this chapter that it in fact is Kant's conception, and when I originally developed it some years ago, I thought that it was not. But as the next chapter, Chapter 5, suggests, Kant's conception is at least in spirit very similar to what I advocate here. The chapter also includes a defense of my understanding of acting from duty against a popular objection put forth by Bernard Williams, sometimes referred to as the "one thought too many" objection.

Chapter 5 examines Kant's account of acting from duty and of moral worth. We know that actions cannot, on Kant's view, have moral worth unless they are done from duty; but what about overdetermined actions, actions done from both duty and some inclination? Can they have moral worth? In the course of addressing this question it becomes apparent that the question itself is in need of scrutiny. What exactly is an overdetermined action, anyway? Should we be bothered if the answer to the moral worth question is 'No'? Chapter 5 does several things at once: (1) It shows that the notion of an overdetermined action needs refinement and refines it accordingly, introducing a distinction between overdetermined actions and what I call "hybrid actions," a distinction crucial for assessing the textual evidence for and against the possibility that overdetermined actions can, on Kant's view, have moral worth. (2) It shows that the question of overdetermined actions having moral worth may lead us astray insofar as we aim to understand Kant's ethics. (3) It shows that Kant does not hold that if an agent was inclined at t_1 to do x, her doing x at t_1 cannot have moral worth. (4) It suggests that many generations of Kant's readers have been wrong to suppose that it is unfortunate if Kant does not allow that overdetermined actions may have moral worth. (5) It suggests that Kant's readers (and, in particular, teachers of Kant's ethics) have exaggerated the importance to his moral philosophy of his claims that action A does, and that action B does not, have moral worth, and it points out that his discussion of moral worth plays a strategic role in the argument of *Groundwork* I and needs to be read accordingly. Most important, (6) Chapter 5 argues that despite initial appearances, the value that Kant attaches to acting from duty attaches primarily not to actions done from duty as a primary motive—

to individual actions prompted by the thought 'This is morally required'—but to governing one's conduct by a commitment to doing what
morality asks. This is important because one conclusion of Chapter 4 is
that the objections stick only insofar as it is acting from duty as a primary
motive that is treated as having special value. They miss their target if the
value attaches primarily to governing one's conduct by a commitment to
duty (or, as I there put it, to duty operating as a secondary motive).
Insofar as it is the latter, not the former, that is of primary value in Kant's
ethics, he is not vulnerable to the criticisms examined in Chapter 4.
Although Kant's texts support my claim, there is certainly room for
disagreement about how the relevant passages should be read. But even
if the textual evidence is not decisive, this much is clear: Kant has no basis
for attributing (and no need to attribute) value to individual actions done
from duty (or to acting from duty as a primary motive) that does not
attach to acting from duty as a secondary motive.

Too short to be a chapter, the second interlude points out that in
couching my examination of criticisms in the terms in which they are
usually couched, specifically, in terms of *motives*, I have given the critics
an undeserved edge. The term 'motive' evokes a theory of agency quite
different from Kant's and, in generating this confusion, adds some force
to the critics' objections. The initial appeal of the objections—and the
lingering feeling of many people that Kant's emphasis on acting from
duty is extreme—may be due in considerable part to this confusion.

Even if everything said in Chapters 4 and 5 is true, a related worry has
not yet been addressed. In so valorizing acting from duty, doesn't Kant
undervalue love, affection, and fellow feeling? True, he does not hold
that an inclination to perform action *A* prevents the performance of *A*
from having moral worth. Moral worth, in other words, is not contin-
gent on the absence of the relevant inclination. But can he recognize that
some inclinations—and some affective responses—are good, and that an
agent devoid of them would be morally deficient? Chapter 6 examines
and evaluates Kant's view in light of these questions. Although it is not
difficult to defend Kant against some common objections—for instance,
that he holds that inclinations are all bad, or that he holds that we are
passive with respect to our emotions and feelings—it is by no means clear
that he accords fellow feeling, love, and affection the value that it seems
is their due. A passage in the *Doctrine of Virtue* asserts that sympathetic
feeling is a duty, yet also speaks favorably of the wise man who, when he
could not help his friend, said "What is it to me?" and (as a very similar
passage in the *Lectures on Ethics* adds) turned coldly away. I examine

this passage and offer a partial defense of Kant, but also grant that he seems to accord value to sympathetic feeling only insofar as and only when it can be used to help another; when it cannot, the agent does well to "turn it off," Kant suggests. Hence the 'almost' in my title. That Kant seems to accord value to sympathetic feeling only insofar as it can be used to help another is one part of Kant's theory (admittedly a very small part) that I do not wish to defend.[8]

BEFORE proceeding to Chapter 1, I note some objections to Kant's ethics which I do not address but which some readers might expect to hear discussed, since they could reasonably be subsumed under the heading of "objections to Kant's emphasis on duty." These are objections which are either based on too patent a misunderstanding of Kant's ethics to merit extended discussion or which have been adequately dealt with elsewhere. They bear mention, however, because the recurring thought, "But why doesn't she discuss this other objection?" might hinder comprehension of the arguments of the present work. I hope that a brief discussion will serve to alert readers to reasons for doubting the seriousness of the objections and will thus remove one set of obstacles to understanding my discussion of the serious objections that are the focus of this work.

One objection is to the value that Kant attaches to acting on principle, where acting on principle is seen to involve applying a rule mechanically and then acting accordingly.[9] There is no doubt that Kant does attach

---

8. I do not mean that it is the only part that I do not wish to defend. But it is the one qualification to my defense of Kant against the charge that he places too much value on acting from duty and too little value on affect.

9. Related to this objection is the allegation that on Kant's view moral deliberation is to be guided, as Lorraine Code puts it, "wholly by universal rules" that preclude sensitivity to context, to differences among the relevant persons, and so on. Thus Code objects (referring to an illustration she developed from Anthony Trollope's novel, *The Warden*): "The presumption that Bold's relationship to the Warden, and his consequent *knowledge* of the Warden's character and circumstances, creates in favor of appealing to *who* the Warden is, is erased in a deliberation guided wholly by 'universal' rules. There is no space to argue that this case is different because of who *this* man is, in his specificity and particularity. Hence the Kantian impartiality principle does not generate an instrument finely enough tuned to translate principle into morally sensitive practice. If wealth in the clergy is a mark of corruption, then it must always be so, without exception" (Code, *What Can She Know? Feminist Theory and The Construction of Knowledge* [Ithaca: Cornell University Press, 1991], p. 75).

A more plausible version of the objection is voiced by Stuart Hampshire: "An abstract morality places a prepared grid upon conduct and upon a person's activities and interests, and thereafter one only tends to see the pieces of his conduct and life as they are divided by

great value to acting on principle, but acting on principle does not entail mechanically applying a rule. This is not how principles, on his view, work. Principles generally underdetermine action and require judgment.[10]

Indeed Kant emphasizes that it is a mistake—a mistake of the immature—to rely on rules.[11] Any approach to practical thinking which shies away from thinking is a form of self-imposed immaturity. "Rules and formulas, those mechanical aids to the rational use, or rather misuse, of his natural gifts, are the shackles of a permanent immaturity." He assimilates reliance on such mechanical aids to a failure to think for oneself. Reliance on rules is one form of that failure. "It is so easy to be immature.

---

lines on the grid" ("Public and Private Morality," in *Public and Private Morality,* ed. Stuart Hampshire [Cambridge: Cambridge University Press, 1978], p. 40). See Barbara Herman's discussion of Hampshire's criticism in her "Integrity and Impartiality," *Monist* 66 (1983): 233–250; reprinted in Herman, *The Practice of Moral Judgment* (Cambridge: Harvard University Press, 1993).

The worry that persons are viewed simply as rational beings and not as the particular persons that they are is expressed by Robin Dillon in her "Respect and Care: Toward Moral Integration," *Canadian Journal of Philosophy* 22 (1992): 105–132. She claims (p. 121) that "although the Kantian formula of persons as ends in themselves is claimed to regard persons as irreplaceable, there is a sense in which Kantian respect does in fact view persons as intersubstitutable, for it is blind to everything about an individual except her rational nature, leaving each of us indistinguishable from every other. Thus, in Kantian-respecting someone, there is a real sense in which we are not paying attention to *her*, for it makes no difference to how we respect her that she is who she is and not some other individual." It is true that a person is worthy of respect in virtue of being a rational being, but it is not true that it makes no difference to how we respect her that she is the particular person she is. In respecting someone as a rational being we respect her as a being who sets ends for herself. Respecting a particular person requires taking her ends seriously and thus attending to what her particular ends are. See Thomas Hill Jr., "Humanity as an End in Itself" in his *Dignity*; and Christine Korsgaard, "Kant's Formula of Humanity," *Kant-Studien* 77 (1986): 183–202.

10. See G 398 and the sections in the *Doctrine of Virtue* (MM) entitled "Casuistical Questions." See also Onora O'Neill, "Kant's Ethics and Kantian Ethics," lecture delivered to the North American Kant Society at the Central Division meetings of the American Philosophical Society, Chicago, April 1991; Henry E. Allison, *Kant's Theory of Freedom* (New York: Cambridge University Press, 1990), p. 165; and Robert B. Louden, *Morality and Moral Theory: A Reappraisal and Reaffirmation* (New York: Oxford University Press, 1992), pp. 113–115.

11. The claim that I am saying Kant rejects should not be confused with the claim that thinking is rule-governed, which Kant of course endorses. To say that it is rule-governed is to say only that it can be explained by rules. Thinking is in this regard like everything else in nature: "Everything in nature, in the inanimate as well as the animate world, happens *according to rules*, although we do not always know these rules" (*Logic* 11/13).

If I have a book to serve as my understanding, a pastor to serve as my conscience . . . and so on, I need not exert myself at all. I need not think, if only I can pay" (*WE* 35–36).

Another objection to Kant's emphasis on duty is that it is supposed to result in a focus on action rather than on character. We can, it is often assumed, only have duties to perform certain actions, not to be a certain kind of person or to have a certain type of character. Although I do not address this claim directly, readers interested in it will notice that some of the discussion in subsequent chapters (Chaps. 2 and 5, in particular) provide strong reasons for thinking that insofar as the contrast makes sense, Kant is at least as concerned with character as with actions.[12] (To ask which concerns him more, however, misleads; he is interested in conduct, which concerns both character and action.) And although he would agree that we cannot have a duty at t_1 to feel happy or to feel compassion at t_1 (or shortly thereafter), we can have a duty to cultivate certain feelings and to become better people. An emphasis on duty as Kant understands it does not steer one away from a concern with character.

The previous objections are closely tied to (and in some instances specifications of) the general objection to Kant's emphasis on duty. A different sort of criticism that needs to be noted so that it will not pop up later and impede understanding is as follows: moral reasoning, it is said, must on Kant's view exclude empirical considerations.[13] That would certainly be a serious objection if it were true; happily, it is not. Morality cannot be grounded in empirical considerations and thus the Categorical Imperative is not to have an empirical foundation, but the application of the Categorical Imperative or the determination of just what morality asks of us often involves, on Kant's view, empirical considerations. This is clear even from the preface to the *Groundwork*. The moral law requires "a power of judgement sharpened by experience" for its application (389). As one would expect, given this statement, Kant's examples of applications of the Categorical Imperative show that he thinks it appropriate to take empirical considerations into account. His examples

---

12. For a discussion of the contrast between character and action and the idea that ethics of virtue are primarily concerned with character while ethics of duty are primarily concerned with action, see my essay "The Ethics of Duty/Ethics of Virtue Debate and Its Relevance to Educational Theory," *Educational Theory* 35 (1985): 135–149.

13. See Williams, "Persons, Character, and Morality" in *Moral Luck* and *Ethics and the Limits of Philosophy*.

make use of such empirical facts as that we are not self-sufficient but rather are beings who often require the assistance of others.[14]

The final two objections to be considered are specifications of the general objection to Kant's emphasis on duty.

The first is that Kant thinks of the moral agent as someone who acts for the sake of duty, and this seems to mean that the Kantian moral agent acts not with the aim of helping another or of fighting social injustice (or, if this sounds too abstract, a very specific social injustice) but with the aim of doing his duty. *Duty* is what the agent is thinking of, not the needs of others or the importance of eliminating a specific social injustice. And this seems far from morally ideal, as well as rather artificial. Surely the moral person is concerned with homelessness, the unfairness of certain laws, the needs of an ailing relative, and not just with some highly abstract notion such as duty.[15]

An improved version of this objection will be addressed in Chapter 4. As it stands, the objection rests on a misunderstanding. It wrongly supposes that Kant expects us to act for the sake of duty, as if our end is simply to do our duty. There is more than one operative confusion here, but the major one is a conflation of acting from duty with acting for the sake of duty. Kant unquestionably places great importance on acting from duty. Just what acting from duty amounts to will be considered later. But one thing that is clear is that one's goal, in acting from duty, need not be to do one's duty. Duty should be our motivating conception and need not be our end. The aim or end can be to save the child who has just darted into the street, or to show concern respectfully without seeming condescending or meddlesome, or to speak both truthfully and sensitively.

Unlike some of the other errors noted here, this one is fairly subtle and

14. See Mary Gregor, *Laws of Freedom: A Study of Kant's Method of Applying the Categorical Imperative in the "Metaphysik der Sitten"* (Oxford: Basil Blackwell, 1963), chap. 1; O'Neill, *Constructions of Reason: Explorations of Kant's Practical Philosophy* (Cambridge: Cambridge University Press, 1989), part 2; Sally Sedgwick, "On the Relation of Pure Reason to Content: A Reply to Hegel's Critique of Formalism in Kant's Ethics," *Philosophy and Phenomenological Research* 49 (1988): 59–80, and "On Lying and the Role of Content in Kant's Ethics," *Kant-Studien* 82 (1991): 42–62; and Louden, *Morality*, pp. 100–103.

15. This view is put forth by, among others, Carol Gilligan in *In a Different Voice: Psychological Theory and Women's Development* (Cambridge: Harvard University Press, 1982), and Nel Noddings in *Caring: A Feminine Approach to Ethics and Moral Education* (Berkeley: University of California Press, 1984).

quite understandable. It is abetted by a very unfortunate mistake in translation in one of the most widely read translations of the *Grundlegung*: H. J. Paton renders *aus Pflicht*, which without question should be translated as *from duty* (or *out of duty*), at crucial points as *for the sake of duty*. My reason for not treating this error at greater length is that it has been adequately dealt with elsewhere.[16]

The next objection is similar to the last. It is sometimes suggested that the Kantian agent is a sort of moral narcissist: his moral concern is with his own moral purity. His focus is inward, on his own goodness, rather than outward, on the needs of others.[17]

The objection finds some grounding in the fact that duties to self are no less central or important in Kant's theory than duties to others. Duties to others are, however, by no means derivative from duties to self, so it would be far-fetched to suggest that the centrality of duties to self in Kant's ethics shows the agent's fundamental concern to be with his or her own purity.[18] That the happiness of others is an obligatory end just as

16. See Barbara Herman, "Integrity and Impartiality," *Monist* 66 (1983): 233–250; reprinted with revision in Herman, *The Practice of Moral Judgment*; and Henry Allison, *Kant's Theory of Freedom*, pp. 102–103 and chap. 10.

17. Given the similarity between this objection and the previous one, it might seem at first that an analogous answer is called for. One might think that the way to address the objection is to say that the end is other-directed but that the motivating conception is inward-looking and concerns one's own moral purity. But this would not do. The critic will maintain that if the Kantian agent's concern to alleviate poverty or to comfort a frightened child is grounded in a more fundamental concern with his or her own purity or goodness, this in effect grants the objection. A concern with one's purity should not be fundamental.

18. This is not to deny that Kant says that were there no duties to oneself there could be no duties to others. He does not claim, however, that the latter derive from the former, but only that "I can recognize that I am under obligation to others only insofar as I at the same time put myself under obligation" (*MM* 417). I thus disagree with Robert Louden, who quotes approvingly the following claim, by Philip Hallie in *Lest Innocent Blood Be Shed* (New York: Harper Torchbooks, 1985), p. 278: "Kant is very careful to point out . . . that what we do to or for others is not central to ethics; the orderly conception of our own souls, our character, is what ethics seeks to achieve, and praises when it succeeds." See Louden's discussion in "Can We Be Too Moral?" *Ethics* 98 (January 1988): 361–378, especially pp. 365–366, and in his *Morality*, pp. 14–16. In addition to citing *MM* 417, Louden cites a passage from the *Lectures on Ethics* which is much stronger evidence for Hallie's assertion but still does not go as far as Hallie's assertion: "Our duties to ourselves rank highest and are the most important of all. . . . A man who performed his duties to others badly, who lacked generosity, kindness and sympathy, but who nevertheless did his duty to himself by leading a proper life, might yet possess a certain inner worth; but he who has violated his duty to himself, can have no inner worth whatever" (*LE* 117–118; cited on p. 13 of *Morality*; Louden's translation). This passage does not support the view that the Kantian

one's own perfection is ensures that the objection does not take hold. It is worth noting, too, that even the end of moral self-perfection involves serious attention to the world and to one's interaction with others: self-improvement would be a hollow project if one did not think about one's effect on others. (It is true that Kant focuses, in explicating the duty of moral self-perfection, on deepening one's commitment to acting as duty requires; but here, too, if the commitment is not to be hollow, one will have to attend to the world. How else will one reflect on what, indeed, duty does require?)

The notion that the Kantian agent is a moral narcissist may be due in part to a failure to read in context Kant's remarks in the *Groundwork* about moral worth, a failure that may lead some to suppose that the Kantian is ever mindful of the moral worth of his actions and further, that the Kantian sizes up others morally and (usually smugly) rates himself or herself in comparison with others. The failure to read Kant's remarks on moral worth in context is addressed in Chapter 5. Here I only point out that Kant's ethics has considerable momentum away from the moral evaluation of others and from measuring oneself relative to others. (The point is quite independent of my suggestion that the importance to Kant's theory of his claims about moral worth is often exaggerated.) This is evident from several considerations, among them the fact that only one's own perfection, not the perfection of others, is an obligatory end. Although we are not to encourage others in their moral depravity—we are not to "see to it that a drunkard is never short of wine" (*MM* 481)—it is not our business to monitor and evaluate other adults and try to make them better people. Recall too Kant's indication in the *Groundwork* that our conception of what is right is not to be relativized to the level of excellence of others' conduct, and his rejection of the use of examples of heroism in moral education partly because such use detracts from the conception of morality as something accessible to everyone and not a matter of heroism or moral prowess.[19] More generally, Kant's ethical writings emphasize self-evaluation and in particular forward-

---

agent is to be fundamentally concerned with tending to his or her soul. We are to be concerned with both our own characters and others' well-being; the most that Kant says in the direction that Hallie and Louden point is that failure in duties to self is worse than failure in duties to others.

19. On this last point, see Chap. 1. On the more general point, see Hill, "Kant's Anti-Moralistic Strain," in his *Dignity*.

looking reflection on one's conduct, not assessment of the conduct of others. As Onora O'Neill has pointed out, the Categorical Imperative is primarily a test for agents to apply to their own maxims.[20]

It is worth noting the gap between one common expectation in contemporary ethics and Kant's approach. Many recent philosophers, particularly in the utilitarian tradition, think that the proper focus of ethics is the question of what our social norms should be. Duty, in their view, is conceptually tied to what we have a right to demand that others do. John Stuart Mill is cited approvingly: "It is a part of the notion of duty in every one of its forms that a person may rightfully be compelled to fulfill it. Duty is a thing which may be *exacted* from a person, as one exacts a debt."[21] In Kant's scheme, what Mill asserts of duty is true only of one type of duty, juridical duty, and juridical duties are the province of *Rechtslehre*, not *Tugendlehre*, that is, of the philosophy of law or right, not of ethics proper. This will be elaborated in Chapters 1 and 2. I mention it now to point out that the rather common misconception that Kant is concerned with judging others and affixing credit and blame may well be due to a failure, when reading Kant, to expunge from one's mind the picture of ethics as positive social morality. An assumption that *this* is what ethics is about, together with the fairly correct perception that Kant's ethics is stern and exacting, may yield the picture of Kant—or of the Kantian—as an intolerant, judgmental moralist.

ONE last preliminary. If there is a wide gap between the Kantian construal of 'duty' and the construal of those who see ethics as positive social morality, the gap is even wider between the Kantian construal and associations with 'duty' that arise from our colloquial use of the word. Our colloquial use of the word 'duty' would not lead one to look favorably on the idea of a moral philosophy in which the concept of duty loomed large. 'Duties' brings to mind paying taxes, returning borrowed items promptly, keeping appointments with students, and attending department meetings. The word 'duties' suggests (among other things) jejune tasks that one performs perfunctorily, many of which are duties in virtue of institutional arrangements and the expectations of one's profes-

20. See O'Neill, *Constructions of Reason*, especially chap. 5.
21. John Stuart Mill, *Utilitarianism* (Indianapolis: Hackett, 1979), p. 47. See also the view of duty affirmed by J. O. Urmson in "Saints and Heroes," in *Moral Concepts*, ed. Joel Feinberg (London: Oxford University Press, 1969). I discuss Urmson's conception of duty in Chap. 2.

sion. We often use the word 'duty' with scare quotes (or a facial expression that suggests scare quotes), indicating that what is called a duty is frequently overrated or mistakenly thought to be morally obligatory. Thus duties are seen not only as relatively unimportant but also as sometimes opposed to what is really right or best. To some, a paradigmatic usage of 'duty' is 'military duty'. This leads many philosophers to be uneasy about duty as a central concept in ethics. When, several years back, I mentioned to a colleague that I was writing an article in defense of acting from duty, he remarked, "Talk of duty always makes me nervous. It reminds me of the Vietnam War and the draft." The following inscription on a monument reflects the notion of duty that many assume is somehow relevant, if not central, to Kant's ethics: "To the sons of the University, who entered the war of 1861–1865 in answer to the call of their country and whose lives taught the lesson of the great commander that duty is the sublimest word in the English language."[22] Such associations, the term 'military duty', and other common uses of the word 'duty' make it easy to forget that 'duty', as Kant uses it, does not stand for something that is imposed from without.

Similar associations color our conception of duty as a motive or incentive. When we think of someone acting from duty, an unattractive figure such as Karenin in *Anna Karenina* comes to mind: someone who, we think, might make a good person with whom to forge a business deal, but not a desirable friend or spouse. We picture someone who supposes that because he does his duty—where duty is construed rather narrowly—his conduct is beyond moral criticism.

Such a focus on duty, it is sometimes said, threatens to blind us to other important dimensions of morality. Without supposing that this could not be the case, I want to stress that the issue has to be examined with a Kantian notion of duty before us, not with our colloquial understanding of 'duty' and 'duties'. There is no justification for evaluating Kant's ethics by substituting current colloquial usage for what Kant meant by 'duty' (i.e., *Pflicht*). 'Duty' in Kant's ethics refers to whatever one morally ought to do. This is easy to forget, especially when we read the word 'duties'. Even more than 'duty', 'duties' brings to mind those many little tasks that (to name a few possibilities) one's religion, one's social or professional or familial role, or the laws of the land demand.

---

22. The inscription is from a monument on the campus of the University of North Carolina at Chapel Hill.

Duties in *this* sense are often morally insignificant, more often morally significant yet legitimately outweighed by certain other considerations, and occasionally immoral. An example of a morally insignificant duty might be a "duty" to fast. Kant was troubled by the conception of morality promulgated by many religions and decried the elevation of morally insignificant acts to the status of duties.[23] Examples of acts that are by no means morally negligible, but at the same time are not infrequently outweighed by other considerations, are keeping one's office hours and promptly returning the little items one has borrowed.[24] Examples of immoral "duties" are turning in runaway slaves in the antebellum South and, more recently, supplying the government with information on people suspected of communist leanings. Given such associations with the word 'duties', it is especially important to remember that 'duties' is simply the plural of 'duty', where the latter refers to whatever one morally ought to do.

I suspect that a good deal of the discomfort that many people have with Kant's emphasis on duty is heightened by their associations with the word 'duty'. But this is not to deny that there are deeper and more compelling reasons for the discomfort. I turn now to the project of examining those reasons.

23. See A 147–148, a passage reminiscent of David Hume's caustic remarks in *A Treatise of Human Nature* and the *Enquiry concerning the Principles of Morals* about "monkish virtue." For a more extended discussion see Kant, *Religion*, bk. 4.

24. See Wolf, "Above and Below the Line of Duty," *Philosophical Topics* 14 (1986): 131–148.

PART I

I

Kantian Ethics and the Supererogatory

❖❖❖

1   The complaint that Kantian morality is in some sense too minimal dates at least to 1793, when Maria von Herbert wrote the following in a letter to Kant:

> Don't think me arrogant for saying this, but the commandments of morality are too trifling for me; for I should gladly do twice as much as they command. . . .
> I console myself often with the thought that since the practice of morality is so bound up with sensuality, it can only count for this world, and with that thought I could still hope not to have to live another life of empty vegetating and of so few and easy moral demands after this life.[1]

Von Herbert might be unique in finding the alleged problem a source of personal despair, but she is not unique in finding Kantian morality objectionably minimal. In his *Friendship, Altruism, and Morality*, Lawrence Blum argues that Kantian ethics cannot do justice to the value of altruism,[2] and in *A Short History of Ethics*, Alasdair MacIntyre claims that Kant's ethics tells us only what not to do:

> The typical examples of alleged categorical imperatives given by Kant tell us what *not* to do; not to break promises, tell lies, commit suicide, and so on. But as to what activities we ought to engage in, what ends we should

1. *Kant: Philosophical Correspondence, 1759–99*, ed. and trans. Arnulf Zweig (Chicago: University of Chicago Press, 1967), pp. 201–202.
2. Lawrence Blum, *Friendship, Altruism, and Morality* (London: Routledge and Kegan Paul, 1980).

pursue, the categorical imperative seems to be silent. Morality sets limits to
the ways in which and the means by which we conduct our lives; it does not
give them any direction. Thus morality apparently sanctions any way of
life which is compatible with keeping our promises, telling the truth, and
so on.[3]

MacIntyre's objection is based on a misreading of Kant's works, or
perhaps too limited an acquaintance with Kant's ethical writings. Even
a cursory reading of *The Doctrine of Virtue* suffices to show that
MacIntyre is mistaken. Blum's claim is more plausible but also ill-
founded, or perhaps (since Blum is primarily concerned to challenge not
Kant's ethics but a loosely related Kantian ethics) based on an understanding of Kantian ethics in which 'duty' is closer to colloquial usage
than to Kant's meaning.

At the same time that some recent theorists have echoed von Herbert's
complaint that Kant's ethics asks too little, others, recognizing that on
Kant's view we *do* have duties to be beneficent, to strive for self-knowledge, to cultivate our natural and moral powers, and so on, take his
theory to demand too much. Different though these criticisms are, they
are not as opposed as they appear. They concur in the view that Kant
expects to get far more mileage out of the notion of duty than it is
reasonable to expect. Both sets of criticisms construe his theory as too
minimal *conceptually* (and one regards it as too minimal with respect to
what it asks of us). Duty, it is said, is just one part of morality (if indeed
it is any part of morality). An ethical theory in which duty takes over is
a severely impoverished theory.[4] Hence the need for a category of the
supererogatory.

But it is not only Kant's critics who take this view. Kant scholars who

3. Alasdair MacIntyre, *A Short History of Ethics* (New York: Macmillan, 1966), p. 197.
4. See Roderick Chisholm, "Supererogation and Offense: A Conceptual Scheme for
Ethics," *Ratio* 5 (1963): 1–14; Paul Eisenberg, "Basic Ethical Categories of Kant's
Tugendlehre," *American Philosophical Quarterly* 4 (1966): 255–269; Joel Feinberg,
"Supererogation and Rules," in his *Doing and Deserving: Essays in the Theory of Respon-
sibility* (Princeton: Princeton University Press, 1970); Philippa Foot, *Virtues and Vices*
(Oxford: Basil Blackwell, 1978); David Heyd, *Supererogation: Its Status in Ethical Theory*
(Cambridge: Cambridge University Press, 1982); Michael Slote, *Goods and Virtues* (Ox-
ford: Clarendon Press, 1983); Michael Stocker, "The Schizophrenia of Modern Ethical
Theories," *Journal of Philosophy* 73 (1976): 453–466; J. O. Urmson, "Saints and Heroes,"
in *Moral Concepts*, ed. Joel Feinberg (London: Oxford University Press, 1969); and
Bernard Williams, *Moral Luck: Philosophical Papers 1973–1980* (Cambridge: Cambridge
University Press, 1982), and *Ethics and the Limits of Philosophy* (Cambridge: Harvard
University Press, 1985).

have sought to defend Kant against the charge that his moral theory is conceptually quite limited have tacitly granted the assumption that any ethical theory that does not recognize a special category of the supererogatory is ipso facto flawed. They have argued either that Kant does have a place in his theory for the supererogatory or that room can be made for it with only minor (and salutary) revisions. I argue against the assumption.[5] The absence of a special category for the supererogatory poses no serious problem, given his understanding of 'duty' and his category of imperfect duties. Moreover, the absence of a category of the supererogatory contributes positively to his theory. The emphasis on duty, together with the demand that agents act from duty in the sense explained in Part II, provides a unity to agency—a unifying thread to the responsible agent's reflections—and this would be disrupted if Kantian ethics were revised so as to recognize the supererogatory.

The chapter is structured as follows. The second section investigates what it is that supererogationists are claiming. In particular, what criticism do they intend when they fault an ethical theory for failing to leave room for the supererogatory? The third section asks whether Kant's ethics leaves room for the supererogatory. Finding that it cannot, I then investigate Kant's reasons for not accommodating it, and suggest that the considerations he adduces should give us pause and prompt us to question the supererogationist thesis. Finally, I ask why it is supposed to be so important to have a special category of the supererogatory and argue that the reasons supererogationists put forth offer no more support for their claim than for distinguishing as Kant does between perfect and imperfect duties.[6]

2   Supererogationists believe there are acts that fit the following criteria: they are beyond duty, and they are morally good and praiseworthy. They are beyond duty in that "they fulfil *more* than is required, *over and above* what the agent is required or expected to do" and thus are optional.[7]

---

5. I do not claim that *no* ethical theory needs the category. It may be important for utilitarianism and other forms of consequentialism which emphasize the maximization of some good. Whether it is will not be considered here.

6. I do not mean to suggest, of course, that Kant is unique in the history of ethics in drawing this distinction. For a history of the distinction prior to Kant, see Wolfgang Kersting, "Das starke Gesetz der Schuldigkeit und das schwächere der Gütigkeit," *Studia Leibnitiana* 14 (1982): 184–220.

7. Heyd, *Supererogation*, p. 1.

This may sound clear enough, but in fact the claim that there are acts of such and such a sort is apt to mislead, since it might be read as a claim that people do *x* or *y*, where *x* and *y* are acts such as donating blood, giving money to the poor, or forgiving someone (to take some of the examples David Heyd gives of supererogatory acts).[8] No one is questioning whether people ever donate blood, and so on. That is not at issue. Nor is the issue (or one of the issues) *why* people do these things, even though on this matter there no doubt is room for discussion and disagreement. The issue between supererogationists and those they oppose is not about whether people act in this or that way. It does not parallel, for instance, debates about whether people ever act altruistically, debates in which the issue concerns what people do and what their real motives are. Rather, the issue concerns *how to classify acts*. The issue arises because theories such as Kant's are criticized for failing to recognize or leave room for the category of supererogatory acts. To evaluate the criticism, we need to ask what it is that ethical theories are (according to these critics) supposed to do, and whether the requirement is a reasonable one. Is an ethical theory ipso facto flawed if it fails to recognize this category? (And what counts as recognizing the category?)

That this is the issue emerges only through a haze (particularly since some writers have confused the claim that supererogatory acts are of value with the claim that classifying the acts as supererogatory is of value).[9] The clearest indications are these: Heyd explains that one of his book's aims is "to show that supererogation is a distinct and determinate

---

8. Heyd, *Supererogation*, p. 2.

9. Heyd, for example, offers the following as an argument for the social value of recognizing the category of supererogatory acts: "There is a famous Talmudic saying, 'Jerusalem was only destroyed because judgments were given strictly upon Biblical law and did not go beyond the requirement of the law'. . . . It expresses epigrammatically our common moral disapprobation of societies in which superogatory behaviour is rare, societies which do not recognize the value of action beyond duty. We usually regard a social organization or a group that does not encourage supererogatory action (let alone that fails to leave room for it) as morally deficient" (*Supererogation*, p. 178). Which is it that we commonly disapprove of: the fact that conduct of the sort that is often classified as supererogatory is so rare, or a failure to classify such conduct as supererogatory? It is the former, not the latter. And what is alleged to have been a problem in Jerusalem is that people were not encouraged to go beyond minimal morality, i.e., that they were not encouraged to do more than what was strictly required. The alleged problem is *not* that they were not encouraged to view acts that are good from a moral standpoint but not strictly required *as supererogatory*, rather than view them as (for instance) acts that fall under a principle of imperfect duty.

class of moral action deserving of moral scrutiny, and that there are both theoretical and moral reasons for treating these acts as belonging to a separate category." He emphasizes that "one criterion of the acceptability of a theory" is its "treatment of supererogation," and he says that supererogation cannot "be accounted for . . . by a theory which takes duty as exhausting the whole realm of moral behaviour."[10] And in his classic "Saints and Heroes," J. O. Urmson calls for a two-tiered ethical theory that sharply separates the supererogatory from duty: "Thus as moral theorists we need to discover some theory that will allow for both absolute duties, which, in Mill's phrase, can be exacted from a man like a debt, to omit which is to do wrong and to deserve censure, and which may be embodied in formal rules or principles, and also for a range of actions which are of moral value and which an agent may feel called upon to perform, but which cannot be demanded and whose omission cannot be called wrong-doing."[11]

In short, the supererogationist holds as a condition of adequacy for any ethical theory not only that it recognize the possibility (and actuality) of certain acts that go beyond what is morally required and are morally praiseworthy but also that it treat these acts as constituting an independent category, independent in the sense that their value cannot be explained in terms of duty. I refer to this as the 'supererogationist thesis'. The thesis is about how to view such acts, and how to categorize them within ethical theory.

On what grounds can one argue that a category is or is not needed in ethical theory? The territory is murky and ill-charted but, taking a clue from David Heyd, I think that we can say this much: a category is needed in ethical theory either for its explanatory value or because it is

---

10. Heyd, *Supererogation*, pp. 1, 10, and 3.

11. Urmson, "Saints and Heroes," p. 67. The views that I attribute to Urmson throughout this book are based solely on his "Saints and Heroes." In a more recent article he takes a different stand: "I deplore the introduction of this term ['supererogatory'], which has a clear use in theology where it belongs, into moral philosophy, and regret having, just once, used it in that way myself." And: "I wish to dissociate myself . . . from those who speak as though there was a special variety of acts called supererogatory. . . . It seems to me that 'supererogatory' is an unnecessary blanket-term used to cover a number of types of moral action which are as worthy of distinction from each other as they all are from duties and obligations" (Urmson, "Hare on Intuitive Moral Thinking," in *Hare and Critics: Essays on "Moral Thinking"*, ed. Douglas Seanor and Nicholas Fotion [Oxford: Clarendon Press, 1983], pp. 167–169). Just how much of "Saints and Heroes" he means to repudiate is not clear (particularly since he does not actually use the term 'supererogatory' in that piece).

practically valuable, valuable for (among other things) self-direction, moral education, and the flourishing of a community.[12]

In denying the supererogationist thesis, I shall first of all be asserting that the value of supererogatory acts *can* be explained in terms of duty, and *is* thus explained by Kant.[13] Supererogationists will no doubt respond that I do not recognize their special value, and they are partly right: I do not believe the acts to have the special significance that supererogationists attribute to them. The value they do have can be captured, and perhaps better captured, without the category of supererogatory acts. I will be claiming that most of the (meaningful) theoretical work for which the category of the supererogatory is thought necessary can be handled by distinguishing between imperfect and perfect duties.[14] The remainder is handled by shifting our attention away, at the appropriate point, from action to character (see Sec. 6). I will not be denying that there are acts that can (contextually, and as acts, not as act-types) be labeled "supererogatory." But it is the wrong thing to focus on; it is not something that ethical theory should emphasize. Supererogatory acts do not form an ethically useful or theoretically interesting kind.

---

12. These are considerations that Heyd offers in support of supererogationism. See Sec. 5, below.

13. By 'duty' I here mean duty as Kant understands it, not as supererogationists understand it. One might wonder, as indeed an anonymous referee has, whether the disagreement between Kant and the supererogationists is merely terminological. Although there certainly is a terminological disagreement, it reflects deeper disagreements that concern the nature of moral constraint, its proper place—especially its pervasiveness or lack thereof—in our lives, the relation between moral constraint and freedom, and related matters, which I take up in Chap. 2.

The referee suggests, however, that what Kant means by 'perfect duty' is what supererogationists mean by 'duty', so couldn't Kant therefore be viewed as a supererogationist, since he holds that there are acts that go beyond perfect duty (and are meritorious)? In reply, I note first that what supererogationists mean by 'duty' is rather different from what Kant means by 'perfect duty', since perfect duties can require a person to sacrifice her life (e.g., to refuse to bear false witness even if she knows that will mean imminent death). But even if 'perfect duty' meant for Kant what 'duty' means for supererogationists, it would be misleading to regard him as a supererogationist. For although he holds that there are acts that are good to do yet beyond perfect duty, just as supererogationists hold that there are acts that are good to do yet beyond duty, the following difference remains: Kant holds that we are morally constrained to perform some such acts, while supererogationists do not. That this is a significant disagreement will emerge in this chapter and the next.

14. For an indication of why I add "meaningful," see the final paragraphs of this chapter.

BEFORE turning to the question of whether Kant's ethics leaves room for the supererogatory, we should take note of some differences among supererogationists. The differences concern the conditions under which an act is supererogatory. We may in fact distinguish two types of disagreements concerning these conditions.

First, supererogationists may differ (as may their critics) as to *what is morally required*. One might hold that we have only negative duties; acts of helping others are beyond the call of duty. Another might hold that although we are morally obligated to help others if we can do so at very little cost to ourselves, we are not obligated to go to much trouble to help others. Yet another supererogationist might maintain that only acts of tremendous self-sacrifice are supererogatory.

Second, supererogationists may, and in fact do, differ as to the conditions under which an act is *morally good*. An act does not qualify as supererogatory simply by being "optional," that is, neither required nor forbidden. It must also be morally good. But just what it takes to meet this condition is a matter of contention. In the view of some supererogationists, to be supererogatory the act must be performed "from altruistic rather than merely selfish motives."[15] David Heyd takes a different stand: although the intention of the act must be altruistic, that is, "conceived as benefiting another person (or persons),"[16] the motive need not be; it can, for example, be to gain fame. Another supererogationist emphasizes a different requirement: "Genuine supererogatory acts, like genuine acts of gift-giving, are inspired by something like benevolence and love. The saint and the hero in their different ways bestow upon others the free gift of their service." A supererogatory act is "done voluntarily, and out of love," not out of duty.[17]

This brief sketch of differences among supererogationists is merely

---

15. Michael Clark, "The Meritorious and the Mandatory," *Aristotelian Society*, new series, 79 (1978): 29. He uses the word 'meritorious' in this passage, but indicates on p. 23 that he uses 'meritorious' as synonymous with 'supererogatory'.

16. Heyd, *Supererogation*, p. 137.

17. Patricia McGoldrick, "Saints and Heroes: A Plea for the Supererogatory," *Philosophy* 59 (1984): 523–528. The quotations are from pp. 527–528. Although similar to the claim that a supererogatory act must be altruistic, her claim goes further in stressing that a supererogatory act is similar to (genuine) gift-giving in that it is wholly voluntary. (See Chap. 2, Sec. 5, below.)

that; my aim is to indicate that although they share the view I outlined above, they disagree, in some instances, as to the characterization of a supererogatory act and—this is different—as to whether a particular act qualifies. (It is different because we may agree on which acts are F yet disagree over what the criteria for F-ness are, or how to characterize F.) Some of these disagreements will be relevant to our evaluation of the question of whether Kant can accommodate the supererogatory.

Despite their differences, supererogationists are in broad agreement on the following points: (1) A supererogatory act is beyond duty, strictly optional, yet morally good. (2) Its moral goodness is not simply a function of the motive that prompts it; only certain sorts of acts, described without reference to the agent's motive, are even candidates for supererogatory acts. Finally, (3) supererogationists are in agreement as to what sorts of acts are paradigmatic supererogatory acts. These include Urmson's examples of a doctor's leaving home and a comfortable practice to work in a plague-ridden city, and a soldier's throwing himself on a live hand grenade to save his comrades. Also included are Heyd's example of Captain Oates of the Arctic expedition "sacrificing his life so as to secure his friends' survival,"[18] and that of Europeans, not targeted for extermination by the Nazis, hiding in their homes those who were so targeted.

With these preliminaries out of the way, I turn to the question of whether Kant's ethics leaves room for the supererogatory. I begin by examining an argument put forth by Thomas Hill Jr., from which I will build my case that Kant has no need for a special category of supererogatory acts.[19]

---

18. Heyd, *Supererogation,* p. 2.

19. Another Kant scholar who seeks to defend Kant by arguing that he has room for the category of the supererogatory is Onora O'Neill (then Nell). In a brief section of her book, *Acting on Principle: An Essay on Kantian Ethics* (New York: Columbia University Press, 1975), she suggests that attention to the fact that, for Kant, some but not all obligatory acts have moral worth discloses that Kant does have room for the category of the supererogatory. She argues as follows: "If one defines supererogatory acts as those which go beyond duty in the sense of doing *more* than is obligatory, then it would seem that acts which are obligatory and also morally worthy are acts of supererogation. If, on the other hand, like Eisenberg, one defines supererogatory acts as acts which though not obligatory are morally worthy, then Kant also can allow for these" (p. 96). The problem with this argument is that it takes the mark of a supererogatory act to be its moral worth. This is problematic both because of Kant's particular account of moral worth of actions and because it does not locate correctly what, on supererogationists' views, is distinctive about supererogatory acts.

For Kant, an act is morally worthy if and only if it is done from duty. But the mark of

3 In his very illuminating "Kant on Imperfect Duty and Supererogation," Hill argues that attention to Kant's classification of duties discloses that he can recognize the category of supererogatory acts.[20] Although I follow, by and large, his reading (and tidying up) of Kant's classifications and agree that they show Kant's ethics to be "less rigoristic than commonly thought,"[21] I do not think he establishes that Kant can accommodate the supererogatory. In the end he can locate a space for the supererogatory only by pressing Kant's ethics into a mold very alien to Kant, though very familiar to twentieth-century philosophers. In itself this need not be an objection, since it is certainly valuable to propose a friendly amendment to a major thinker's view, that is, an alteration that improves the view while leaving most of it intact (including, of course, what is central to it). I argue, however, that it is by no means clear either that the proposed modification improves Kant's ethics or that it leaves most of it intact.

In discussing Hill's argument I follow his explanation of Kant's distinction between perfect and imperfect duties rather than encumber this already complex discussion with an examination of exegetical questions concerning imperfect duties. That examination is postponed until Chapter 3, where I take up the question of how much latitude imperfect duties permit.

Hill tidies up Kant's classification by recognizing a subclass of imperfect duties, "wide" imperfect duties.[22] The class of supererogatory acts,

---

a supererogatory act is not that it is done from duty, or from anything else which we might hold to be an especially good motive. Although in the view of some supererogationists an act cannot qualify as supererogatory *unless* it is performed from the right sort of motive, others deny that this is required. In the first instance, furthermore, what they see as "the right sort of motive" is not the motive that, on Kant's view, confers upon an act moral worth.

Moreover, despite their disagreements concerning the moral goodness of acts, no supererogationists hold that an act's being performed from the right sort of motive *suffices* to render the act supererogatory. The mark of a supererogatory act is that it is strictly optional from the standpoint of duty; optional yet morally good, where its goodness is not determined simply by the motive.

20. Thomas E. Hill Jr., "Kant on Imperfect Duty and Supererogation," in his *Dignity and Practical Reason in Kant's Moral Theory* (Ithaca: Cornell University Press, 1992), pp. 147–175.

21. Ibid., p. 148.

22. Kant's terminology is looser than this, as Hill recognizes. The exegetical difficulties are brought out in Mary Gregor, *Laws of Freedom: A Study of Kant's Method of Applying the Categorical Imperative in the "Metaphysik der Sitten"* (Oxford: Basil Blackwell, 1963), chap. 7; in Paul Guyer, *Kant and the Experience of Freedom* (Cambridge: Cambridge University Press, 1993), chap. 10; as well as in Hill's "Kant on Imperfect Duty."

he suggests, is to be located among the wide imperfect duties. Wide imperfect duties differ from perfect duties in two respects. First, wide imperfect duties—indeed, all imperfect duties—are first and foremost duties to adopt a maxim or embrace a particular end.[23] Whereas perfect duties prescribe the actions we are to take (or omit), imperfect duties prescribe "only the *maxim of the action* . . . not the *action itself*" (*MM* 392).

Second, wide imperfect duties allow latitude not allowed to perfect duties. Hill distinguishes three types of latitude. Principles of wide imperfect duty allow each of the following:

(a) room for judgment in deciding whether or not a given principle is relevant to a particular situation . . . ,

(b) freedom to choose various ways of satisfying a principle in a particular situation once we decide that the principle applies [and]

(c) freedom to choose to do *x* or not on a given occasion, as one pleases, even though one knows that *x* is the sort of act that falls under the principle, provided that one is ready to perform acts of that sort on some other occasions.[24]

Principles of other imperfect duties—for example, duties of self-respect—allow latitude only of the types described in (a) and (b). Principles of perfect duties do not admit of latitude of the third type, and they allow less latitude of types (a) and (b) than do principles of imperfect duty. Thus, a principle of wide imperfect duty, for example, a principle of beneficence, not only leaves open what it is that I am to do when I act beneficently; it also permits me to omit altogether to act beneficently in certain circumstances in which I have an opportunity to help someone, provided that I act beneficently in other circumstances, and that I really have adopted a maxim of beneficence. Similarly for a principle of developing my talents. In contrast, principles of "narrow" imperfect duties, for example, duties to respect others, allow only the first type of latitude.

To sum up: imperfect duties, unlike perfect duties, are primarily duties to adopt a maxim. In addition, principles of wide imperfect duty allow greater latitude than do either perfect duties or narrow imperfect duties. They allow us to omit some actions that fall under the principle in question.

23. "Imperfect duties . . . are only *duties of virtue*," a duty of virtue being "an *end that is in itself a duty*," i.e., a duty to adopt a particular end (*MM* 390, 381).

24. Hill, "Kant on Imperfect Duty," p. 155.

To comprehend more fully the distinctions between perfect and imperfect duties and between wide and narrow imperfect duties, we should turn our attention to a more basic distinction in Kant's moral philosophy, the distinction between juridical and ethical duties.

The distinction between juridical and ethical duties is along one dimension quite crisp. Ethical duties do not entail corresponding rights to exercise compulsion; juridical duties (or "duties of *Right*") do (*MM* 383). Ethical duties, whether perfect or imperfect, imply no corresponding right to coerce us to fulfill them; indeed, it is impossible to coerce someone to fulfill an ethical duty. It has to be impossible, since the constraint entailed by an ethical duty is *self*-constraint (*MM* 380), and it has to be self-constraint because otherwise one would not, in acting morally, act freely. (This is tied to other differences: the constraint entailed by juridical duties can be merely external, while that entailed by ethical duties is internal; and while the doctrine of right dealt only with outer freedom [*MM* 380], ethics is concerned with inner freedom.)

This is the cleanest way of differentiating ethical from juridical duties. The other differences are scalar, and plot not only the juridical/ethical distinction but also the distinctions between perfect and imperfect duties and between narrow and wide imperfect duties. All three distinctions can be understood in terms of (1) the extent to which the duty is primarily a duty to perform an action, and the extent to which it is instead a duty primarily to embrace an end, and (2) the degree of latitude that a particular duty has.

If we envision a scale ranging from the most narrow duties to the widest, juridical duties are the narrowest and wide imperfect duties are the widest. Juridical duties are duties to perform particular actions; they involve no requirement that one's maxim in performing them be this rather than that, that one's end be that rather than this. By contrast, "Ethics does not give laws for *actions* (*Ius* does that), but only for *maxims* of actions" (*MM* 388). The distinction is less tidy than the quote suggests; in the case of wide imperfect duties, ethics gives laws only for maxims, and provides only very indirectly and with great latitude any indication as to what actions one is to perform. Narrow imperfect duties, as explained earlier, leave less latitude; perfect duties leave still less, and although even here ethics gives laws directly for maxims (requiring that one have or adopt certain ends) and not actions, the actions indirectly prescribed are more easily specifiable.

In sum, juridical duties, perfect duties, narrow imperfect duties, and wide imperfect duties differ primarily in degree of latitude. But in addition, juridical duties differ from ethical duties in that the former imply corresponding rights to exercise compulsion.

We return now to Hill's attempt to locate supererogatory acts among those that fulfill wide imperfect duties. He does not simply equate them with acts that fulfill wide imperfect duties. One reason why a simple equation would not do is that there are circumstances where an act that fulfills a wide imperfect duty will be mandatory ("e.g., if one who has continually neglected to help others is faced with his last opportunity").[25] The best candidate for a supererogatory act, Hill says, is an act that

(a) is of a sort commended by a principle of wider imperfect duty,
(b) is motivated by a sense of duty (or, perhaps, respect for moral reasons),
(c) is neither forbidden nor required by another, more stringent duty . . . ,
(d) is in a context where no alternative is required by more stringent duty and there is at least one alternative that is neither forbidden by more stringent duty nor commanded by other principles of wide duty, and
(e) is done by an agent who has adopted the relevant principle of wider imperfect duty and has often and continually acted on that principle.[26]

Has Hill shown that Kant has a place for supererogatory acts? That depends on what is meant by saying that Philosopher X has a place for supererogatory acts. One might mean that Philosopher X can, without inconsistency, recognize that there are particular acts that, in certain circumstances, it is good but not morally required to do. Alternatively, the speaker might be claiming something more, namely that Philosopher X can, without inconsistency, treat the category of the supererogatory as supererogationists ask that it be treated. In the first and weaker sense, Hill has shown that Kant has a place for supererogatory acts. Even this

---

25. There is a puzzle here: If I have continually neglected to help others, can I fulfill a principle of wide imperfect duty by helping someone now, when I see that it is my last chance? If I have never helped anyone until now, it is hard to claim that I have adopted a maxim of beneficence. It is not as if one could easily just fail to come across, or hear of, someone in need. One would have to go to considerable trouble to avoid occasions for acting beneficently. For an act of helping others to fulfill a principle of imperfect duty in the conditions Hill describes, it would have to be the case that the agent recently underwent a moral "rebirth," only then adopting a maxim of beneficence. He would have to have undergone a moral rebirth for his act of helping others, in the example, to fulfill an imperfect duty.

26. Hill, "Kant on Imperfect Duty," pp. 168–169.

needs qualification, however. Hill has shown that there are acts which it would be good to do but which one is not morally required to do—provided that 'acts' is understood to mean particular acts, not act-types. To the extent that Kant can recognize supererogatory acts, these are acts that can only be specified by reference to the particular context, including not only the agent's motives but also her past performance and her principles. We cannot, on the Kantian scheme as explicated by Hill, say that acts of helping others or acts of heroism are supererogatory; whether or not they are depends on the factors just mentioned.

Before taking further measure of the gap between what Hill has shown and what supererogationists want, we should note what his discussion clearly does establish. Urmson sought to show that some phenomena ("facts of morality," as he put it) simply cannot be accounted for by "this threefold classification"—of the morally required, the permitted, and the forbidden—or by "any classification that is merely a variation on or elaboration of it."[27] He cites saintly and heroic acts. Precisely because they are saintly and heroic, they seem not to fit into any of the three categories. Hill's exegesis makes plain that Kant's theory, clearly a "variation on or elaboration of" that threefold classification, *does* have a place for heroic and saintly acts. Dealing with them contextually, it treats them neither as duties nor as merely permitted but (except in circumstances where they are impermissible) as ways of (to put it loosely) fulfilling imperfect duties. More accurately, they are ways of living in accordance with the principles or maxims that the imperfect duties enjoin us to adopt.

Hill's detailed presentation of Kant's classifications demonstrates that a theory based on the threefold classification can be considerably more intricate than Urmson suggested. It also throws into relief that in at least one important respect Kant's classifications are richer than Urmson's. In addition to providing a place for the type of acts just mentioned, Kant's classifications allow one to distinguish between duties that can be exacted from one (the juridical duties) and those that cannot be (the ethical duties). By contrast, Urmson recognizes only the former type of duty.[28]

This is not to say that Hill has shown that Kant's theory is adequate to what Urmson terms "the facts of morality," but only that it can deal

27. Urmson, "Saints and Heroes," p. 60.
28. Urmson would not, however, recognize all juridical duties as duties, since some demand more than he would think it reasonable to demand.

with heroic and saintly acts in a more sophisticated and subtle way than Urmson recognized. To demonstrate that Kant can recognize supererogatory acts in this weak sense is thus not yet to satisfy the supererogationists. To see what objections they might have, let us look again at Hill's conditions (a)–(e). Many would object to conditions (b) and (e) on the ground that they overemphasize acting on principle. I think that all supererogationists would reject the stipulation that to be supererogatory an act must be performed from a sense of duty. Even if this were modified, as Hill parenthetically suggests, from "a sense of duty" to "respect for moral reasons," the requirement would very likely continue to be thought inappropriate by many. As noted earlier, Heyd explicitly allows that the motive may be a desire for fame, stipulating only that the intent must be altruistic. Although many supererogationists insist, contrary to Heyd, on a particular sort of motive, they too would object to (b) [and probably (e)], not primarily as too restrictive but as positively *disqualifying* the act, showing it to fail to be supererogatory. For them a supererogatory act involves an element of spontaneous giving. That spontaneity is undercut if the act is guided by the thought that it is in accordance with—a way of living by—the principles of imperfect duty. As supererogationists see it, it is rather like a child deciding to make a present for her mother, thinking to herself that she will, as a Campfire Girl, thereby earn a colorful bead to sew onto her Campfire jacket. The warmhearted gesture no longer seems to be quite that; the goodness of giving freely to another has been—as a supererogationist might see it— sullied by the thought that so acting meets certain requirements.

We might try revising Hill's criteria accordingly. But in addition to being an unpromising maneuver (since (e) would have to be altered in a way that would not square with the idea of locating the supererogatory among imperfect duties), it would at best solve only a small part of the problem. The real difficulty is that supererogationists are trying to get the discussion of heroic and saintly acts away from duty, but the Kantian analysis keeps pulling what is supposed to be "beyond" duty back under the rubric of duty. To satisfy supererogationists, one would have to show that Kant does not just have a cubbyhole somewhere for supererogatory acts but is able to accord them a proper place, and thus proper regard. Their idea is not that you are under no moral obligation right now to perform acts they think of as supererogatory provided that you perform acts of this sort on other occasions. It is not enough that you are under no obligation to perform such acts *right now*; you are to be under no obligation *ever* to perform such acts. Even if conditions (b) and (e) were waived, the Kantian approach would not be what supererogationists want. Supererogationists do not want supererogatory acts to be thought of as just one way—even an exceptionally admirable way—of abiding by the principles of imperfect duty; they want us to see such acts as *beyond* duty.

Hill realizes this, I think, for he notes that condition (b) seems to require that "one can do something supererogatory only if he mistakenly thinks that it is his duty." He proposes a modification of Kant's position: "In reply we might suggest that it is not an unreasonable extension of Kant's position to say that what is required for moral worth is not a motive to do one's *duty* but a motive to do what is demanded *or encouraged* by moral considerations" (my emphasis). The nature of the proposal becomes clearer when he takes note of a similar difficulty concerning (e). "How, one may wonder, can I be going 'beyond duty' if I am guided by a principle of duty?" His response underscores his view that Kant's terminology does not aptly express his true position.

> Kant's terminology of "imperfect" and "perfect" duty does confuse the issues. It is as if Kant started to work out a moral theory on the model of legal-like strict duties, and then, discovering that there is more to morality than duty, still retained the old labels for types of duty rather than spoil the symmetry of his theory by changing to more natural expressions. For example, what Kant is concerned to say about beneficence is (i) it is a duty to adopt a maxim of beneficence, and therefore (ii) it is a duty to promote the happiness of others sometimes, but also (iii) when one has satisfied these minimum and rather indefinite requirements, one may promote their happiness or not, as one pleases, but to do so with the proper motive will always be of positive moral worth. Kant tried to say all of this with his restrictive terminology of duty when it could be put more simply by making an early distinction between what is obligatory and what is merely good to do.[29]

Hill is suggesting that Kant would do better to distinguish between what is obligatory and what is merely good to do. His proposal would have the effect of narrowing the scope of duty so that certain acts that Kant sees as fulfilling our imperfect duties count instead as supererogatory. Is this a proposal that Kant would (or should) welcome?

The proposal, we should note, would still not satisfy many

29. Hill, "Kant on Imperfect Duty," p. 172.

supererogationists. As noted above, it recognizes supererogatory acts only contextually. Whether one has performed a supererogatory act will depend not just on the act but also on one's past conduct. In addition, the act must be performed from "the proper motive" to count as supererogatory; condition (b), it appears, is left intact. Keeping these points in mind, let us turn to the question of whether Kant would (or should) welcome Hill's proposed revision, a revision that would at least go *some* way toward satisfying the supererogationist.

4 One set of reasons for thinking that Kant would reject Hill's proposal—and, more generally, any proposal to allow a place in his theory for a category of supererogatory acts—can be gleaned from the Methodology of the *Critique of Practical Reason*. Kant is concerned in that section with the question of how "we can make the objectively practical reason also subjectively practical" or, in other words, how "we can secure to the laws of pure practical reason access to the human mind and an influence on its maxims" (*PrR* 151). After proposing that "educators of youth" present their subjects with examples from biographies, so that "by comparing similar actions under various circumstances, they could begin to exercise the moral judgments of their pupils in marking the greater or less moral significance of the actions," Kant remarks:

> But I wish they would spare them examples of so-called noble (super-meritorious) actions, which so fill our sentimental writings, and would refer everything to duty only and the worth which a man can and must give himself in his own eyes through the consciousness of not having transgressed his duty, since whatever runs up into empty wishes and longings for unattainable perfection produces mere heroes of romance, who, while priding themselves on their feeling of transcendent greatness, release themselves from observing the common and everyday responsibility as petty and insignificant.[30]

Lacking the glamour of heroic deeds, "everyday responsibility" may seem petty and insignificant, unworthy of our attention. Kant points out that a focus on the supermeritorious may lead us to release ourselves from routine moral requirements. One can imagine various ways this might happen: such moral requirements may just not capture our attention; they may not motivate us, because we associate morality with

30. *PrR* 155. See also R 48–49/44.

spectacular deeds and see everyday moral requirements as trivial, not even part of *real* morality; or we may regard ourselves as special, too great to bother with jejune moral requirements. ("You criticize me for yelling at you and the kids after a hard day at work? You?! All you do is stay home with the kids, when I risk my life daily as a cop!")

Although Kant does not develop the point, his observations suggest the danger that one may come to feel that supererogatory acts substitute for moral requirements. Worse yet, it may be very tempting so to substitute (at least if one chooses supererogatory acts of the nonheroic, nonsaintly variety). One can puff up with self-satisfaction at having done something "extra" for someone; it is not as easy to feel smug and superior about doing what, one believes, anyone in those circumstances is morally required to do.

Kant's own concern is slightly different, blending two worries: (1) We may pride ourselves on feelings of transcendent greatness, substituting apparently meritorious feelings—"empty wishes and longings for unattainable perfection"—for action. (2) We may release ourselves from everyday responsibility because we think we are special, too great for such trivialities.

The first is a version of a familiar theme in Kant's ethics, bound up with his antiromanticism: instead of taking action, we content ourselves with noble sentiments. Thus, instead of helping the needy, we feel sorry for them (perhaps so intensely sad that we feel that we cannot bear the sadness, and must stay away from subjects that remind us of the needy). We suppose that we are very good people because we feel so sad for them. This is wrong. We should not think that because our sentiments are noble, our "hearts in the right place," our characters and conduct are as they should be. Although we are not virtuous if we merely do what is right, we are also not virtuous if we merely feel as we should, without troubling to help.

In Chapter 6 I will discuss this theme in connection with Kant's claim that we have a duty to cultivate our sympathetic impulses. I will say no more about it here, because the point that Kant develops from it in his remarks on moral education and the supermeritorious poses far less serious problems for the supererogationist than do the other concerns that are suggested by the same passages. Another concern should be added to those discussed. If moral education emphasizes heroic deeds, morality may seem too remote and, for the most part, optional. This is closely tied to Kant's conviction, reiterated throughout the second

Critique, that the motive of duty is weakened by romantic enthusiasm for "actions called noble, magnanimous, and meritorious" (*PrR* 157). The thought behind this remark is suggested by the following passage:

> The mind is disposed to nothing but blatant moral fanaticism and exaggerated self-conceit by exhortation to actions as noble, sublime, and magnanimous. By it people are led to the illusion that the determining ground of their actions is not duty, i.e., respect for the law. . . . This law always humbles them when they follow (obey) it, but by this kind of exhortation they come to think that those actions are expected of them not because of duty but only because of their own bare merit. (*PrR* 84–85)

The danger is that people will see morality as something that makes a claim on them only because they are special (noble, meritorious). Either they will not see themselves as constrained by morality, regarding themselves instead as volunteers; or they will see themselves as constrained, but only because of their merit—a version of noblesse oblige.[31] Morality will seem optional or, alternatively, incumbent only on the noble. Thus there are two dangers, and they are heightened by the fact that not everyone will see himself or herself as noble—and thus morality may seem to be something that concerns only others. Indeed, if identified too closely with heroic feats, morality might come to be thought of as a sort of spectator sport, or perhaps as a profession. It would be one of a number of fields in which those with a special gift for it might excel, but one that is beyond the reach of most.[32] This is, of course, very much at odds with Kant's conception of morality as within everyone's reach and incumbent on all.

Some might dismiss Kant's worries about an emphasis on the supererogatory, deeming them silly and far-fetched. I don't think that they are silly, and indeed, reflection on our own society lends some evidence to the concern that supererogatory acts may be seen as more important than, and perhaps as substituting for, morality's requirements.[33] According to popular, although usually unarticulated, dogma, a

31. See *PrR* 82 for remarks on viewing oneself as a moral volunteer.

32. Interestingly, David Heyd sees it as an argument in *support* of supererogation that "supererogatory action breaks out of the impersonal and egalitarian framework of the morality of duty" (*Supererogation*, p. 175).

33. The notion that the special merit of supererogatory acts could cancel out the moral "debt" incurred by a failure to fulfill a moral requirement was implicit in medieval Church doctrine, according to which the penitent could be absolved without fulfilling his penance (provided that he gave money to the Church, joined the Crusades, or did whatever else the current conditions for indulgences stipulated). Aquinas and Bonaventure emphasized that

husband need not feel guilty about treating his wife more like a pet than
a person if he buys her expensive gifts; and (something of an extension of
this) we need not worry too much about how badly underpaid secretaries
are since we have Secretaries' Week. (And it is much more fun to give a
present to those in an inferior role than to try to bring it about that they
cease to occupy an inferior position!) To take a different example, we all
know that extreme poverty and social injustice abound, and most of us
believe that they are not ineradicable; but to offer some surplus food or
old clothes to the poor is much easier and less threatening than working
to alter the conditions that make poverty and inequality social institutions. Acts of charity toward those who occupy an inferior social and
economic position have their own distinctive gratification.

In developing this point I have in mind a passage from the *Doctrine of
Virtue*. In the section on beneficence Kant queries:

> Having the means to practice such beneficence as depends on the goods
> of fortune is, for the most part, a result of certain men being favored
> through the injustice of the government, which introduces an inequality of
> wealth that makes others need their beneficence. Under such circum-
> stances, does the rich man's help to the needy, on which he so readily
> prides himself as something meritorious, really deserve to be called benefi-
> cence at all? (*MM* 454)[34]

I take it that Kant would be all the more worried if alongside (or instead
of) the imperfect duties we had a category of supererogatory acts. For
although the imperfect/perfect distinction may make it easy for us to
regard some of our duties as wide and imperfect when in fact the
sociohistorical underpinnings of the situation indicate that we may well
have something closer to a duty of justice (a perfect duty), at least it offers
no special temptation to dismiss them as not really duties at all.[35]

---

the penance was not canceled but paid: the debt was paid from the Church's treasury,
which stored the extra merit from the supererogatory acts of Jesus, Mary, and the saints.
See P. F. Palmer, "Indulgences," in the *New Catholic Encyclopedia*, vol. 7 (1967), pp. 482–
484. David Heyd has an interesting discussion of the theological issues concerning
supererogation in chap. 1 of his *Supererogation*. As he points out, Kant's thinking was
undoubtedly influenced by Martin Luther's attack not only on the system of indulgences
but on the underlying doctrine of supererogation.

34. See also n. 1 in the Methodology (*PrR*); *E* 490–491/104–105; and "Duties Towards
Others" in *LE*.

35. In the *Doctrine of Right* Kant defends taxing the wealthy to "provide the means of
sustenance to those who are unable to provide for even their most necessary natural needs"
(*MM* 326). The wealthy have "acquired an obligation to the commonwealth, since they
owe their existence to an act of submitting to its protection and care, which they need in

It may seem unfair to supererogationists to allude to ubiquitous abuses of the notion, even if they are ubiquitous, and are the very sorts of abuses Kant worried about. After all, an argument against an abuse of a notion is not a good argument in favor of giving up the notion. If we firmly reject the suggestion that one stores up 'credit' through one's supererogatory acts and if heroism is not emphasized too much in moral education, why suppose that we need to abandon the category of the supererogatory?

To be sure, this argument has merit. But it should also be borne in mind that it is not an easy matter to reject, as a culture, a self-serving (and barely articulated) belief; in this case, the notion that good deeds make up for failure to take morality's requirements seriously.[36] And in a society like ours which encourages self-indulgence, self-flattery, and competitiveness, a "point-system" of morality, with its suggestion that one can (especially if one has money) buy one's way out of morality's requirements through acts of "generosity," may be difficult to resist.[37] This is surely relevant to the issue at hand. As noted, whether or not we need a category of the supererogatory is to be determined primarily by its explanatory value and its practical value; and the points above are clearly relevant to the latter. In sum, although they do not show that we must reject the category of the supererogatory, these considerations provide reason for insisting on hearing just why it is supposed to be so important to recognize a special category of the supererogatory. But before canvassing the supererogationist arguments, we have other Kantian objections to consider.

---

order to live; on this obligation the state now bases its right to contribute what is theirs to maintaining their fellow citizens" (*MM* 326). Kant emphasizes that this sustenance is to be provided for "by way of coercion, by public taxation, not merely by *voluntary* contributions." He includes under the heading of voluntary contributions "lotteries, which produce more poor people and more danger to public property than there would otherwise be, and which should therefore not be permitted" (*MM* 326).

36. Nor is it clear that supererogationists always want this to be rejected. Indeed, Heyd suggests that although we should reject one platform of the Church doctrine on supererogation, i.e., that moral 'credit' can be transferred from one person to another, "the model itself may serve—*mutatis mutandis*—as an illustration of what is meant by 'merit', namely, a certain surplus which is credited to the agent" (see Heyd, *Supererogation*, p. 140). Thus, the central idea that the agent has earned 'extra credit' persists.

37. Cf. Feinberg's discussion of a point-system conception of morality in "Supererogation and Rules." See also Mordecai Nisan, "Moral Balance: A Model of How People Arrive at Moral Decisions," in *The Moral Domain: Essays in the Ongoing Discussion between Philosophy and the Social Sciences*, ed. Thomas E. Wren (Cambridge: MIT Press, 1990), pp. 283–314. Nisan argues that our moral deliberations reflect a point-system conception of morality.

The second set of objections brings us to the heart of the matter, for they oppose dividing what Kant means by 'duty' into what one really must do and what, as Hill puts it, it would be good to do. Kant's opposition to such fragmentation is not, to my knowledge, ever explicitly stated, but it can easily be extrapolated from the texts. First, and related to the objections mentioned above, such fragmentation makes much of morality *optional*. It introduces a division, a fence around what "I may choose, as I please," separating it from what I "have to" do. I have done "my duty" (conceived, following Hill's suggestion, more narrowly than Kant wanted it); now my time, my choices are all mine (except, of course, for the constraints of perfect duties). Any other attention to morality is, for me, strictly optional.

This is all quite alien to Kant's ethics. There is no clear line of demarcation between what I must do, morally, and what is nice but morally optional. Nor does Kant attempt to trace such a line of demarcation. To do so he would have to give up a central thesis: that we have a duty to strive to perfect ourselves morally. This duty, which we cannot escape by being "good enough," underlies our other imperfect duties. To give it up would be to alter, quite radically, the structure of his moral scheme. I will say more in Chapters 2 and 3 about the role of this duty in the overall structure. Here I simply document that he does hold that we have such a duty.

One might have thought that moral self-improvement would be, on Kant's view, just one of various ways of honoring the imperfect duty of perfecting oneself. Since he includes under the heading of self-perfection cultivating "the powers of the body," improving one's memory, and so on, we might expect that one does not neglect the end of self-perfection if, say, one chooses to focus on developing one's mathematical talents and to let one's character develop or rot as it may. But in fact he specifies that we have a duty to strive to be morally better. "However evil a man has been up to the very moment of an impending free act . . . it was not only his duty to have been better . . . it is *now* still his duty to better himself" (R 41/36). In the *Doctrine of Virtue* he asserts that we have a duty to be virtuous and declares that "the first command of all duties to oneself" is to "*know* (scrutinize, fathom) *yourself* . . . in terms of your moral perfection" (MM 441).[38] ("Only the descent into the hell of self-knowledge can pave the way to godliness" [MM 441].) And, to give an

---

38. See also *PrR* 33.

example of a somewhat more specific requirement to better ourselves morally: under the heading "On the duty of love to other men" he writes that "we have an indirect duty to cultivate the compassionate . . . feelings in us" (*MM* 457).

Because we have a duty to improve ourselves morally—because we are not permitted to become complacent about our characters—the imperfect duties cannot be seen as admitting of a plateau, a point beyond which more conduct of the same sort is supererogatory. As Warner Wick remarks, the imperfect duties "not only allow us considerable leeway in achieving their objectives, but they are indefinite in the further sense that what they demand is also without assignable limits. We may never say, 'There, I have at last done all that I ought to do for other people.'"[39] Similarly, we are never to decide, "I'm now such a good person that the duty to improve oneself morally no longer applies to me."

The central difference between this approach and that taken by supererogationists lies not in the deeds required, but in the fact that imperfect duties are primarily duties to have certain maxims (the having of which will then direct one's actions to some extent, but in no very determinate way). The difference can be brought out by noting a subtle tension in Hill's account of what Kant "is concerned to say about beneficence." After saying that "it is a duty," on Kant's view, "to adopt a maxim of beneficence," and that this entails a duty of promoting the happiness of others sometimes, Hill says that according to Kant, "when one has satisfied these minimum and rather indefinite requirements, one may promote their happiness or not, as one pleases."[40] But it is not entirely as one pleases; if it were, virtue would be optional and the duty to improve oneself would be incumbent only on those who, morally speaking, are especially derelict. Morality would indeed be minimal.

On Kant's picture one cannot both have a maxim of beneficence and regard one's "work" as over. This is not because having the maxim of beneficence entails the odd mind-set of Susan Wolf's moral saints, who strive to do as much good as possible and to make their every action as virtuous as possible.[41] But although a maxim of beneficence does not require that one seek to maximize with respect to the happiness of others,

39. See his introduction to Immanuel Kant, *Ethical Philosophy* (Indianapolis: Hackett, 1983), p. li.

40. Hill, "Kant on Imperfect Duty," p. 172.

41. Susan Wolf, "Moral Saints," *Journal of Philosophy* 79 (1982): 419–439. See also R. M. Adams's reply, "Saints," *Journal of Philosophy* 81 (1984): 392–400.

neither does it permit one to say, 'Ah, I've met my weekly quota; now I can relax'. Having this maxim is incompatible with drawing a line around one's "own life" or "own projects" and seeing morality the way one might see mowing the lawn (or as a child might see doing his homework or performing his Boy Scout deeds): as something to get out of the way.

SOMEONE might suggest that we can avoid the egocentric, self-satisfied approach without completely rebuffing the supererogationist. We can do so if we retain Kant's category of imperfect duties for routine, nonheroic beneficent acts, while relegating to the supererogatory the spectacular deeds (on which Urmson laid so much emphasis): hurling oneself onto a live hand grenade in order to protect one's buddies, rushing into a burning building in the hopes of saving the people in it, leaving one's home and comfortable medical practice to work in a plague-ridden area, and so on.[42] This would, in effect, narrow the scope of the supererogatory but at least recognize the category.

This revised proposal is an improvement over the original. It preserves the notion that we continue to have a duty to strive to be virtuous even if we are, morally speaking, well above average, and it recognizes duties to help others. But it limits those duties, for it says that we need not go to any considerable trouble to be virtuous or to help others. The assumption here seems to be that if acts are only hard enough for us, they should be regarded as optional.[43] This assumption needs to be examined.

Many people no doubt accept this assumption and believe that any decent ethical theory will honor it. But there are good reasons, which Elizabeth Pybus develops in a discussion of Urmson's "Saints and Heroes," for questioning the wisdom of building such an assumption into moral theory. Pybus notes that there are a great many acts (not just those for which people are given special medals) which require considerable courage. Take, for instance, the agoraphobe who does an elderly neighbor's shopping. She "is just as brave as the heroic soldier" and "might even find the death threatened by the grenade less frightening." The relevance of this observation becomes apparent when we remind ourselves of what is at issue and what questions we should be asking.

---

42. The first and third examples are from Urmson, "Saints and Heroes."
43. It does not logically require the assumption, but its motivation derives from it.

Since what is at issue is whether ethical theory needs to recognize a category of supererogatory acts, we need to ask whether acts of a certain sort, for example, acts that require great courage, are, as a class, beyond duty. As Pybus says, "We should not ask whether the action of throwing oneself on a grenade is beyond the call of duty, but whether actions of a certain sort, viz., very brave ones, are beyond the call of duty. And they are not. Clearly we cannot slide out of doing our duty by saying that we are not brave enough. Sometimes we may be excused for a loss of nerve, but we cannot remain cowards all our lives, and use that as an acceptable excuse for fulfilling only the basic requirements of morality."[44]

The case is all the clearer when we look at other moral requirements, for example, to be just or beneficent. Imagine someone saying, "I'm sorry; I'm just not the giving type. That may be easy for others; I'm just selfish, so you can't expect me to help you in times of need." Or: "Fairness isn't my forte. It's unreasonable to expect it of me when it's so hard for me, so contrary to my nature. Give me something easier to do." As Pybus points out, and as Kant held, morality is pervasive: we cannot just complete certain chores (picking the ones that best fit our temperament), and then be off the hook.

Still, someone might suggest, perhaps the assumption *should* be accepted, if suitably understood so that only very difficult deeds count as too difficult, and therefore optional. (On this suggestion, helping others in times of need would not generally qualify as too difficult, even for the very selfish.) After all, the objection continues, isn't that assumption the essence of Kant's celebrated principle, " 'Ought' implies 'can' "?

The answer to this is an unequivocal *No*. Kant's famous principle *is* often cited as support for a claim that we must not regard too much as our duty, but his point was not the contraposition of the dictum—that if we cannot do *x*, we have no duty to do *x*—but rather that if we ought to do it, we *can* do it. "When the moral law commands that we *ought* now to be better men, it follows inevitably that we must *be able* to be better men" (R 50–51/46).[45] He was calling not for a shrinking of duty but for a recognition that we are much more capable than we suppose, and that usually we are not honest with ourselves if we say "I just couldn't help it" or "It's too much for me." Far from endorsing the assumption that acts

44. Elizabeth Pybus, "Saints and Heroes," *Philosophy* 57 (1982): 193–199. The quote is from p. 198. In citing this passage I am uneasy about "basic." That I would have put the word in scare quotes may reveal a difference between Pybus's views and mine.

45. See also R 47–48/43, and PrR 159.

that are very difficult for us should be regarded as optional, Kant's principle emphasizes that *difficult* does not mean *impossible*.

The conflict between the assumption and Kant's ethics runs still deeper. To regard all acts that are very difficult for me as acts that I cannot perform would be, on his view, to undermine my freedom (more specifically, to act as if my particular fears, desires, and aversions positively preclude that I perform certain acts, and therefore to act as if I am not free). In Arthur Miller's *The Crucible*, John Proctor refuses on pain of death to provide a public "confession" to witchcraft, realizing that to confess would lend an air of legitimacy to the Salem witch trials. To apply here a point that Kant makes in the second *Critique*: we may not know whether we would act similarly in such circumstances but we know that we could, and in recognizing that we are capable of so acting we recognize our freedom. Kant says the following concerning someone asked to imagine that he is threatened with death by his sovereign unless he makes "a false deposition against an honorable man whom the ruler wished to destroy under a plausible pretext": "that it would be possible for him [to refuse] he would certainly admit without hesitation. He judges, therefore, that he can do something because he knows that he ought, and he recognizes that he is free—a fact which, without the moral law, would have remained unknown to him" (*PrR* 30).

THE reason mentioned above for rejecting Hill's amendment to Kant's ethics focuses on the fact that one may not, on Kant's view, adopt a policy of never doing anything to help others which one finds extremely difficult or distasteful. In that sense, saintly and heroic acts are, as a class, not beyond duty. But there is yet another sense in which they are not beyond duty, and this consideration provides further reason for believing that Kant would reject Hill's proposal.

The sense of duty is supposed to govern all of our conduct, unifying and harmonizing our various aims and maxims. But if we recognize as a special category acts that are beyond duty, this would tend to limit the scope, and thus the contribution, of the sense of duty. The sense of duty alerts us to moral questions concerning admirable conduct, to issues we are otherwise likely to miss. If heroic and saintly acts are viewed as beyond duty, they seem to be, as good acts, off in a realm unto themselves. We tend not to weigh their merits against potentially competing considerations, nor to ask whether the actions are in conflict with some duty. More importantly, we do not expect the agents to do this; indeed, hesitation or caution about such acts is thought of, rather, as showing a lack of bravery.[46] In the domain of nonheroic supererogatory acts there is a similar (although somewhat weaker) expectation that these acts are always good to do. After all, they are nice, well-intentioned and (let us suppose) backed by real goodness; what could be objectionable?[47] The problem is that sometimes acts that seem and perhaps *are* noble and meritorious (or just plain nice) are contrary to duty. Heroic acts will sometimes violate a duty to oneself, and favors done (unbidden) for others may leave them with an unwanted sense of having burdened us, of being indebted to us, or (as when I help the child next door too much with her homework) with too little self-sufficiency.

Acts of heroism are typically thought of as off in a realm unto themselves, and it is no wonder that they are. We admire the qualities that enable a person to dive in midwinter into the Potomac in an effort to save the victims of a plane crash. And we are grateful that people with such qualities (courage, willingness to risk their lives to help others, etc.) exist. The fact that we (correctly) admire and appreciate such people is, however, no reason for thinking that their heroic actions are inevitably right. Suppose (imagining a case different from the actual one of 1982) that the would-be rescuer is almost certain to drown, as well as not to save anyone. (If this isn't good enough, suppose the agent is as likely to impede the person in danger of drowning as to help him.) As Kant points

---

46. Traditionally, and still in vogue in some circles today, the word for this has been 'effeminacy'. The idea that it is unmanly to have second thoughts about, e.g., rushing into a burning building to rescue someone, may lurk behind the assumption that such acts are invariably good.

Judging from the philosophical literature on supererogation, there appears to be a link between supererogation and the traditional male domain. The favorite examples of supererogatory acts—e.g., a soldier throwing himself on a hand grenade—tend to be those that exhibit a remarkable degree of some masculine virtue, or a virtue, masculine or not, expressed in the context of traditionally masculine activity. Not only are feminine virtues dramatically underrepresented, Heyd (and earlier Urmson) explicitly discounts a mother's "great sacrifice for her child." It is not "strictly speaking" supererogatory, Heyd explains, because it pertains "to the sphere of natural relationships and instinctive feelings (which lie outside morality)" (*Supererogation*, p. 134).

47. Often the function of moral principles and reflection is thought to be that of a corrective to "defective" tendencies and impulses: cowardice, malice, spite, and so on. I discuss this view in Chap. 4. One of Kant's contributions was to emphasize that moral scrutiny is needed even with respect to acts of kindness. No acts should be thought of as, in that sense, beyond duty.

out, the mere fact that an act is self-sacrificial and admirable does not entail that it is good to do or that one ought ideally to do it.[48]

We need, in short, to disentangle the admirable from the right. A mode of conduct may be admirable in that it points to a virtuous character trait, and yet wrong. An act may be right, though not particularly admirable. An emphasis on the supererogatory makes it difficult to keep the two distinct.

In the foregoing I have presented a number of reasons for thinking that inclusion of the category of the supererogatory in Kantian ethics would be undesirable.[49] Although in some instances these considerations may seem pertinent only for Kantian ethics and perhaps moving only to Kant, some of the objections have, I think, broader application and appeal. Their compellingness, however, must be weighed against considerations that support inclusion of the category of the supererogatory in ethical theory. Are there reasons for including it which outweigh the objections presented above?

5   One common argument is that an ethical theory without the category, such as Kant's, fails to accord with our commonsense intuitions and with our ordinary use of the word 'duty'. Appealing to "common

48. At *MM* 423 Kant begins his casuistical questions concerning suicide by asking: "Is it murdering oneself to hurl oneself to certain death (like Curtius) in order to save one's country? Or is deliberate martyrdom, sacrificing oneself for the good of all mankind, also to be considered an act of heroism?" *Vigilantius* suggests much graver misgivings about sacrificing one's life for the sake of others: "It is permissible to risk one's life, where there is a danger of losing it, but I can never be allowed to sacrifice my life intentionally or to kill myself in fulfillment of a duty to others. For example, Curtius's throwing himself into the pit in order to preserve the Roman people is contrary to duty; a soldier who opposes enemy forces, on the other hand, is merely risking his life, just as the sailor, fisherman, and other people with dangerous occupations are risking their lives" (*V* 629–630). I am grateful to Mario von der Ruhr for help in translating this passage. See also *PrR* 158.

49. There is, however, some indication that Kant was willing at least at one point to recognize supererogatory acts and indeed to use the label. Vigilantius recorded in his notes on Kant's lectures that Kant used the expression '*opus supererogationis*'. The claim in which the expression is said to have occurred is a curious one. According to Vigilantius, Kant claimed that while parents are obligated to feed their children, to educate their children to the point where they can support themselves is an *opus supererogationis*. (He went on to say, according to *Vigilantius*, that therein lies the basis for the duty of gratitude that children have to their parents: in the fact that the parents performed this *opus supererogationis*.) ["Die Erziehung der Kinder aber bis zu ihrer Selbstversorgung, d.i. eine so geordnete Bildung, dadurch Kinder mit ihrem Zustande Zufriedenheit und Wohlgefallen an ihrer Existenz erhalten, ist ein opus supererogationis der Eltern" (*V* 670).]

opinion," Paul Eisenberg states that many of the actions or modes of conduct which Kant regards as duties "are in fact . . . acts of supererogation."[50] One of his examples is the duty (or alleged duty) to promote the happiness of others. Appeal to common opinion is often dubious; on issues of whether we have to promote the happiness of others or whether it is optional, common opinion is decidedly suspect. This is one area where ethics should hope to do more than articulate the common opinions of what is, in our case, a rather self-centered and ungenerous society.

Other arguments turn on the importance of maintaining minimal standards of moral decency and community harmony while also recognizing personal autonomy and the need, on the part of individuals, not to be overburdened by societal and moral demands. Urmson offers the following five reasons "why our code should distinguish between basic rules, summarily set forth in simple rules and binding on all, and the higher flights of morality of which saintliness and heroism are outstanding examples":

1. It is critical that certain moral demands be given a "special status" and that "exceptional pressure" be exerted to secure compliance to them.
2. "Basic duties . . . must be . . . within the capacity of the ordinary man."
3. "A moral code . . . must be formulable . . . in rules of manageable complexity," and rules regarding when one must nurse sick neighbors or help out in leper colonies cannot be so simply formulated.
4. "A line must be drawn between what we can expect and demand from others and what we can merely hope for and receive with gratitude when we get it."
5. It is "better that pressure should not be applied" when not necessary, that is, when no "fundamental matters" are concerned.[51]

There are a number of problems with Urmson's arguments, most notably that they seem to apply more to club rules than to ethics. Unless

50. Eisenberg, "Basic Ethical Categories," pp. 267–268. It has become common to speak as if there is nothing problematic in the supposition that one condition of adequacy for moral theories is that they must not make excessive demands on us. For an insightful discussion of this notion of "excessive demands," see Norman Care, "Career Choices," *Ethics* 94 (1984): 283–302, especially sec. 5; reprinted in Care, *Sharing Fate* (Philadelphia: Temple University Press, 1987).

51. Urmson, "Saints and Heroes," pp. 70–72.

we grant that morality is a matter of "codes" and that for it to be *S*'s duty to φ, it must be appropriate for someone or other to apply pressure to secure *S*'s compliance, (3) and (5) are beside the point. Since (4) begs the question, we are left with (1) and (2). Now, (1) and (2) are plausible.[52] Indeed, if we leave out the bit about exerting pressure, a Kantian would find them unobjectionable.[53] But although plausible enough as claims, they offer no more support for inclusion of the category of the supererogatory in ethics than for leaving things as Kant left them. They support recognition of imperfect duties as much as they support the thesis in whose defense they are put forth.[54]

The same holds for some of David Heyd's arguments. He defends supererogationism on the grounds that "society cannot require of the individual every act that would promote the general good, and . . . the individual has the right to satisfy his wants and to achieve his ends and ideals regardless of their social utility (with some obvious limitations, of course)."[55] We needn't examine the argument for this claim, for if successful, the claim provides as much support for the thesis that ethical theories should distinguish imperfect duties from perfect duties as it does for the supererogationist thesis that it purports to establish.[56] Our imperfect duties do not require that we subordinate all of our other ends to the general good.

52. I here ignore a difficulty with (2) but take it up in the next chapter: just what does Urmson mean by "within the capacity"? His attempt to clarify (2) only complicates matters, for he gives as examples of rules that ask more than the ordinary person (or man?) is capable of the prohibition laws in the United States and the gambling laws in Britain. But surely it is not beyond the capacity of the ordinary person (assuming that the ordinary person is not supposed to be an alcoholic) to abstain from liquor and dice! Urmson gets into this difficulty through his conflation of moral demands with social and legal demands.

53. Although a Kantian would find them unobjectionable, the Kantian and Urmson accept (2) for rather different reasons. They both accept (2) because 'ought' implies 'can'; but they understand that famous principle differently. Urmson's point is that we must take care lest we count as a duty something that is too hard. Kant's point, as I pointed out in Sec. 4, is that if we ought to do it, we can do it: *difficult* does not mean *impossible*.

54. For further discussion of problems with Urmson's arguments, see, in addition to Chap. 2 of the present work, Heyd, *Supererogation*, pp. 166–167, Clark, "Meritorious and Mandatory," pp. 27–29; and Pybus's "Saints and Heroes."

55. Heyd, *Supererogation*, p. 166. Michael Clark offers a similar argument in "Meritorious and Mandatory."

56. Heyd's argument rests on a false dichotomy between two conceptions of a morality of duty: "a system of requirements aiming at the maximization of general good or happiness" and "a means of securing some minimal conditions of cooperation and justice" (*Supererogation*, p. 174). Kantian ethics, which he presumably counts as a "morality of duty," is neither.

But Heyd also claims that "supererogation can be proved to have moral value by pointing out the freedom of the individual involved in purely optional choice, the social cohesion resulting from supererogatory behaviour and the rationality of voluntary altruistic behaviour."[57] Insofar as performance of imperfect duties is not purely optional, this claim (or part of it) would seem to provide an argument for supererogation stronger than the correlative argument for imperfect duties. It rests, however, on the controversial (and in the context of our discussion, question-begging) assumption that freedom is incompatible with, or at least diminished by, moral constraint. Kant of course denies that there is a conflict between freedom and moral constraint. On a Kantian view, the fact that supererogatory acts are purely optional while imperfect duties are not is of little relevance.[58]

Heyd also suggests that social cohesion results from supererogatory behavior. A member of a group, he explains, "shows that he has an interest in his fellow members which is deeper than his contractual commitments, or than the personal benefit he can draw from his membership in the group" when he does "more than is required." This, in turn, improves the relations between the members of the group: the relations "become more friendly, personal, and based on good will."[59] Two points are in order here. First, it is clear that many acts that fulfill imperfect duties will equally express this willingness to do more than the bare moral minimum. Second, his claim rests on a familiar but questionable picture of obligations. We tend to assume that obligations can best (or only) be seen on a contractual and individualist model, where one regards one's obligations as a sort of burden that one must undertake in order to get what one wants. This is indeed the way contemporary philosophy and contemporary American commonsense morality typically see obligation, but it may not be the best way. In *Kant's Moral Teleology*, Thomas Auxter draws a striking contrast between the con-

---

57. Heyd, *Supererogation*, p. 166. I do not discuss the claim about the rationality of altruistic behavior. I find no argument or explication of it in Heyd, unless it is (despite what he says) part of an argument for the claim that a particular argument against supererogation is unsuccessful, rather than an argument that supererogation has positive moral worth.

58. Heyd also puts forth the following consideration: "Such a freedom allows for the exercise of individual traits of character and for the expression of one's personal values and standards of moral behaviour" (*Supererogation*, 175). But imperfect duties equally allow for this.

59. Heyd, *Supererogation*, p. 179.

notations of 'obligation' and those of the German equivalent, *Verbindlichkeit*:

> In English the sense of obligation is a "requirement that compels," "an action imposed by which one is bound or restrained," or "a constraining power." The source of this requirement, compulsion, imposition, or constraint may be law, society, or conscience, but the effect is the same: one is bound (in a negative sense) to do something because one is forbidden to do otherwise. The essence of obligation is constraint. Yet the meaning of *Verbindlichkeit* is not restricted to this idea of constraint. While it is possible to speak of ourselves as being bound to do something in a negative sense (that is, as being bound, tied, and *constrained* to do something), it is also possible to think of the relation as a positive one. In this sense we are united, connected, or combined with others; we are joined and linked to them. Here the meaning of "bound" is positive. . . . Moral (that is, rational and autonomous) activity is the basis for the tie we feel with others.[60]

Thus, not only is it not the case that the category of supererogatory acts is needed instead of (or in addition to) that of imperfect duties in order to promote a sense of community; the very notion of duty may have a special contribution to a sense of community which supererogation lacks.

In sum, none of the arguments in favor of recognizing a special category is compelling.[61] It is tempting to think that whatever initial appeal they have is due to ignorance of, or inattention to, the alternatives. Compared with an ethical theory that requires that one always do as much good as one possibly can, Urmson's vision of a two-tiered theory is quite attractive. But compared with a scheme that classifies acts we often think of as supererogatory under the heading of duty and that treats them as ways of fulfilling imperfect duties, the two-tiered approach loses some of its appeal. In the next chapter we will take up this matter, asking whether something other than inattention to or ignorance of the Kantian alternative motivates the supererogationist view.

60. Thomas Auxter, *Kant's Moral Teleology* (Macon, Ga.: Mercer University Press, 1982), pp. 163–164.

61. Another work one might consult here is Gregory Mellema's *Beyond the Call of Duty: Supererogation, Obligation, and Offense* (Albany: State University of New York Press, 1991). A supererogationist, Mellema does not directly argue for recognizing the category of the supererogatory but does seek to explain the "anti-supererogationist impulse." See chaps. 5 and 6.

6   There is, however, a more powerful argument to consider, not for full-blown supererogationism, but for a qualified, contextualized form of it, similar to that suggested by Hill. I have in mind the view that certain acts should be seen as supererogatory provided not only that the act itself is of a certain type but also that the agent's character and past conduct meet certain conditions. More fully, the view is that given the agent's character and in particular, given that she adopted the relevant maxim and acted in a way expressive of that maxim, a particular act that she performed should (provided it is of the right sort) be seen as supererogatory. The argument I will develop suggests that unless we speak in terms of supererogatory acts—unless we see acts of this sort, and in this context, as supererogatory—we fail to capture something meaningful; and likewise, an ethical theory that does not recognize supererogatory acts, at least in this contextualized way of recognizing them, will fail to capture and do justice to certain moral phenomena.

To develop the argument, I will borrow, out of context, an observation that Heyd offers in his chapter on Kant's ethics. He notes, "If x and y are both actions which equally fulfill a certain imperfect duty D, then it is true that we may perform *either x or y*. . . . But although Kant says nothing about it, there is the possibility of doing *both x and y*. And doing so is clearly meritorious and praiseworthy."[62] His observation suggests that we need to be able to discriminate between the following two sorts of cases. Imagine Jill and Maria, both of whom have adopted a maxim of beneficence. Both, that is, really care about the welfare of others; neither is someone who just tries to fulfill a minimal requirement so that she can get on with the things she really cares about. Although the latter stance is inconsistent with having a maxim of beneficence, there are many different ways of living, all consistent with having that maxim. Jill helps others often, but she does not make the sacrifices of time and energy that Maria makes. Maria volunteers at a rape crisis center. Jill does not turn her back on needy people and is sensitive to the needs of others, but she does not go out of her way to involve herself in activities of the sort that Maria takes part in. In addition, Jill tends not to take notice of others' needs except when she is personally acquainted with the people in question, or when a crisis such as a famine on a distant continent receives

<hr>

62. Heyd, *Supererogation*, p. 63. Michael Stocker makes a similar point in his "Supererogation and Duties," in *Studies in Moral Philosophy*, ed. Nicholas Rescher, American Philosophical Quarterly Monograph Series, 1968.

much more attention in her community than faraway crises usually receive.

If we do not single out supererogatory acts, how can we pay due regard to instances in which someone does far more to fulfill an imperfect duty than do many others who themselves cannot be faulted for having too legalistic and minimalist a conception of what they ought to do? In each case they really do have the right spirit about what they are doing; they are not trying to get duty or morality "out of the way." They take it seriously; they do not treat it the way most of us treat, say, housecleaning. And, we are assuming, neither Maria nor Jill is primarily aiming to impress others or to buttress a personal sense of moral superiority. In such a case, we surely need to have a way of according a special moral status to some of Maria's actions. What better way than by deeming her actions supererogatory?

This argument is compelling only if we are unimaginative. The strategy is first of all unnecessary. There is another way to recognize the special goodness of Maria's conduct. But the strategy is not only unnecessary, it is even inadequate to meet the problem at hand. Which acts will count as supererogatory? Only the really time-consuming ones? Or perhaps the ones she finds most unpleasant? Or the ones most of us would find especially difficult or unpleasant? None of this looks promising. Furthermore, how are we to distinguish the Marias from the Mother Teresas?[63] These may seem to be small, isolated, perhaps procedural problems; but I think that they are more than that. They are symptomatic of a general misdirection. The supererogationist approach assumes that we need a way to accord a special moral status to certain *actions*. But is this really what is needed? No. What deserve special recognition are their characters. It is not that some particular actions of Maria's should be characterized in a way that sets them apart from her other actions and from Jill's actions; what is ultimately impressive is the *character* that Maria's decision to work on an emergency hot line reflects.

Long before Urmson wrote "Saints and Heroes" we have had available

---

63. I follow the custom in the contemporary literature on moral excellence and related topics of citing Mother Teresa as a moral exemplar, but I do so with misgivings. Should someone who publicly opposes birth control and abortion be treated in moral philosophy as a paradigmatically morally excellent person? I certainly do not want to endorse that view, nor, I imagine, do most other philosophers who cite her as a moral exemplar. Rather, we are focusing on her altruism and ignoring her stands on birth control and abortion, and are thus speaking of a somewhat fictionalized Mother Teresa.

to us another way of according special moral status to the conduct of a Maria or a Mother Teresa: we speak of their virtues, of their character, of their remarkable commitment to good causes. Can we consistently speak this way and be Kantians? I see no reason to think we cannot. It is true that the emphasis that Kant places on virtue as "the strength of man's maxims in fulfilling his duty" (*MM* 394) or as "fortitude . . . with respect to what opposes the moral disposition within us" (*MM* 380) lends itself better to recognizing the virtue of someone who fulfills a perfect duty in the face of enormous cost to himself than to discerning the special goodness of Maria as contrasted with Jill, or Mother Teresa as contrasted with either of them. But his notion of virtue is suited to the latter, as well: virtue is revealed by the extent to which, and the way in which, one fulfills such duties of virtue as participating actively in the fate of others (*MM* 457). Kant says that it is not so much a matter of "the degree to which one follows certain maxims" but rather of "the specific *quality* of the maxims" (*MM* 404), and this captures the difference between the Marias and the Jills. Although Maria and Jill both adopt maxims of beneficence, their more specific maxims differ, and some of their differences reflect a differing degree of virtue.[64]

It might be objected that doing as I propose would not really be any different from emphasizing supererogatory acts. After all, won't recognition of a virtuous character be based on the judgment that the person has performed supererogatory acts? The objection, I believe, oversimplifies the relation between our appraisals of individual acts and our judgment that the agent has a virtuous character or character trait. First, though the fact that *S* performs supererogatory actions provides some evidence of virtue, it does so only in conjunction with information about *S*'s motives, aims, and values—information gleaned only from observing her non-supererogatory actions as well as the supererogatory ones, and,

---

64. This is a delicate point. Although Kant's ethics provides a basis for saying that Maria is more virtuous than Jill and that Mother Teresa is yet more virtuous, it is a singular advantage of the Kantian approach that it does not encourage us to rank virtuous people or virtuous lives and does not make it easy to recognize slight differences in degree of virtue. There are many ways of being virtuous and though we must not be complacent and must strive to be more virtuous, it is not the case that—either as agents or as theorists—we should have a determinate picture of the best (exemplified by the life of a particular saint or hero) and measure ourselves accordingly. I develop this point toward the end of Chapter 2. For a suggestion of a Kantian basis for recognizing differing degrees of virtue, see Stephen Engstrom, "Conditioned Autonomy," *Philosophy and Phenomenological Research* 48 (1988): 435–453, especially secs. 3 and 4.

more generally, from observing her conduct. So, the fact that the agent performs supererogatory acts does not by itself provide much evidence of virtue. Second, a well-founded judgment that the agent is virtuous need not be based on a claim that she has performed supererogatory acts. The basis might be, rather, that she fulfills perfect duties at enormous cost to herself, and in circumstances where most of us would not fulfill such duties. Or, again, the basis might be that she does more than most people, or goes to more trouble than do most people, to fulfill her imperfect duties; more generally, it might be that she takes them much more seriously. A judgment that a person is virtuous may, but need not, have as part of its basis a judgment that she (often) performs supererogatory acts.

Recall too the difficulty of determining that *now*, beginning with *this* act, the agent is doing more than is required by principles of imperfect duty. This difficulty further undermines the notion that a judgment that the agent's conduct reveals generosity or deep commitment to a worthy cause should be based on the judgment that she has performed a supererogatory act.

In sum, an attribution of virtue may, but need not, be based on a judgment that the person has performed a supererogatory act; and if it is, it should not be based only on that judgment. Clearly then, a judgment that someone has a certain virtuous character trait is not a disguised judgment that she has performed, or often does perform, supererogatory acts.

It might be said that the judgment that someone has performed a supererogatory act is in some important sense more basic or "natural" than a judgment that she is generous or in some other way virtuous. If it does seem more basic, this could be due to the fact that much of twentieth-century ethics has, until quite recently, neglected character and virtue, and has attempted to say all that we want to say about morality through judgments of actions. For this reason it may be more familiar to us to locate the goodness in the act, but that is no argument for continuing to do so. I see no other reason for taking the judgment that an act is supererogatory to be more basic. I am not claiming that judgments about character are more basic than judgments about acts; for though that claim is plausible, it also seems plausible to claim that a judgment that a particular act is right, or that it is wrong, is more basic than a judgment about a person's character. I don't mean to take a stand on that question. By contrast, the claim that judgments that an act is supererogatory are more basic than judgments about character *does* seem implausible.

I turn now to a second possible objection. One might wonder if the reasons for being wary of categorizing acts as supererogatory don't also apply to the view I propose.

Let us recall the problems and briefly consider whether a Kantian view gets around them. As I indicated earlier, a problem with the category of supererogatory acts is that it invites the notion that a large part of morality is beyond moral scrutiny. It does so in two different ways. First, it suggests that acts of beneficence and other acts standardly classified as supererogatory are strictly "extras," not morally mandatory. Because they are optional, self-criticism and moral scrutiny of one's omission of such acts would generally be inappropriate (unless one felt that one had a special "calling" to morality). Second, inclusion of a special category of supererogatory acts in ethics invites the assumption that admirable and apparently unselfish acts which are more than we ordinarily expect from people are certain to be morally unobjectionable.

The Kantian view avoids both of these problems. Its position is that the happiness of others is an obligatory end and that one must, therefore, embrace a maxim of beneficence, but that it is impossible to say exactly what one must do accordingly. How much one must do and precisely what, cannot be said; but one must care, and the caring must be practical, not "pathological."[65] I must *do* something, not content myself with feeling moved. "Doing something" is not optional. Thus the Kantian view avoids the first problem.

It steers clear of the second problem in the following way: if we accord a special moral status to the character of a Mother Teresa rather than to the impressive actions, we avoid the tendency to suppose that actions that exhibit a remarkable and morally good character trait must be right. Acts such as those of tremendous fortitude or self-sacrifice impress us because they reveal a strength of character which most of us lack. If the act is not obviously objectionable, we tend to bestow on it the label 'supererogatory'. It is more than could be asked or expected, and it displays something admirable. Yet it may nonetheless be morally questionable. If we direct our moral admiration toward the character trait rather than toward the action, this confusion can be avoided, since a

---

65. For a discussion of the distinction, see Susan Mendus, "The Practical and the Pathological," *Journal of Value Inquiry* 19 (1985): 235–244.

character trait can be good without it being the case that any act that displays it is morally unobjectionable.[66]

IN conclusion, I think that Kant was right to set aside a category of imperfect duties for those duties that are such that there is no clear answer to the question "When have I fulfilled them?" and for the fulfillment of which one must adopt a maxim. This category supplies much of what ethicists have wanted from the category of the supererogatory. The rest—with one exception—is better captured by evaluation of character than by recognizing a special category of actions that go "beyond" duty. The exception, the one thing that talk of virtue and imperfect duty does not capture, is something that I do not see to be of much importance. This is the bare goodness of the act, *independent* of what it tells us about the agent's character. Without the notion of the supererogatory we cannot speak of an action's being extraordinarily good except by talking about what it suggests concerning the agent's character. It is rare, I think, that we have occasion to do so. Not that there is never occasion; if it is possible to act heroically, or extremely generously, but *out of character*, we might wish to speak of the greatness of the act, without believing that the act shows the person to be great or otherwise virtuous. I am not convinced that this is so; it seems odd that there is no explanation of the remarkable act that shows something admirable about the agent. Of course we can construct cases where the act clearly does not show greatness: Urmson's example of the soldier who throws himself on a live grenade to save his buddies could be embellished so as to say that the soldier planned to commit suicide all along and saw this as a terrific opportunity to do so without causing his family the particular grief that a suicide usually causes (and without depriving them of his life insurance benefits).[67] It might be asserted that now we have a heroic deed which does not show greatness of character. But I maintain that though the act is optimific and shows wonderful considerateness and resourcefulness, it is no more heroic than the usual suicide.

66. This confusion is not always benign. It invites, among other things, paternalistic intervention. Kant's remarks about the need for respect to check love are apropos. See *MM* 448–453.

67. Richard Henson so revised the example (though to make a somewhat different point) in his comment at the 1985 Eastern Division meetings of the American Philosophical Association on an early version of what became this chapter.

Recognizing the possibility that there *may* be cases in which the act was truly great, yet out of character, I am not urging that we seek to eliminate the term 'supererogatory' from our philosophical vocabulary. But I think everything else that we want to capture with the term 'supererogatory' is better captured by talk of imperfect duty and virtue.[68]

One's views on the subject of this chapter will have quite a lot to do with how broadly one wants to understand duty. If one favors a narrow concept of duty, one's views will be quite different from mine. But what should now be clear is that we need not start from the premise that room must be left in every ethical theory for the supererogatory, and then tailor our concept of duty accordingly.

68. As I observed above in Sec. 1, supererogationists differ as to whether an act can be supererogatory regardless of the agent's motive, or whether an altruistic motive is needed before the act can qualify as supererogatory. Thus, Heyd writes that although the intent must be altruistic, the motive need not be; it can, for example, be to gain fame (*Supererogation*, pp. 115 and 137). In contrast, Michael Clark, indicating that he uses 'meritorious' as synonymous with 'supererogatory', specifies that "the sacrifice will not be meritorious unless made from altruistic rather than merely selfish motives" ("Meritorious and Mandatory," pp. 23 and 29). Supererogationists accepting the first position are particularly unlikely to find my proposal congenial, since it does not encourage attending to the bare supererogatory act.

2

Minimal Morality,
Moral Excellence,
and the Supererogatory

⬦▪⬦

1   In the last chapter I defended Kant's ethics against the charge that because it does not and cannot accommodate the category of supererogatory acts, it is a failure, and I defended it by challenging the assumption that any ethical theory that does not recognize a special category of supererogatory acts is ipso facto flawed. I tried to show that a Kantian treatment of acts that contemporary moral philosophers usually classify as supererogatory may well be preferable to the contemporary approach. The last part of that chapter canvassed the supererogationists' arguments and concluded that there are no compelling reasons for favoring their approach to Kant's. This raises the question: What explains the disagreement between supererogationists and the Kantian? Repeatedly those defending the need for a category of the supererogatory implicitly assume that the only alternative to their view is a position according to which every act they see as supererogatory is morally required. If they realized that this assumption is false, would they embrace Kant's position? Presumably not. What objections would they have to the Kantian approach?

Because supererogationists have not addressed this matter,[1] it will take considerable probing through their claims and arguments to figure out just what objections they would have, and what underlying disagreements motivate the objections. That is the task of the present chapter. I want to give fuller expression to the supererogationist point of view and

1. One exception is Richard McCarty, whose work I discuss in Chap. 3.

to compare the approach to character and moral excellence taken by supererogationists with that suggested by Kant's writings.

2   We may take as our point of departure J. O. Urmson's criticisms in "Saints and Heroes" of theories such as Kant's which, he claims, do not do justice to saintly and heroic acts. To recapitulate: the theories criticized are those that classify all acts as either forbidden or permissible, and, if permissible, either obligatory or not. That is, they recognize actions that are obligatory, actions that are permissible but not obligatory, and actions that are wrong. "To my mind," Urmson writes, "this threefold classification, or any classification that is merely a variation on or elaboration of it, is totally inadequate to the facts of morality; any moral theory that leaves room only for such a classification will in consequence also be inadequate."[2] The "facts" he refers to are those suggested by the title of his article—essentially, that there *are* saintly and heroic acts.[3] These acts go *beyond* duty, and thus are not obligatory; but they are not simply permissible acts either, since they have a moral value that merely permissible acts lack. They thus seem, as he suggests, to lie outside the threefold classification.[4] To accommodate such acts and to

2. J. O. Urmson, "Saints and Heroes," in *Moral Concepts*, ed. Joel Feinberg (London: Oxford University Press, 1970), p. 60.

3. One might think that the relevant facts are that there are saints and heroes, and that Urmson is criticizing ethical theories for failing to recognize the special goodness of such people. That it is the acts, not the people, whose special goodness these theories are said not to recognize is evident from a clarification he makes concerning the type of heroism and saintliness that does, and the type that does not, show the threefold classification of actions to be inadequate. A person may be called saintly or heroic if (either effortlessly or with abnormal self-control) she does her duty in contexts in which inclination or self-interest would lead most people not to do it; alternatively one may be called saintly or heroic if she performs actions that are far beyond the limits of her duty. Actions in the first type of situation, he says, "fall under the concept of duty" and therefore do not challenge the threefold classification; but actions of the second type do not, and thus do challenge the classification. But if his concern were with character, not action (i.e., if his complaint were that moral theories leave no room for recognizing the goodness of saintly or heroic characters, rather than that they leave no room for recognizing the goodness of heroic or saintly acts), the two types of saintly or heroic acts would challenge such moral theories equally. There would be no ground for saying that heroism or saintliness of the first type can be accommodated by the threefold classification, whereas heroism or saintliness of the second type cannot be.

4. Urmson, "Saints and Heroes," p. 60. Urmson's opening line, "Moral philosophers tend to discriminate, explicitly or implicitly, three types of action from the point of view of moral worth" (p. 60), reveals a confusion. The classification of permissible, obligatory, and forbidden is made *not* from the point of view of *moral worth* but of rightness. In blurring

recognize their value, an ethical theory must have, in addition to the usual three categories, a category of supererogatory acts.

To get a handle on what is at issue, it may be helpful to locate Urmson's claim in the context of a wider discussion: How can we see to it that morality is neither too minimal nor excessively demanding? One way, generally viewed now as a crucial part of the solution (whatever the remainder of the solution may be) is to *keep duty from constituting all of morality.* The reasoning goes like this. If duty is allowed to comprise all of morality, one of two things happens. Either morality is too minimal—this happens if 'duty' is construed narrowly as referring, primarily if not exclusively, to institutional duties, duties of an office, and duties we incur through making promises and appointments or taking vows; *or*, it is argued, morality is excessively demanding—this happens if 'duty' is understood broadly, since then, it seems, everything that we ideally should do, that it would be *good* to do, and that we are (by any stretch of the imagination) capable of doing, it is our *duty* to do.[5]

To see to it that morality neither asks too much nor offers too little, we accept, according to this line of thinking, a narrow construal of duty and recognize the category of the supererogatory, viewing it as sharply distinct from duty. In short, we accept Urmson's recommendation. Morality thus divides into two parts. One part tells us what we have to do, and at the same time indirectly assures us that we are under no obligation to do anything more; the other provides us with something to admire, praise, and, if we are so inclined, emulate. Thus morality *offers* more than a minimum, by indicating what is praiseworthy, but does not demand "too much," since what is required is only that we fulfill the minimal requirements.

As indicated in the previous chapter, I think that the purposes (I should say, all the worthwhile purposes) for which the category of supererogatory acts is thought to be necessary can be accomplished without it

---

the distinction between moral worth and rightness, Urmson makes theories based on the threefold classification look more impoverished than they are by suggesting that the classification gives the theory all it has to say about the character behind the action, *as well as* all that it has to say about the action's deontic status.

5. For an example of the narrow construal of duty—one so narrow that the qualifier 'primarily, if not exclusively' could be omitted—see Joel Feinberg, "Supererogation and Rules," in Feinberg, *Doing and Deserving: Essays in the Theory of Responsibility* (Princeton: Princeton University Press, 1970), pp. 3–24. I include the qualifier since some supererogationists do not accept as narrow a conception of duty as Feinberg's.

and, more generally, without dividing morality up in the way suggested. Kant's ethics, despite the fact that it is often thought to be proof that we need a category of supererogatory acts, offers an alternative way of accomplishing these purposes. Consider the purpose emphasized by Urmson. Kant's ethics keeps saintly and heroic acts (as well as more jejune acts of lending a hand) from being either merely permissible or in every case morally required. It also keeps morality from being minimal— it certainly does not equate morality with adhering to negative rules, despite periodic accusations that it does just that.[6] Kant's ethics clearly does not do that; it tells us what our obligatory ends are, and gives some direction as to what we must do accordingly (e.g., cultivate certain dispositions in ourselves). So it is not minimal; and at the same time, it is, arguably anyway, not excessively demanding. It does not tell us that we must, for example, subordinate all of our other ends to the end of promoting the happiness of others.

Kant's ethics thus serves as a reply to the argument, sketched above, that if duty is allowed to comprise all of morality, either it renders morality too minimal—this is the risk if 'duty' is construed very narrowly—or it makes morality too demanding—this happens if 'duty' is understood broadly so as to entail that whatever it would be good to do, we have a duty to do (provided we are not absolutely incapable of doing it). 'Duty' can be understood broadly without being understood *that* way; and thanks to the category of imperfect duties, a morality of duty can have a rather different shape than is usually supposed.[7]

3   Why don't supererogationists realize this? An examination of their arguments invites the guess that they never thought about Kant's imperfect duties. David Heyd writes, for example, that "supererogation provides moral agents with the opportunity of exercising and expressing virtuous traits of character, of acting altruistically, and of fulfilling their individual ideals—opportunities which are denied to them in the sphere of the morality of duty and obligation."[8] But that is not true of a Kantian

6. See, for example, Alasdair MacIntyre, *A Short History of Ethics* (New York: Macmillan, 1966), p. 197.

7. As noted earlier, David Heyd speaks as if a morality of duty must be either "a system of requirements aiming at the maximization of general good or happiness" or "a means of securing some minimal conditions of cooperation and justice" (Heyd, *Supererogation: Its Status in Ethical Theory* [Cambridge: Cambridge University Press, 1982], p. 174). Kant's morality of duty clearly is neither of these.

8. Ibid., p. 10. Another example: "Supererogatory action may contribute to the strengthening of social bonds and augment the feelings of a close-knit community. For by

morality of duty: it in no way denies moral agents any of these opportunities. Given the abundance of arguments like Heyd's, and remembering that the *Doctrine of Virtue* was not available in English until 1964 and still is not well known among philosophers who are not Kant scholars, a Kantian with missionary zeal might be tempted to believe that if only supererogationists knew about Kant's imperfect duties and the shape that they give to his ethics, they would change their view. But in fact some supererogationists clearly do know Kant's *Doctrine of Virtue*—indeed David Heyd's thoughtful chapter on Kant and supererogation indicates that he has made a serious study of it. Still, they might, as Heyd seems to at times, forget to take the Kantian option into account when they are arguing for supererogationism. So the possibility remains that they champion supererogationism because of insufficient attention to the alternatives. Without ruling out this rather uncharitable and arrogant hypothesis, I hope to uncover in their writings assumptions about morality and moral excellence that explain why they would, even if fully aware of the Kantian alternative, reject it.

Why then, do they—or, if they do not speak to it, would they—reject the Kantian approach? The first layer of the explanation is this: the Kantian approach asks supererogationists to view supererogatory acts in a way they won't countenance—as acts that, though not required, are ways of fulfilling imperfect duties. In contrast, the supererogationist is committed to the view that, in Heyd's words, "Acts which go beyond the call of duty are in *no* way obligatory. They are not imperfect duties, or less stringent duties; nor are they just a type of duties entailing no corresponding rights."[9] The problem is that the Kantian approach un-

---

doing more than is required a member of a group shows that he has an interest in his fellow members which is deeper than his contractual commitments, or than the personal benefit he can draw from his membership in the group" (ibid., p. 179).

Some arguments put forth by supererogationists actually better support the Kantian approach than supererogationism. For example, Heyd writes, "But even if a society (or an institution) could survive if its members no more than adhered to the requirements and rules of behaviour, it would be morally deficient. Our objection to such a society is analogous to our judgment of an individual who never forgives, who is never charitable in his dealings with others, and who always and without exception insists on his rights" (ibid.). Right! We would object to such a person, because we think that people have a duty to be charitable and forgiving. (How could we object if we thought it supererogatory to be charitable and forgiving?)

9. Ibid., p. 125. Cf. p. 57, where with reference to the distinction in Kant's ethics between duties of virtue and juridical duties, Heyd writes, "The failure of this distinction to accommodate supererogation is due to the fact that it is a distinction *within* the concept

mistakably does not entail that all acts of a certain sort count as "beyond duty." It is not even consistent with it. I cannot say, if I accept it, "I've performed some kind acts, so performing any further kind acts is supererogatory"; or "I've perfected what I take to be my chief talent—my gymnastic skills—so I've fulfilled my duty to perfect myself and never have to demand anything of myself by way of self-perfection in the future." The attitude evinced by those statements is inconsistent with embracing as ends the happiness of others and my own perfection.

The Kantian approach cannot provide even a highly contextualized division of the sort just indicated, between what is required and what is supererogatory. Much less can it offer the clean division that Urmson insists on. According to Urmson, "A line must be drawn between what we can expect and demand from others and what we can merely hope for and receive with gratitude when we get it; duty falls on one side of this line, and other acts with moral value on the other, and rightly so."[10] Since we need to know what we can expect and demand from others (and they of us), we need to know pretty precisely what our duties and their duties are. Kant's ethics does not offer such precision concerning our duties. *Some* duties can be spelled out fairly precisely, but by no means all.

The explanation offered thus far as to why supererogationists would reject Kant's approach clarifies their stand, but does not explain it. We want to know why, when Kant clearly does not think it important to draw a line between the mandatory and the supererogatory, supererogationists think it so important. The answer will have to unfold slowly, but we can start with this: A large part of the disagreement can be traced to differing views of duty and of the nature of moral constraint and its relation to freedom. Very generally, supererogationists view duty and morality legalistically, whereas Kant does not. They see the source of morality to be external to us, moral requirements to be a burden, and the experience of being subject to moral requirements to be that of having something more or less onerous demanded of one in the name of society. On Kant's view, by contrast, the moral 'ought' *is* properly experienced as a constraint, but not as a constraint imposed on us by others; the constraint is internal, as is the source of morality. Furthermore, moral

---

of moral duty. Supererogation is recognized only as a class of acts, which although obligatory, cannot be externally exacted. But there is no place for supererogation in the sense of moral acts which are not duties *at all*."

10. Urmson, "Saints and Heroes," p. 71.

constraint is not, according to Kant, a constraint on our freedom; supererogationists, by contrast, generally hold that it is.

Now I'll try to do three things at once: fill in the rough sketch I just gave, provide evidence that supererogationists hold these views, and indicate some differences among supererogationists. Bear in mind that I am not claiming that supererogationists have to hold any or all of these views, or even that all as a matter of fact do. I am trying to tease out of their arguments for supererogationism (arguments that generally support Kantian ethics as well as the view they are arguing for) some motivation for favoring supererogationism over the Kantian approach. I'll start with Urmson.

4   As we saw in Chapter 1, Urmson writes that our "moral code"— and that term is significant—"should distinguish between basic rules, summarily set forth in simple rules and binding on all, and the higher flights of morality." His arguments in favor of regarding all morally good action that goes beyond minimal duties as supererogatory are mostly based on considerations of what will best secure compliance with what he calls "basic duties"—those duties whose fulfillment is crucial if life is not to be, as he puts it, brutish and short. He worries that if more is presented to us as morally mandatory, we will be less willing to fulfill our basic duties. One reason he gives is that the "ordinary man" may be unable to do what is presented as duty, if duty encompasses more than minimal duty; and should this happen, "a general breakdown of compliance with the moral code would be an inevitable consequence; duty would seem to be something high and unattainable, and not 'for the likes of us'." Another reason is that "a moral code . . . must be formulable in rules of manageable complexity," and, he thinks, rules explaining in what circumstances one should, for example, nurse sick neighbors, cannot be formulated simply enough to pass the test.[11] If the code is too

---

11. Ibid., pp. 69–70; p. 70; pp. 70–71. There is tension in Urmson's view. Duties are to be exacted like debts; compliance with them by all is indispensable, etc. Yet he speaks of persons who do their duty "in contexts in which inclination, desire, or self-interest" or "terror, fear, or a drive to self-preservation" would lead most people not to do it. People who do their duty in such contexts do so "as a result of exercising abnormal self-control" (p. 61). Here it does not seem that duties are to be exacted like debts, etc. His examples bear this out: the "unmarried daughter" carries out her "duty" of "staying at home to tend her ailing and widowed father"; the "terrified doctor" heroically does his "duty": he stays by his patients in a plague-ridden city (p. 61).

complicated, people will not comply with it; so it is better to stick with the basic rules, which, he believes, can be formulated reasonably simply.[12]

Another argument that Urmson offers appeals to the nature of duty. It is "part of the notion of a duty that we have a right to demand compliance from others."[13] Indeed, we "have no choice but to apply pressure on each other to conform" to duty. Duty is to be exacted like a debt, and failure is to be censured.[14] It is no wonder, given this notion of duty, that duty should be thought to be something quite unpleasant and something to be kept in check.

One might infer from these quotations that the point of morality, on Urmson's view, is to keep us from killing one another, or from making life brutish and short by some other means. That would not be accurate. It is one of morality's aims, but he emphasizes that it should not be the only one. Morality should also inspire and ennoble (as it would not if it were merely a morality of duty, in his sense of 'duty'), and it should do so by recognizing, or providing a basis for recognizing, special goodness. But these two aims or functions of morality—the minimal one and the lofty one—are sharply separate. By contrast, there is no such division in Kant's ethics. One might think that such a division is generated by Kant's distinction between duties we can be compelled to perform and other duties—that is, between juridical duties and duties of virtue—but that is not the case, since the latter are still duties. Morality cannot be seen from a Kantian perspective as having these two distinct aims. For a Kantian,

12. As Michael Clark has pointed out, it is by no means clear that Urmson's test of simplicity is a reasonable one, nor that the rules he thinks of as basic pass it. Clark observes, "A rule requiring everyone who passes a serious motor accident to give help would . . . tend to be self-defeating, since too many helpers are often as bad as none. But there are certainly many occasions when people ought to help victims in motor accidents and would be wrong not to do so. There is no reason why this moral requirement should not be laid down in a rule which indicates that it is unnecessary . . . to give help when enough people are already doing so, and that what counts as 'enough' is a matter for common sense in the face of the particular circumstances. . . . If there were a special difficulty about formulating moral rules which are easily intelligible, it would apply as much to rules about mandatory acts as to injunctions to nurse lepers and the like." Clark, "The Meritorious and the Mandatory," *Proceedings of the Aristotelian Society*, New Series, 79 (1978/79), pp. 27–28.

13. Urmson, "Saints and Heroes," p. 71.

14. Ibid., p. 70. The sentence takes the form of a conditional—"If we are to exact basic duties like debts, and censure failure, such duties must be . . . within the capacity of the ordinary man"—but it is clear from the context that he is affirming the antecedent. See also p. 71: "It is part of the notion of a duty that we have a right to demand compliance from others even when we are interested parties."

part of being moral is striving to be better. There is no category of being "minimally moral" without that. Indeed, the category of "minimally moral" makes little sense on a Kantian view. This is an important difference between the Kantian and the supererogationist views, and we will return to it later.

5   Although supererogationists have chastised Urmson for his arguments—Millard Schumaker, for example, remarks that they "are more appropriate to jurisprudence than to moral philosophy"[15]—they too see morality legalistically.

David Heyd does not speak in terms of moral codes and favors a defense of supererogationism that is not keyed to the goal of ensuring compliance with minimal morality. But in its own way, Heyd's defense is legalistic. It relies on analogies to law; in particular, he likens moral constraint to legal constraint. He writes, for example, of "good acts" being "imposed on us as legal or moral duties." In the same section he speaks of moral and legal compulsion as if they involve compulsion in roughly similar ways. This occurs when he compares supererogationists to those who wish to restrict Good Samaritan legislation and says that "both parties hold that compulsion (legal and moral respectively) is in itself bad." The claim, as well as the terminology, is significant: moral compulsion is, like compulsion in general, a bad thing, something to be kept to a minimum. Being morally required to do x is rather like, indeed perhaps an instance of, being coerced to do something. There is, he says, an "analogy between the limits of the legal enforcement of morals and the limits of moral duty," and the analogy "rests on the view that both the law and the morality of duty are means of achieving certain basic aims (such as security, social interaction, and basic justice), but should be kept confined to these vital functions."[16]

Heyd indicates that he does not accept Urmson's narrow, institutional notion of duty.[17] That his (and Schumaker's) notion of duty is, however, fairly narrow is evident from the following. Their discussions reveal an assumption that aligns them with Urmson and distances them from Kant, namely, the assumption that x is not wrong unless it wrongs someone. Heyd, following Schumaker, writes that "refusal to do a favour cannot

---

15. Millard Schumaker, *Supererogation: An Analysis and Bibliography* (Edmonton: St. Stephen's College, 1977), p. 13.

16. Heyd, *Supererogation*, p. 178; p. 176; p. 177.

17. Ibid., pp. 134–35.

be criticized as morally wrong." The reason? "We can ask for a favour, but never claim it."[18] But of course it does not follow from the fact that no one can claim a favor as one's due that it is never morally wrong not to do a favor (or never criticizable as morally wrong). It follows only from that fact together with the assumption that unless someone can claim to be wronged by x, x is not morally wrong (or cannot be criticized as morally wrong).

From the foregoing it is fairly clear that enthusiasm for supererogationism is not based only (if at all) on ignorance about the alternatives. It is based on a conception of (a) duty as entailing corresponding rights, (b) moral constraint as burdensome in roughly the way that legal constraint is, and (c) a "morality of duty" as something that interferes with individuals' lives and that should be prevented from interfering more than is absolutely necessary. Nonetheless, someone might argue, it could still be that at least some of these views—for example, that our duties are to be kept to a minimum—are based on an assumption that the only alternative is a "maximal" morality, perhaps a crude utilitarian position such as that we must at all times maximize the general happiness. Perhaps the motivation for the assumptions outlined is a supposition that there is no viable alternative. Although this would be a strained explanation of some of the assumptions, it will be worthwhile to take up the challenge by probing more deeply into why moral constraint is thought to be a rather bad thing.

At one level the answer is clear: It is not just that we dislike moral constraint; rather, moral constraint is seen as a bad thing because it limits freedom and autonomy, and these are manifestly *good* things. Heyd's chief argument in favor of supererogationism is that freedom and autonomy are at stake; and just as people should be "legally free to do certain morally wrong actions," so should they be "morally free not to be virtuous."[19] Freedom and autonomy are the cornerstone of Michael Clark's defense of supererogationism as well, and they also play a role in Schumaker's arguments.[20]

18. Heyd, *Supererogation*, pp. 148–49; Schumaker, *Supererogation*, p. 17.
19. Heyd, *Supererogation*, p. 177.
20. Urmson also seems to appeal to freedom at one point, when he writes: "We have no choice but to apply pressure on each other to conform in these fundamental matters; here moral principles are like public laws rather than like private ideals. But free choice of the better course of action is always preferable to action under pressure, even when the pressure is but moral" ("Saints and Heroes," p. 71). However, he is appealing to freedom from social pressure, and thus his concern is rather different from that of Heyd, Schumaker, and Clark.

At another level the answer is unclear. To what value(s) are Heyd, Clark, and Schumaker appealing when they speak of autonomy and freedom? Is it autonomy in the sense of self-government and self-direction? Or do they mean freedom as license, that is, freedom to do what one wants to do in the absence of constraints? This matters, because only the latter would give them reason to champion supererogationism over the Kantian approach—and even then only if moral constraints count as constraints of the relevant sort. If it is autonomy as self-government that they have in mind, this would be some confirmation for the hunch that they have no basis for preferring their approach to Kant's.

To see this, consider first a passage that appeals to autonomy. Seeking to explain what gives a person "the moral right to refrain" from supererogatory acts, Clark writes that the answer "is to be given in terms of the independent value of personal autonomy, the value of freedom to control and plan one's life and to choose the style in which one lives." But there is no loss of freedom to control and plan one's life if the acts thought of as supererogatory are instead classified as ways of fulfilling imperfect duties (except, of course, for the loss entailed by the fact that one is not free to neglect imperfect duties entirely). Clark continues: "It is a precondition of this freedom that a man should have a reasonable chance of knowing what future constraints there will be on his personal projects and mode of living so that he can arrange his life accordingly. If he must, for example, always do his utmost to maximize the happiness of others, whoever they are, then his moral right to conduct his life in his chosen way, and his capacity to predict future constraints, are severely restricted."[21] This precondition Kant's ethics certainly satisfies, given the latitude allowed by the imperfect duties. The problem that worries Clark is one that plagues some utilitarians, but not Kant.

Insofar as autonomy is the value appealed to in arguing that morality must include a category of the supererogatory lest it ask too much of us, the argument is a weak one. It supports supererogationism no more than it supports the Kantian approach. Kant's conception of morality, with its very open-ended imperfect duties, does not limit self-government. We are enjoined, on Kant's ethics, to perfect ourselves and to promote the happiness of others, but how we do this is left to us—thus allowing, and indeed requiring, self-government. Far from encroaching on autonomy, in the sense of self-government, Kantian morality can more plausibly be said to "increase" it (by demanding it), since the agent must really *govern*

---

21. Clark, "Meritorious and Mandatory," p. 29; pp. 29–30.

herself, not simply obey specific moral injunctions. On the supererogationist view, by contrast, everything beyond compliance with those minimal injunctions is optional—and this, one might say, leaves relatively little room for self-government, although plenty for liberty as license.

Compare the appeal to autonomy, thus understood, with an appeal to liberty as license. Liberty as license seems to be what Heyd has in mind when he says that people should be, as quoted above, "morally free not to be virtuous" and asserts that "the value of supererogatory acts consists [in part] in their being totally optional and voluntary."[22] His suggestion seems to be that even viewing oneself as obligated to embrace the ends of the happiness of others and one's own perfection involves an undesirable element of constraint. It is preferable, on this view, that a choice, for example, to donate blood, be optional *not only* in that no one can claim as his due that you give blood, and you do not act wrongly if you do not (depending on your other conduct), but also in that you are not guided by a view that you morally ought to promote the well-being of others. Needless to say, this contrasts sharply with Kant's view.

Although Heyd's position is somewhat unclear, no guesswork is needed to ascertain that Schumaker champions liberty as license, and defends supererogationism accordingly. In his monograph on supererogation, he contrasts viewing "man . . . as being perpetually forced to do this or that thing on pain of otherwise being in the wrong" with viewing him as "essentially a free agent doing whatever he will except when specific situations generate specific obligations."[23] Despite the fact that the former view would not aptly depict Kant's position, his espousal of the latter view throws into relief the conflict with Kant's ethics. As Schumaker sees it, part of freedom is that one is much of the time completely unconstrained by moral considerations. One is free to do what one will "*except*" (to repeat) "*when specific situations generate specific obligations.*" Not so, on Kant's view. The reason is not that one must always be doing whatever will do the most good, but that on a Kantian view morality, and in particular duty, is not confined to specific obligations, specific times, places, and subject matter. My duty, for instance, to respect other human beings constrains me all the time and shapes how I perceive the world—what I notice, what I think about, and

22. Heyd, *Supererogation*, p. 9.
23. Schumaker, *Supererogation*, p. 35.

so on.[24] It entails that I ought never be malicious, manipulative, coercive, and so on, and this requires that I be attuned to signs that what I am doing might in fact be manipulative, or that my enthusiastic invitation to a friend ("I *really* hope that you'll join us! Without you there, it just won't be fun. I'm making your favorite dish") may leave her too little opportunity to decline and thus involve an element of coercion. Though there is no value in being obsessively worried about such possibilities, the point is that one must be attuned to such moral signs not just in specific situations, but in general.

So whereas the Kantian missionary, who thinks that supererogationists would convert once they understood Kant's ethics, finds some support in the fact that Clark appeals to considerations of autonomy which support the Kantian approach as much as the supererogationist one, Schumaker's and Heyd's remarks suggest that there is more to their insistence on a category of the supererogatory than inattention to alternatives. Their remarks help to locate a conflict between their approach and the Kantian's, since Kant of course denies that moral constraints limit freedom. Schumaker's discussion suggests another dimension to the position that moral duty should be kept to a minimum: Not only should moral constraints not ask too much of us in terms of effort and sacrifice; they should also be subject to bracketing so that unless we are among those for whom morality is a vocation, they do not loom large in our lives. Instead, like onerous tasks, they can be confined to certain situations and otherwise be off our minds.

Insofar as this view is held by supererogationists, it helps provide a basis for adhering to supererogationism (by which I mean not an argument, but a basis as opposed to a failure of imagination or scholarship). Not only, the idea seems to be, should our lives be free of moral requirements that exact large sacrifices, but, in addition, even moral constraints of a less demanding sort should be kept from permeating our lives. Moral requirements are seen as a sort of intrusion on one's life, perhaps a bit like the task of calculating one's taxes: as something necessary, but definitely to be kept to as minimal a task as possible. This

24. I am borrowing a thought from Christine Korsgaard, who writes in "Morality as Freedom": "One of the things that we expect of a person who has an end is that she will notice facts that are associated with that end in a certain way, and things that bear on the promotion of the end will occur to her" (p. 44). In *Kant's Practical Philosophy Reconsidered: Papers Presented at the Seventh Jerusalem Philosophical Encounter*, ed. Yirmiyahu Yovel (Dordrecht: Kluwer Academic Publishers, 1989), pp. 23–47.

compartmentalization fits nicely with the separation of morality's two functions—to keep life from being as brutish and short as it would otherwise be, and to inspire and ennoble—and with the division of morality into minimal morality and moral excellence.

6 While Heyd, Schumaker, and Clark appeal to freedom or autonomy as the ultimate basis for so dividing morality, Urmson's rationale is rather different. His argument, in essence, is that if life is not to be brutish and short, we must divide morality into the basic duties and the "higher flights" of morality.

Recall Urmson's argument that if our moral code demanded of us something beyond the capacity of ordinary people, ordinary people would take the code less seriously, for they would see duty as "something high and unattainable, not for 'the likes of us'." A "general breakdown of compliance with the moral code would be an inevitable consequence."

The argument is odd for many reasons, but there are two matters that especially merit our attention. First, the argument seems to suppose that our moral capacities are fixed and thus that we have no obligation to improve ourselves. Second, Urmson does not consider the possibility that people, ordinary or not, might have duties to do acts of type x, where type x is varied enough that they can fulfill the duty in many different ways. He assumes that duties leave no significant leeway as to how they are to be fulfilled.

The assumptions emerge when we examine his argument and take notice of the curious suggestion that ordinary people are not capable of doing more than their minimal duty. That is the suggestion if he means 'capacity' literally, and if the argument is to support the view that morally good acts and activities beyond minimal morality are to be regarded as supererogatory. For the notion is that we ordinary people cannot improve our characters so as to press beyond our "limits." We just cannot be very generous, or cannot curb our greed, lust for power, and other wayward appetites more than "this much"—whatever that amount is. We are not responsible for our moral weaknesses and character flaws, or, at least, we are not responsible for ameliorating them. This seems to be Urmson's argument, if he means 'capacity' literally. However, it is possible that he doesn't mean 'capacity' literally, and in fairness we should consider an alternative reading.

6.1   On the alternative reading, Urmson is asserting not that ordinary people are literally incapable of doing more than minimal duty but only that they *cannot be expected* to bring themselves to do more. This is a possible reading (though not, I think, a likely one), given his use of 'bring themselves': "It would be silly . . . to say . . . 'This . . . you . . . must do', if the acts in question are such that manifestly but few could bring themselves to do them." The worry, thus understood, is not that they could not do it if they willed to, but that they cannot be expected to will to do so. This alternative reading is supported by Urmson's illustration of the dangers of asking more than can be expected of ordinary people. He offers the following "parallel from positive law": "The prohibition laws asked too much of the American people and were consequently broken systematically; and as people got used to breaking the law a general lowering of respect for the law naturally followed; it no longer seemed that a law was something that everybody could be expected to obey."[25] It would be very odd to suppose that the prohibition laws asked something of people that it was beyond the ability of the ordinary person to do (assuming that the ordinary person is not an alcoholic). The example is not odd on the interpretation just suggested.

But we now have another puzzle: if the reason why ordinary people cannot be expected to do more than minimal duty is not that they (we) are literally incapable of doing more, *why is it* that we cannot expect more of them (ourselves)? Reflection on Urmson's example of prohibition suggests the following answer: people may judge that what is asked of them is not worth the effort or sacrifice. The reason may be partly that they find it too difficult and partly that they think that what is asked of them should not be asked of them. The effort or sacrifice is more than is warranted. So perhaps what Urmson means is that the code asks not what it would be impossible for the ordinary man to do, if he really willed to do it, but asks *more than the ordinary man will judge to be worth the effort.*

If this is the problem, however, the solution need not be what Urmson suggests. Rather, the solution is to cleanse what goes by the name 'morality' of its silly requirements, so that what is asked is, although plenty difficult at times, unquestionably important. The solution is not to tailor morality to what people find easy enough to do. (And as Michael Clark notes, "what people find themselves able and willing to do may well be influenced by what is generally expected of them."[26])

---

25. The quotes from Urmson are from "Saints and Heroes," p. 70.
26. Clark, "Meritorious and Mandatory," p. 27.

So this alternative reading of Urmson's remarks about capacity brings us back to the points made earlier. If the reason why ordinary people cannot be expected to do more than "minimal duty" is that they believe themselves constitutionally incapable of doing more, we should not endorse that belief, but challenge it. If the problem is with what is advertised as morality—silly requirements put forth as the requirements of morality—let's correct that and not use it as an excuse for saying that morality itself must not be demanding. This is, interestingly, something that Kant thought needed correction, particularly insofar as the requirements of certain religions are thought of as moral requirements. This is prominent in *Religion*; but a passage in *Anthropology* is particularly appropriate here, since it emphasizes that when people are unwilling to exert the effort or make the personal sacrifice to do something asked of them, it sometimes is because they reasonably judge the thing asked of them to be not so much difficult as stupid.

> What vexations there are in the external practices that people attribute to religion . . . ! The merit of piety is located precisely in the fact that these practices serve no purpose, and in the mere submission of the faithful to patiently letting themselves be tormented by ceremonies and rites, penances and mortifications of the flesh (the more the better). This vassalage is *mechanically easy* (for no vicious inclination need be sacrificed in it). But to a thinking man it is bound to be *morally most troublesome* and irksome.—So when the great moral teacher of the people said, "My commands are not hard," he did not mean that we can fulfill them without much exertion; for as commands that require pure dispositions of the heart, they are in fact the hardest possible commands. But for a reasonable person they are still infinitely easier than commands to be busy doing nothing . . . . For a reasonable man finds what is mechanically easy very difficult, when he sees that the trouble it involves serves no purpose. (*A* 148)

6.2   More needs to be said about the notion that ordinary people cannot be expected to do more than minimal duty. The idea seems to be that we divide into two groups, the ordinary and the extraordinary, and while the latter can be saintly or heroic, the rest of us cannot be expected to do more than return what we borrow, refrain from beating people up, and the like. Whether this is the best interpretation of Urmson's view in "Saints and Heroes" is, as noted, not clear; but it is worthy of mention in any event since it does seem to motivate some defenses of supererogationism and historically has played a prominent role in religious ethics.[27]

The "two groups" idea contrasts sharply with Kant's view of people as equals and as capable of doing whatever morality requires. That we are all capable of this is asserted, among other places, in a dramatic passage in the second *Critique*.

> Suppose that someone says his lust is irresistible when the desired object and opportunity are present. Ask him whether he would not control his passion if, in front of the house where he has this opportunity, a gallows were erected on which he would be hanged immediately after gratifying his lust. We do not have to guess very long what his answer would be. But ask him whether he thinks it would be possible for him to overcome his love of life, however great it may be, if his sovereign threatened him with the same sudden death unless he made a false deposition against an honorable man whom the ruler wished to destroy under a plausible pretext. Whether he would or not he perhaps will not venture to say; but that it would be possible for him he would certainly admit without hesitation. (*PrR* 30)

6.3   Kant's view might strike some as romantic nonsense (although he of course saw it as antiromantic). The "two groups" idea, or some variant thereof which retains the notion that many or most of us are not capable of anything beyond "basic duties," may seem the more plausible one. After all, someone might argue, there *are* acts and activities, typically thought of as supererogatory, that some of us cannot bring off. The misogynist would be a dreadful rape crisis counselor, and the judgmental moralist would probably be abysmal at talking sympathetically with an ex-rapist racked by guilt. To take a rather different example, the non-swimmer cannot, no matter how strong his will, swim to the middle of the lake to save someone's life. Let's face it: we differ in our moral talents and in skills relevant to acting morally. Many of us cannot swim well and cannot perform surgery at all. You may be much more compassionate and sensitive than I, and I may be so lacking in sensitivity that it is pointless for me to try to comfort the bereaved or bolster the self-esteem of a chronic self-hater.

27. William Frankena appeals to and discusses it in his "Moral Decency," unpublished manuscript.

But at most this shows that there are *particular* good deeds that cannot be our duties. It does not show that *nothing* which is not a minimal, basic duty can be morally required of us.[28] The point here is that incapacity with respect to particular good deeds does not disprove the claim that one is morally obligated to do something more than "minimal" duty—it does not, for instance, disprove the claim that one has an imperfect duty to promote the happiness of others. If I am hopelessly bad at comforting people, perhaps I could still be helpful in other ways—maybe by helping to repair a neighbor's lawn mower or running errands for a friend who is ill. Absent from Urmson's discussion is any consideration of the possibility that we have open-ended duties, such as Kant's imperfect duties, to do what we can, given our abilities, talents, and proclivities, beyond minimal duty.

There is another point to make here.[29] Those of us who are very insensitive or lacking in compassion do not thereby acquire a *right* to be nasty and malicious, or even an *excuse* for our ill treatment of others. So it is hard to see why it should serve as a reason for limiting our duties to help others (much less serve, as Urmson's argument would have it, to limit everyone's duty to help others). As I argued in the previous chapter, our character flaws should not serve as excuses for immoral conduct or moral laziness. They are not, generally, to be regarded as permanent disabilities. Although it may well be true of some of us that we could never make ourselves paragons of compassion, surely there is something

28. Notice too that if it shows that there are particular good deeds that cannot be our duty, since we are incapable of performing them—swimming to the middle of a lake to rescue someone or helping someone overcome depression—they are not supererogatory for us, either. If I really cannot do x, x is not something which it would be good for me to do but which I do not really have to do. If I cannot swim, it is no more the case that I ideally should but do not have to swim to the middle of the lake (or that it would be good if I would do it, though I do not have to), than it is the case that I am obligated to do so.

29. The point is also made by Christopher New, who brings out how little mileage one can get from the uncontroversial point that x should not be required of a person if the person is incapable of doing x: "Saintliness and heroism are not duties for those who cannot be saintly and heroic. But, similarly, honesty and temperance are not duties for the kleptomaniac and the alcoholic; for honest and temperate are things they cannot be. That would be a poor reason for saying that honesty and temperance should not be laid down as duties at all. They are duties for those who can be honest and temperate. . . . It may be retorted that the alcoholic and kleptomaniac—and for that matter, the inveterate pick-pocket and habitual liar—have at least a duty to *try* to be temperate and honest. But this argument can be applied to saintliness and heroism too—have we not all a duty to try to become saintly and heroic, to resist the pull of selfishness and fear as much as we can?" (New, "Saints, Heroes, and Utilitarians," *Philosophy* 49 [1974]: 181).

that we can do to improve our characters—we can learn to be more sensitive, learn to be better listeners, learn not to point out to people that they have brought on their own ruin, and so on. In other words, not only is it odd to suggest that our inability to perform certain acts thought of as supererogatory should excuse us from performing any; we also let ourselves off too easy if, recognizing that we are insensitive and lacking in compassion, we simply *give up* on trying to lend a sympathetic ear and instead do something we find easy, like giving someone a present. This is the second conspicuous omission from Urmson's argument: there is no suggestion that we might have a duty to *improve* our characters, no thought that perhaps we should regard our characters not as fixed but as something that we are responsible for shaping.

7   It is time to pull together the various observations about what supererogationists suppose, or at least appear by omission to suppose, and see how, if at all, the observations combine to explain why supererogationists would not accept the Kantian way of dealing with the acts they think of as supererogatory.

First, there is the narrow conception of duty, slightly narrower on Urmson's view than on others. Duties, Urmson says, are to be exacted from a person like a debt. They entail corresponding rights, and the right-holder should be in a position to ascertain whether his rights are being violated. A duty to improve one's character, or a duty to promote the happiness of others (but not necessarily as much as possible) is in neither case a duty the fulfillment of which can be readily evaluated. And in those circumstances where its nonfulfillment is manifest, there is no one whose right is violated by its nonfulfillment, no one, that is, who has any claim to its fulfillment. Insofar as Heyd and Schumaker also hold that one cannot act wrongly without wronging someone, the latter reason for regarding Kantian imperfect duties as poor imitations of real duties would apply to them too. After all, if I fail to try to become a better person, there is no one who could claim to have been wronged by this particular failure of mine (even though many would have reason to believe that they are *worse off* than they would be if I were a better person).

The supererogationists' stand on duty does not by itself really explain why they would reject the Kantian approach if they gave it serious consideration. They might reasonably be expected to consider abandoning their notion of duty unless they had some independent grounds for

favoring it or for rejecting the Kantian treatment of acts they think of as
supererogatory.

The second reason, however, is more deeply entrenched. They view
moral constraints as burdensome and as something to be kept to a
minimum. Although this view *could* rest solely on the conception of duty
just explained, the claim seems instead to rest on the view that moral
constraints are not just unpleasant but are impediments to freedom. Just
what supererogationists mean by freedom is not entirely clear, but insofar as they mean freedom from constraints on doing what we might
wish to do, and include moral constraints among these, their position
would not incline them favorably toward Kant's approach. I find the
suggestion that an act is more purely optional if it is not guided by moral
considerations unpersuasive, and likewise the suggestion that we act
more freely if we are not guided by moral considerations. But the point
here is that one who held this view, together with the belief that the more
free we are, the better, would have strong reasons for rejecting Kant's
approach.

Schumaker's remarks hint at another aspect of this view: moral considerations should intrude into our lives as little as possible (unless, of
course, we choose to be more than minimally moral). The thought is, I
take it, not just that our decisions should not be constrained by the
demands of obligatory ends, but that we should not have to be thinking
about morality. Moral requirements should be specific, not open-ended.
We should be able to forget about them much of the time. I bring this out
because it clashes so sharply with the Kantian picture. One reason why
supererogationists would, I think, find Kant's scheme of duties repellent
is that they attach no value to being a self-legislator and to setting one's
ends, if these ends are ancillary to one's obligatory ends. The task of
being moral, as opposed to the results of people being moral, they seem
to regard as of no value (except instrumentally). It is best if people can
abide by morality's requirements as a matter of habit, without having to
pay much attention to what it is we are to do, and why. (This, inciden-
tally, may be part of the motivation for Urmson's claim that a moral code
"must be formulable in rules of manageable complexity.") To act
morally from habit would on Kant's view be a real loss, not (as is
sometimes thought) because it would be easy, when it is supposed to be
painful—it isn't—but because it would be rote and would not involve
one as an agent. Kant writes in the *Metaphysics of Morals* that "if the
practice of virtue were to become a habit the subject would suffer loss to

that *freedom* in adopting his maxims which distinguishes an action done from duty" (*MM* 409). And in the *Anthropology*: "We cannot define *virtue* as *acquired aptitude* for free lawful actions; for then it would be a mere mechanism in the exercise of our forces. Virtue is, rather, *moral strength* in pursuing our duty, which never becomes habit but should always spring forth, quite new and original, from our way of thinking" (*A* 147).

8   All of the views I have listed as supererogationist serve to support the picture of morality as dividing into two parts, minimal morality and moral excellence. They are bolstered, furthermore, by a key assumption, namely that we are not responsible for our characters. (Alternatively, they may bolster it; here, as elsewhere, it is hard to determine which assumption is more fundamental.) Our obligations are to act in certain ways—to perform certain "external" actions, not to change ourselves. And lurking behind that view *may* be a belief that many, even most, people just cannot be more than minimally moral—though I imagine that many supererogationists would repudiate that claim.

I suspect, in fact, that there is a different assumption that motivates the view that we have no duty to improve ourselves. This is an assumption that is not noted above and does not emerge in the works I have been citing. It is a view about moral excellence, an assumption about ranking people (or rather, types of people) and determining which sort of person is morally the very best. It is easier to explain if I first present what I take to be Kant's view.

For Kant, there are many ways of being a good person, and no clear best. The plurality of moral excellence is guaranteed by the open-endedness of the imperfect duties, and by the fact that we have two obligatory ends, not just one, and neither takes precedence over the other. The great musician—assuming that she does not neglect her imperfect duty to promote the happiness of others—*might* be just as good a person as Mother Teresa. (Or perhaps we should say this: they are both good people, and there is no reason to try to say who is better and little basis for making a comparison.) Because there is no clear best, the imperfect duty that we try to make ourselves better is not as demanding or intrusive as it might otherwise seem.

In contrast, the obligation to make oneself a better person is very intrusive if there is basically just one path for the virtuous to take, so that one is not acting as a truly virtuous person would if, say, one remains an art historian rather than going to an impoverished area of the world to help set up a medical clinic. The assumption that being morally very good means being very self-sacrificial, devoted to the welfare of others, and, furthermore, devoted to helping in certain stock ways colors much of moral philosophy. To take one example: Susan Wolf's well-known article "Moral Saints" paints a monotonic picture of what moral saints would be, as if they would all be fairly similar, and assumes that "a necessary condition of moral sainthood would be that one's life be dominated by a commitment to improving the welfare of others or of society as a whole."[30] To take another: Owen Flanagan, in his "Admirable Immorality and Admirable Imperfection," writes, "The talented student of the sitar who spends several hours a day practicing is doing something admirable, as well as developing an admirable trait. Whereas he violates no moral requirements by diligently practicing, he does what is less than morally ideal. He could after all be spending his time doing what Mother Teresa does."[31]

My point is not to call attention to these as bizarre claims or assumptions. Quite the contrary. The point is that these are widely held assumptions, not thought of as controversial. Kant's view is the one that strikes most of us as strange. Perhaps it is because most philosophers think that there is a fairly clear "morally best" that it is thought that an obligation to try to become a better person would not let us live our own lives. Insofar as supererogationists hold these assumptions, this would go quite far in explaining specifically why they do not ever speak of duties to seek to improve ourselves and, more generally, why they would not find Kant's way of dealing with supererogatory acts congenial.

So do we have a reply to the Kantian missionary who thinks that there is no ground for supererogationists' rejection of or lack of interest in Kant's alternative to supererogationism? I think we do—not a ground in the sense of a good argument for rejecting the Kantian alternative, but still a ground of sorts, rather than simply confusion or ignorance. Of

30. Susan Wolf, "Moral Saints," *Journal of Philosophy* 79 (1982): 419–439.
31. Owen Flanagan, "Admirable Immorality and Admirable Imperfection," *Journal of Philosophy* 83 (1986): 52. Another instance can be seen in Greg Trianosky's "Supererogation, Wrongdoing, and Vice: The Autonomy of an Ethics of Virtue," *Journal of Philosophy* 83 (1986): 26–40. Trianosky writes: "Moral saints and moral heroes are typically people who are always willing to help those in need, even at great risk or inconvenience to themselves. . . . We may think of such noble and selfless individuals as more or less faithful renditions of an ideal type, which I will call *the fully virtuous person*" (p. 31).

course, my aim has not just been the apparently friendly one of defending supererogationists against the missionary's assertion. I have also aimed to lay bare the reasons for supererogationism—reasons, that is, other than those that equally well support the Kantian approach—and to show how the latter gives a unified conception of how we ought to conduct ourselves, whereas the supererogationists, whether because they believe many people to be incapable of more than minimal morality or because they believe we are not responsible for shaping our characters, offer a two-track theory in which minimal morality and moral excellence are sharply separated.

Interlude

❖❖❖

Before leaving the topic of the previous chapter, it may be helpful to list several ways of thinking about character, moral excellence, and duty, and the duties we have with respect to character and moral excellence. This will clarify the views we have been discussing and situate them in a broader perspective. I list them, not with the plan of returning to the list later, but rather to clarify the views by distinguishing them from their near relatives and to provide a sketch, albeit incomplete, of the range of views that can be taken on these issues.

1   One view is the Kantian line as I have presented it: that we should not try to draw a line and say we have a duty up to this point but not beyond, and that everything beyond is supererogatory. Instead, the position is that in addition to having some very definite duties (perfect or narrow duties), we also have open-ended duties that require us to adopt the ends of the happiness of others and our own perfection but do not direct us as to just what, or how much, we must do in virtue of these ends. (They do, however, specify that we have a duty to improve ourselves morally.) Although this is the view that I have presented so far, I will consider in the next chapter the possibility that it is not accurate and will conclude that in fact it does need a slight revision in the direction of "rigorism"—more specifically, in the direction of the second view.

2   The second view is really a sketch of a constellation of possible views. Like the first, it is anti-supererogationist and purportedly Kantian. It holds that we have obligatory ends and that imperfect duties are open-

ended in the sense that the duties do not dictate exactly what we are to do and leave considerable latitude. But unlike the first view, it holds that we are to promote the two obligatory ends as much as we possibly can, in whatever ways we can best make our contribution. (The view would have to be clarified, since there is the question of how to balance the two ends. Different ways of balancing them would yield a variety of views.) Or again, the view could hold that we have a duty to make ourselves as virtuous as possible, again allowing for a variety of ways to do this, and it could cash out "as virtuous as possible" in a number of different ways—in terms of how often, how much effort we go to, and so on.

3 A third view might be thought of as a variant on the second. It is a view that Kant seems at times to be taking, though I follow Mary Gregor and others in thinking that it is not his position.[1] The view is that while the imperfect duties allow considerable latitude, the only permissible reason (other than genuine incapacity, or the requirement of a perfect duty) for omitting to do something that falls under a principle of imperfect duty is that we are doing something *else* that falls under a principle of imperfect duty. However, according to this view (unlike the last) it need not be the case that what we are doing instead *better* promotes others' happiness or our perfection. The idea here is that the justification for omitting to help someone, for example, is that we are helping someone else and cannot help both. It contrasts with the first view, which does not so limit the justification for omitting to help someone, and it contrasts with the second view (or, rather, one version of it) in being less strict: for the second view suggests that we must select courses of action that *most* promote the end, and the third view does not ask that.

4 A fourth view is again anti-supererogationist, but this time not at all Kantian. It is straightforwardly consequentialist and is advanced by

1. Mary Gregor, *Laws of Freedom: A Study of Kant's Method of Applying the Categorical Imperative in the "Metaphysik der Sitten"* (Oxford: Basil Blackwell, 1963), chap. 7. See also Thomas E. Hill Jr., "Kant on Imperfect Duty and Supererogation," in his *Dignity and Practical Reason in Kant's Moral Theory* (Ithaca: Cornell University Press, 1992), pp. 147–175. Although I share Gregor and Hill's view that this is not Kant's position, I disagree with them regarding a passage that they take to be strong evidence for their view. As I explain in Chap. 3, I do not think that the "fantastic virtue" passage (*MM* 409) is strong evidence against the third view because it is phony virtue, not "excessive" virtue, that Kant is criticizing.

Christopher New: we should always do as much good as we possibly can.[2]

5 The second, third, and fourth views demand more of agents than does the first. A fifth view is, like the first three views, fairly Kantian, but it demands less than do any of the views listed. It holds that we have imperfect duties, and they require us to have certain maxims and to act accordingly, but it denies that the imperfect duties (or anything else) require that we strive to be morally better. That is, it interprets the imperfect duties as offering a bit more latitude than I suggested, in that we may act in accordance with the imperfect duties while essentially taking our characters to be simply what they are, not for us to shape. So, according to this fifth view, if I am a caustic, irascible sort of person, I of course still have a duty to promote the happiness of others, but since I can do so even with my unfortunate personality—perhaps I can donate money to worthy causes, or water the neighbor's garden while he is on vacation—that is good enough. I need not try to change myself; I need not try to be more gentle, even if I do cause people close to me a lot of (avoidable) misery. On this view, moral excellence is very much optional. The attitude taken toward one's character is, I think, more like Urmson's than like Kant's view.

Notice that this view need not omit altogether the imperfect duty to develop our talents, since 'talents' encompasses a great deal: musical talents, skills at hunting, athletic excellence, and so on. However, it omits the imperfect duty to improve ourselves morally and, in doing so, dilutes the imperfect duties that it does recognize. Insofar as I am permitted to take my character as a given, I can treat as beyond my capacity a lot of activities that would help others or develop my talents.

6 A sixth view attempts to marry the supererogationist approach to Kant's ethics. Suggested by Hill's paper, "Kant on Imperfect Duty and Supererogation," it accepts the distinction between perfect and imperfect duty and holds that we have imperfect duties of just the sort Kant said, but at the same time holds that as long as we perform some acts (perhaps quite a few) of the sort indicated by the principles of imperfect duty, any

2. Christopher New, "Saints, Heroes, and Utilitarians," *Philosophy* 49 (1974): 179–189.

further acts of this sort are supererogatory. That is, it leaves room for the supererogatory in Kant's ethics, or seeks to make room for it, by designating that there does or can come a time, for an individual, when she has fulfilled an imperfect duty; after such a time, acts of that sort are supererogatory.

There are many ways in which the sixth view, which more closely resembles the first view than any of the other views, might be worked out.

6a   We might say that after a period of time, fulfillment of imperfect duties must be "renewed": acts of helping others cease to be, as a class, supererogatory. We must again perform some acts of that sort; if we do not, our actions would belie our claim to have the happiness of others as an end. After performing many such acts, acts of that sort are once again supererogatory. This might be labeled the *renewal* version of the view.

6b   Alternatively, we might say, as was suggested in the initial sketch of this view, that once we have performed enough such acts of promoting the happiness of others, all such acts are supererogatory. Call this the *home-free* version of the view.

Both the renewal and the home-free versions could be divided further to reflect differences regarding how acts are counted, and whether all acts count equally or instead are classified in terms of degrees of risk and sacrifice. Views that do take risk or sacrifice into account could be further divided as to whether degrees of sacrifice and risk are measured relative to the individual or against a more generic standard.

6c   A third version of the view that tries to marry supererogationism and Kant's ethics is less actional: it holds that I have a duty to make myself virtuous, but only up to a point; once I am reasonably virtuous, striving to be more virtuous is supererogatory. The view might go on to say that my duties to develop myself in other ways and to promote the happiness of others fall under the heading of the duty to be more virtuous and are correspondingly circumscribed. It is not as if once I am reasonably virtuous, I no longer am obligated ever to help others, or not obligated until some years have elapsed; as a virtuous person, I *do* help others. On the other hand, since I no longer have a duty to strive to be more virtuous, I do not have any duty to try to shape my character so as better to promote the happiness of others. This is, I think, the most interesting and most plausible of the versions of the view that present it as involving a threshold and as saying that once I have reached *this* or done *this much*, the rest is supererogatory (or, as in the first version, supererogatory at least for a while).

6d   A fourth version of the view involves a dividing line of a different sort: "Easy" acts of helping others are not as a class supererogatory but are best classified as ways of fulfilling an imperfect duty in the way that I described earlier and summed up under view 1. However, difficult acts of helping others *are* as a class supererogatory. Heroic and saintly acts are entirely beyond duty.

All four, (6a) through (6d), are versions of a hybrid view that recognizes imperfect duties but says that beyond a threshold, they become supererogatory.

7   A seventh view is a position which Heyd pinpoints in order to reject and which Urmson seems to hold in "Saints and Heroes." The position is that because most of us are not capable of doing more than φ, and yet it is imperative for survival, or for minimally civilized survival, that we do φ, it is best to limit our duties to φ and to regard all the rest as beyond duty.

8   An eighth is the position that Heyd takes: even if we are all capable of doing more than φ, and even if the risks and costs of doing more than φ are not great, still everything beyond φ should be treated as optional, for reasons of freedom, autonomy, and community, and especially the value of giving absolutely freely. (I believe Clark and Schumaker accept this, too.)

It may be helpful to contrast the supererogationist stands, (7) and (8), from two positions that have something in common with them but are more radical. Both are suggested (but not endorsed) in a paper by William Frankena, entitled "Moral Decency," and are forms of what he calls *moral decentism*.[3]

9   On this view, morality requires or advocates nothing more than being morally decent. All it asks or even "wants" of us is that we be morally decent. This is similar to views taken by supererogationists but is not quite the same, given the "or even 'wants' of us." It is hard to

3. William Frankena, "Moral Decency," unpublished manuscript.

motivate. One way to motivate it, or at least imagine how someone might find it plausible, is to imagine that a great many of us are such that invariably, if we try to be better than morally decent, we botch it badly, causing great harm. Of us, one might argue, morality does not even want more than moral decency, given our dreadful limitations. Another is to imagine a religious view to the effect that it would be arrogant of us to strive to be more than morally decent; greater goodness is strictly for the gods.

10   A more understandable view is that morality does ask and want more of us than moral decency, but we (a very large majority of us) should not even try to comply. With slight modification, this is Susan Wolf's view in "Moral Saints."[4] The thought is that if we were morally excellent, that would be, in various ways, something of a shame; we can be more excellent if morally we are not quite excellent. If we are only morally decent, not better than morally decent, one barrier to excellence in general is removed; so for that reason it is better to be morally decent than to be morally excellent.

This list serves to give some indication of the array of views that one might take on the subject. It is to that end that I have listed them, and also to clarify the view presented by comparing it to some close cousins. My aim in Chapter 2 was to arrive at a deeper understanding of the disagreement between Kantians and supererogationists than was possible in Chapter 1, and to highlight features of the Kantian view regarding character and moral excellence that tend to go unnoticed. This interlude further highlights those features.

4. Susan Wolf, "Moral Saints," *Journal of Philosophy* 79 (1982): 419–439.

3

Latitude in Kant's Imperfect Duties

◅◆►

1 The list in the first interlude of various positions concerning moral character and the scope of duty is a reminder of some unfinished business. Up until now I have, to avoid unmanageable confusion, postponed addressing the question of just how much latitude there is in Kant's imperfect duties. By and large I followed Hill's explanation of Kant's distinction between perfect and imperfect duties (though my discussion of imperfect duties at times betrays a slightly sterner, or less latitudinarian, view than the one Hill seems to attribute to Kant). In this chapter I explore the question of latitude and consider the possibility that an altogether different reading from the one I laid out in Chapter 1 might be in order.

We need first to be clear on what is not controversial. As explained above, Kant's imperfect duties are duties to adopt certain obligatory ends—the ends of one's own perfection and the happiness of others. Indirectly they require us to perform acts of a certain sort (what sort and how specific a sort have to be left open at this point in our discussion), since it is not the case that we have these ends if we do not act accordingly. If I do nothing whatsoever to develop my talents, it cannot be the case that I have as one of my maxims, 'Perfect thyself'. This much is clear; and it is clear that the wide imperfect duties (and, in fact, all imperfect duties) allow latitude as to just *what* we are to do. How I seek to promote others' happiness, which talents I will especially seek to cultivate, and what sort of morally excellent person I strive to be are matters to be determined partly by chance, but to no small degree by my choice. But latitude has another dimension as well, as the following passage indicates.

(A) [Since] the law can prescribe only the maxim of actions, not actions themselves, this is a sign that it leaves a latitude (*latitudo*) for free choice in following (complying with) the law, that is, that the law cannot specify precisely in what way one is to act and how much one is to do by the action for an end that is also a duty. (*MM* 390)

Imperfect duties allow latitude with respect not only to *what* we do but also to *how much* we do.

Just how much latitude do Kant's imperfect duties leave us? Even if we ignore the *Lectures on Ethics*, where the perfect/imperfect distinction is identical to the juridical/ethical distinction, Kant's texts suggest several views. The standard view, insofar as there is one, is that taken by Hill in "Kant on Imperfect Duty and Supererogation." That view is that besides requiring one to adopt the obligatory ends, the imperfect duties require only that one "act accordingly, at least sometimes, if he gets a chance". Hill explains: "imperfect duties allow us to do what we please on some occasions even if this is not an act of a kind prescribed by moral principles and even if we could on those occasions do something of a kind that is prescribed. For example, though we have an imperfect duty of beneficence we may sometimes pass over an opportunity to make others happy simply because we would rather do something else."[1]

Readings according to which the imperfect duties demand more than this merit consideration. Let us consider a rigorist view that has been discussed in the literature (though not distinguished from other possible rigorist positions) and label it R_1.

R_1 Imperfect duties do not allow us to omit performing an act of a kind they prescribe *unless*, in those circumstances, we perform another act of a kind they (or perfect duties) prescribe. In other words, the only permissible reason for not performing an act that falls under a principle of imperfect duty is (a) that one is performing another act which falls under a principle of imperfect duty or (b) that one is performing an act required by a perfect duty.

This position is suggested by the sentence that immediately follows passage (A), above. Kant cautions:

(B) But a wide duty is not to be taken as permission to make exceptions to the maxims of actions, but only as permission to limit one maxim of

1. Thomas E. Hill Jr., *Dignity and Practical Reason in Kant's Moral Theory* (Ithaca: Cornell University Press, 1992), chap. 8. The quotations are from pp. 150 and 152–153.

duty by another (*e.g.*, love of one's neighbor in general by love of one's parents), by which in fact the field for the practice of virtue is widened. (*MM* 390)

According to R_1, the only permissible reason for not performing an act that falls under a principle of imperfect duty is that one is either performing another act that falls under a principle of imperfect duty or fulfilling a perfect duty. This does seem, at least initially, to be a plausible reading of (B); the point of the example might reasonably be said to be that the latitude of imperfect duties does not license us just to forego—for no particular reason—an opportunity to help someone but only licenses foregoing such an opportunity because it is impossible *both* to help that person *and* to help another.

Following Mary Gregor, Hill argues against the rigorist interpretation, citing passages that conflict with it and suggesting another reading of (B).[2] One passage he cites is the "fantastic virtue" passage.

(C) But that man can be called fantastically virtuous who allows *nothing to be morally indifferent (adiaphora)* and strews all his steps with duties, as with man-traps; it is not indifferent to him whether I eat meat or fish, drink beer or wine, supposing that both agree with me. Fantastic virtue is a concern with petty details [*Mikrologie*] which, were it admitted into the doctrine of virtue, would turn the government of virtue into tyranny. (*MM* 409)

The passage might be thought to conflict with the rigoristic interpretation of (B) by claiming that one can be too virtuous. The fantastically virtuous man might be thought, that is, to be someone who constantly strives to help others or to perfect himself. But this would be a misreading of the passage. He is not someone who is or tries to be "too virtuous"; in fact, "really to be *too virtuous*," Kant writes, "would be almost equivalent to making a circle too round or a straight line too straight" (*MM* 433n). "Fantastic virtue" does not refer to excessive virtue; virtue does not, according to Kant, admit of excess any more than a circle admits of excessive roundness.[3] It refers, rather, to phony virtue. The

2. Ibid., pp. 151–153; and Mary Gregor, *Laws of Freedom: A Study of Kant's Method of Applying the Categorical Imperative in the "Metaphysik der Sitten"* (Oxford: Basil Blackwell, 1963), pp. 107–112.

3. It is true that in the footnote just quoted Kant uses the words 'fantastic' and 'fantasy' in connection with virtue in a way that might seem to support the hunch that fantastic virtue is excessive virtue. Just before the sentence quoted, he says that virtue ("in its

fantastically virtuous man is someone who sees virtue (or the possibility of being virtuous) where it is not. He sees some things that in fact are morally indifferent as if they were not morally indifferent. He is not someone who takes imperfect duties too seriously but someone who makes a fetish out of trivial things (what to eat and drink, and when), wrongly thinking them to be morally nontrivial.[4] (This is the same "fetishism" that Kant criticizes briefly in the *Anthropology* and extensively in the *Religion*.[5])

Nonetheless, this passage is in some tension with the rigoristic reading of (B). For on that reading, a person is, as Hill puts it, "never free from obligation unless it is impossible for him to do something for the happiness of others or towards the development of his own talents." Insofar as "it is virtually always possible to do something for others' happiness or to develop one's talents, the rigoristic interpretation leads to the conclusion that there is virtually nothing morally indifferent, contrary to what Kant says."[6] The rigoristic reading of (B) does not entail that a choice between beer and wine, or fish and fowl, is itself a moral issue; so in that sense it does not entail that these are not morally indifferent. What it does, rather, is limit—rather drastically, one might argue—the moments of one's life in which one is free to do something that does not promote others' happiness or one's own perfection.

The point should not be exaggerated. It is not as if one could not, on the rigorist reading, spend an evening socializing (over wine or beer). It

---

perfection") "is an ideal which requires us to approximate to this end but not to attain it completely, since the latter requirement surpasses man's powers and introduces a lack of sense (fantasy) into the principle of virtue." The point here, however, is not that one who strives to be as virtuous as possible errs, but only that a requirement that we completely attain perfection would be "fantastic." And the footnote very explicitly rejects the notion that one can be too virtuous.

4. One could, of course, plausibly argue that what to eat is in some respects *not* a trivial matter on the grounds that it is wrong to eat meat or that by consuming certain goods, one thereby supports industries, institutions, and practices which are at best morally dubious— e.g., the practices of Nestlé Company of marketing infant formula to the world's poorest people, despite overwhelming evidence that because of unsafe water, illiteracy (hence inability to read the directions), and poverty (hence inability to afford the formula, on which, having weaned their young from breast milk, mothers become dependent), the result is mass starvation. We could easily present a wealth of such examples, but this would not be to the point: though important in their own right, these issues do not bear on the question of interpretation at hand.

5. See, for example, R 168–169/157 and 174/162, and A 127.

6. Hill, *Dignity*, p. 152.

is not as if that would be ruled out in favor of instead doing something to promote others' happiness or develop one's talents. Depending on one's personality, spending an evening with friends presumably would count as doing something that promotes others' happiness. R_1 (unlike R_2, presented below) does not say one has to do *as much as possible* at all times to promote others' happiness or one's perfection. Quite a lot of activities—reading a reasonably good novel or magazine, taking a walk with one's child, cooking a reasonably nutritious and savory meal for friends—would qualify as activities that promote others' happiness or one's perfection. Still, some acts would not, for example, taking a nap that one does not need. On R_1, one should instead read or exercise or listen (attentively) to an opera, or invite a friend out for ice cream. This, one might argue, leaves too little room for morally indifferent acts. It means that an act either fulfills a perfect duty, is in accordance with an imperfect duty, or else is wrong—unless there just was not anything one could do, in those circumstances, to promote others' happiness or one's own perfection. And this, while not in direct conflict with what Kant says in the fantastic virtue passage, is in some tension with it.

This is, I think, rather meager evidence against the rigoristic interpretation of (B). But there are other passages, also cited by Hill, which are in direct conflict with it.[7]

> (D) Lawgiving reason . . . includes me as giving universal law along with all others in the duty of mutual benevolence, in accordance with the principle of equality, and *permits* you to be benevolent to yourself on the condition of your being benevolent to every other as well. (*MM* 451)

On R_1, considerations of my well-being, unlike those of my perfection or of the well-being of Sam, would not be a permissible reason for omitting to help Sandy. But passage (D) makes it quite clear that it *can* be a permissible reason. It does not justify foregoing altogether to help others, but it allows me to weigh in considerations other than those of others' happiness or my perfection when I choose whether or not, in particular circumstances, to opt for a course of action of helping another person (or

7. Gregor's version of the rigorist interpretation is different from (and weaker than) R_1, and is not in conflict with (D). The version of rigorism that she considers does not, she writes, "deny that there is a place in the moral life for choice that is, in a sense, arbitrary" (*Laws of Freedom*, p. 105). I am not considering this putative version of rigorism, because it seems to allow so much latitude as to cease to be rigoristic.

improving myself). The passage is particularly strong evidence against the rigoristic interpretation since it states a position quite central to Kant's theory. We are all equals; there is no ground for regarding as morally irrelevant one's own happiness.[8]

Still another passage in conflict with R_1 is the following, from the introduction to the *Doctrine of Virtue*:

> (E) I ought to sacrifice a part of my welfare to others without hope of return because this is a duty, and it is impossible to assign specific limits to the extent of this sacrifice. How far it should extend depends, in large part, on what each person's true needs are in view of his sensibilities, and it must be left to each to decide this for himself. (*MM* 393)

It is not clear what Kant means by 'true needs', but this need not detain us. The passage indicates that latitude does not merely concern freedom to choose *which* acts to perform by way of fulfilling imperfect duties; yet that is the most that latitude would encompass if R_1 were correct. A passage at *MM* 392 also bears this out, and indeed shows more. It shows that the imperfect duties allow latitude as to how far we go—not just how much, if anything, we do right now—with respect to an obligatory end.[9] The duty to promote one's natural perfection is "of wide obligation," Kant writes.

> (F) No rational principle prescribes specifically *how* far one should go in cultivating one's capacities (in enlarging or correcting one's capacity for understanding, *i.e.*, in acquiring knowledge or skill). (*MM* 392)

8. Recall that the reason Kant offers as to why we have no duty to promote our own happiness—and he offers it repeatedly—is that we seek it anyway. His claim *is* puzzling, since as Bishop Butler stressed (and as Kant at some moments notes, e.g., *G* 399), people sometimes fail, either deliberately or because of carelessness or recklessness, to promote their own happiness. My point, however, is not to evaluate his claim but to emphasize that he offers no other reason why we have no duty to promote our own happiness. It is not that it is somehow "less right" to promote our own happiness than it is to promote that of others; nor is the promotion of our own happiness grudgingly permitted, or permitted as a reward for, or in exchange for, good behavior.

9. One might dispute this by arguing that Kant means, in (F), only that how far one should go in cultivating various powers depends on one's particular talents, interests, proclivities, monetary resources, etc.; not that we are under no obligation to do all that we can to perfect some natural talents or other. Although this alternative reading *is* a possible reading, it is a bit forced and does not sit well with the rest of the paragraph. (Why would the next sentence, which notes the "different situations in which men find themselves" begin 'Then too' if the sentence in question itself concerned our different situations?)

There is, in short, a great deal of textual evidence against the rigoristic interpretation of (B).[10] In addition, there is an alternative reading that is no less natural. As Gregor and Hill point out, the passage can be read as saying that we may not altogether *reject* an end of, for example, helping our neighbors on the ground that we are taking care of elderly parents; but we may limit our pursuit of the first end in favor of the second—that is, put much more energy into the latter and relatively little into the former. Kant's cautionary note, on this reading, is not that we have latitude only as to which of various acts of fulfilling imperfect duty we choose (implying that we must pick one, unless somehow there is nothing at all of that nature that we possibly could do right now). Rather, the cautionary note concerns *maxims* or *ends*, not specific actions, and warns that we may not pick just one instantiation of the obligatory end—for example, *my children's happiness* as an instantiation of *the happiness of others*—and dismiss all other instantiations as "not an end I adopt." That I have young children to tend to will sometimes be an adequate reason for not embarking on some particular projects of helping others, but it is no excuse for a policy of turning my back on needy people other than my children (and me).

The point of (B) can be brought out in another way. To adopt an obligatory end I must adopt some subsidiary ends—ends that instantiate the obligatory end. I cannot make the happiness of others my end without making the happiness of some particular persons my end. One might have thought that it would suffice if I made only the happiness of a few people near and dear to me my end and totally neglected that of all others; Kant's remark clarifies that that would not do at all. I may focus primarily on the happiness of a few others, but I may not have a policy of ignoring the needs of all others.

I think that the textual evidence against the rigoristic reading of (B) is strong enough to warrant accepting the alternative reading as the correct one. And because there is no other textual evidence that supports R_1, and (D), (E), and (F) are evidence against R_1, I see no reason to give R_1 further consideration.

10. Gregor points out a further reason for rejecting R_1. Given Kant's characterization of the difference between perfect and imperfect duties, since we find "in the case of perfect duty . . . necessary exceptions to the general prohibition when we admit empirical knowledge of men's circumstances and conditions, we should expect that the latitude present in imperfect duty implies that, when we admit such empirical knowledge, the duty does permit arbitrary exceptions" (*Laws of Freedom*, p. 102).

2   But this does not settle the larger question, namely, whether some rigoristic interpretation of the imperfect duties might be correct. There are other passages that suggest that something like R₁ might be Kant's view. Shortly after the passage cited above (*MM* 392) indicating that how far we are to go in cultivating our natural powers cannot be prescribed, Kant turns to the duty to perfect ourselves morally. His discussion suggests a more limited latitude than was suggested in (F).

> (G) Hence this duty too—the duty of assessing the worth of one's actions not by their legality alone but also by their morality (one's disposition)—is of only *wide* obligation. The law does not prescribe this inner action in the human mind but only the maxim of the action, to strive with all one's might that the thought of duty for its own sake is the sufficient incentive of every action conforming to duty. (*MM* 393)

The following passages also lend support to a rigorist interpretation:

> (H) But to teach a pupil to *admire* virtuous actions, however great the sacrifice these may have entailed, is not in harmony with preserving his feeling for moral goodness. For be a man never so virtuous, *all the goodness he can ever perform is still his simple duty* (R 48/44; my emphasis)
>
> (I) [One cannot], through future good conduct, produce a surplus over and above what he is under obligation to perform at every instant, *for it is always his duty to do all the good that lies in his power.* (R 72/66; my emphasis and brackets)

What sort of rigorism do these passages suggest? Not, I think, R₁ exactly; for all of them contain (though in slightly different ways) a notion of maximization. (G) says that we are to strive with all our might. (H) enjoins performing all the goodness one can; and (I) says it is one's duty to do all the good one can. This suggests that rather than R₁, the rigorist view we should consider attributing to Kant is one that says that we must always do all we can by way of promoting the obligatory ends. Thus:

> R₂ The only permissible reasons for not performing an act that falls under a principle of imperfect duty are (a) that one is performing another act that falls under a principle of imperfect duty, and *one that better promotes* the obligatory ends than does the act in

question (or equally promotes them) or (b) that one is performing
an act required by a perfect duty.[11]

R_2 is stronger than R_1, since according to it imperfect duties require that
we do *as much as possible* to promote the happiness of others and our
own perfection. It asks us to *do the best we possibly can, at all times.*

Although R_2 initially appears to be an interpretation worth taking
seriously, it is marred by an unclarity in (a)—an unclarity that points to
a deeper problem. What is meant by an act that (compared with the act
in question) "better promotes the obligatory ends"? What, in other
words, is meant (in the sentence before R_2) by "we must always do all we
can by way of promoting the obligatory ends"? Are we, at every time t,
to do all we can to promote at t whichever end we can promote more in
that situation? Or, are we to do all we can to promote at t either end?
(Here it is our choice which end we try maximally to promote; our choice
need not be guided by a judgment as to which end we can better promote
in that situation.) In each of these cases, one end is slighted; and that
seems clearly not in keeping with Kant's position that they are both
obligatory ends, neither of which is to be neglected in favor of the other.
The idea would seem to be rather to try to maximize both at once; but it
is hard to see how that could be done—harder even than it is to see what
it would be to determine which act open to me right now maximizes
either end.

None of these views makes much sense, particularly as a view to
attribute to Kant. What I called an "unclarity" in R_2 thus seems not to be
an unclarity that can be corrected, but rather an indication that R_2 needs
to be scrapped. The problem with R_2 appears to have three components:
the temporal element, the element of maximization, and the fact that on
Kant's view there are two obligatory ends (with priority given to neither)
rather than just one. Rather than give up at this point on all rigorist
interpretations, we might see if we can avoid the problem by formulating
rigorist views that lack one or another of these components. We can start
by revising the temporal index:

> R_3 Our imperfect duties require that we do as much as possible to
> promote one or both obligatory ends, but they require this only

---

11. I'll ignore the complication created by the parenthetical 'or equally promotes them'.

over the long run. We do not have a duty at all times to do the best we possibly can.[12]

For reasons to be explained momentarily, it will be helpful to separate out the different forms that R_3 can take.

$R_{3.1}$ Our imperfect duties require that we do as much as possible to promote the end of the happiness of others.

$R_{3.2}$ Our imperfect duties require that we do as much as possible to develop our natural talents.

$R_{3.3}$ Our imperfect duties require that we do as much as possible to perfect ourselves morally.

In each version of R_3 just one obligatory end is mentioned. The requirement with respect to the obligatory end not mentioned in each respective version of R_3 is like that of the standard view: we are required to promote the end but not to seek to promote it as much as possible. (Of course, R_3 could take a form that conjoins two or all of the above.)

The reason for distinguishing these three versions of R_3 is that there is textual evidence against the first two versions which does not bear on the third, and evidence for the third which does not support the first two. (E) is evidence against $R_{3.1}$, and (F) is evidence against $R_{3.2}$, but neither tells against $R_{3.3}$. That is, Kant specifies that the extent to which one is to sacrifice one's own well-being for that of others and how far one is to go in cultivating one's talents cannot be prescribed in a determinate way; but he does not say anything of this sort with respect to how far we are to go in developing ourselves morally. In addition, in his remarks about moral self-perfection Kant not infrequently uses phrases such as 'as much as possible' and, as in (I), 'all the good that lies in his power', which are suggestive of rigorism; but he rarely uses such terms in connection with developing one's natural talents or promoting the happiness of others. This leads to the thought that perhaps R_3 is Kant's view with respect to moral self-perfection, but only with respect to that end; in other words, that $R_{3.3}$ is his position.

12. To appreciate the need for the distinction between R_2 and R_3, see R. M. Adams's "Saints," *Journal of Philosophy* (July 1984): 392–400. Adams challenges the assumption that "the perfection of a person, in at least the moral type of value, depends on the maximization of that type of value in every single action of the person" (p. 393).

Further support for the hunch emerges when we recall (D) and notice that the very strong reasons it provided against attributing rigorism to Kant do not apply to the attribution to him of $R_{3.3}$.

R_1 (and any form of R_2 which required striving, at every opportunity, to maximize happiness for others) clashes with (D). Rigorism of the forms mentioned leaves no room for taking into consideration one's own happiness, and recognizing that it too counts. It leaves no room, that is, for recognizing that I am equal with all others and have a right to pursue my own happiness as long as I am treating the happiness of others as also an end in itself. But this conflict does not arise between (D) and $R_{3.3}$. One might think that it does: it might seem that my happiness should be a reason for limiting, if I wish, my endeavors to become morally better. But that is not a view Kant holds. The point in (D) about one's own happiness is simply that the principle of benevolence is universal and does not exclude the agent. My happiness is *someone's happiness*; I am not to discount it.

> I want everyone else to be benevolent toward me . . . ; hence I ought also be benevolent toward everyone else. But since all *others* with the exception of myself would not be *all*, so that the maxim would not have within it the universality of a law, which is still necessary for imposing obligation, the law making benevolence a duty will include myself, as the object of benevolence, in the command of practical reason. (*MM* 451)

Kant's reasoning makes it plain that (D) has no bearing on $R_{3.3}$.[13]

Now, it must be admitted that the interpretation I have offered does not square with all of the relevant passages. Both (H) and (I) do suggest a more rigorist reading. I doubt, though, that any interpretation would fit neatly with every relevant passage, and if we are forced to slight some passages, (H) and (I) are the clear choice. Whereas the other passages speak directly to the question of latitude, (H) and (I) do not. (The point of the passage from which [H] is taken is that we should not teach a pupil to admire virtuous actions, for to wonder at a virtuous act "is a lowering of our feeling for duty, as if to act in obedience to it were something extraordinary and meritorious." The paragraph in which [I] occurs

---

13. It does have some bearing on $R_{3.1}$. Although it is consistent with $R_{3.1}$ that I now and then take my happiness into account and allow such considerations to outweigh, on those occasions, the considerations in favor of doing all that I can to promote others' happiness, if I do so very often I will be in violation of $R_{3.1}$.

argues against the notion that one can, through good deeds, store up moral credit that can then erase one's moral debts.)

It might be thought that it was unnecessary to introduce a third version of rigorism (R_3); why did we not simply break down R_2 into $R_{2.1}$, $R_{2.2}$, and $R_{2.3}$, corresponding to $R_{3.1}$, $R_{3.2}$, and $R_{3.3}$? What is the relevance, in other words, of the omission—for this is the difference between R_2 and R_3—of 'at all times'? The reason for omitting this temporal index is apparent when we realize that on $R_{2.3}$ one would be morally required to do as much as one possibly can *at all times* to perfect oneself morally. Yet this is clearly not Kant's position and could not be without a revision in his position so as to give priority to the end of moral self-perfection over the end of the happiness of others. On $R_{2.3}$ it would be wrong to interrupt an activity that promotes self-improvement to do a favor for a friend (assuming that helping the friend does not also promote moral self-betterment). On $R_{3.3}$ this would not be wrong, for it does not ask that at all times we do all we can to improve ourselves morally.

3   If the claims of the last few paragraphs are correct, Kant intends the duty to perfect oneself morally to have less latitude than the duty to promote others' happiness and less than the duty to develop one's natural talents. His wording suggests that we are to do all we can to make ourselves (morally) better people, while it indicates that with respect to the duty to develop our natural talents and the duty to promote others' happiness, how far we are to go is left open. The duty to perfect ourselves morally leaves us considerable latitude as to *how* we are to go about perfecting ourselves—somewhat less latitude than that of either the duty to develop our natural talents or the duty to promote others' happiness, and a bit more than the latitude allowed by the duty to respect others. It allows decidedly less latitude as to *how much* we do than do the first two duties just mentioned, but more than does the duty to respect others, for though we are never morally permitted to *omit* on a given occasion treating others with respect, we need not always do all we can to perfect ourselves morally. In other words, the duty to perfect ourselves morally does not "distribute" to every occasion (every occasion on which it would be possible to do something to perfect ourselves morally); the duty to respect others does.

Where, then, does this leave us? How much latitude do the wide imperfect duties allow? My suggestion is that the standard interpretation is roughly right, but that it needs to be supplemented by a greater emphasis on the fact that we are, on Kant's view, to strive to make ourselves better people—and strive to do so no matter how good we already are. This duty affects how we are to carry out the duty to promote others' happiness. One might think it sufficient to embrace the end of others' welfare, taking it seriously enough to go to some trouble to help others, yet at the same time allowing one's endeavors to be circumscribed by the limitations of one's personality. Thus, if I am easily annoyed or depressed by unhappy people, it would be "good enough" if I sent cheery greeting cards or little presents but avoided seeing or talking with them. Or if I am insensitive and lacking in compassion, and thus lousy at comforting the bereaved or bolstering the self-esteem of a chronic self-doubter, still I can promote the happiness of others in other ways, for example, by donating to charities or watering a neighbor's lawn when he is away.

But this is not really in the spirit of the imperfect duty of making the ends of others one's own. Or to put it differently: the full spirit of it is not brought out until that duty is seen as shaped and "stiffened" by the duty to improve oneself morally. Moreover, the relation goes both ways: the former duty bolsters and gives shape to the duty to improve oneself morally. I am to make myself better and be alert to how I ought to improve. Insofar as I make the happiness of others my end, I will notice, in my self-scrutiny, shortcomings in myself which hurt others (e.g., a tendency to avoid friends when they are ill or depressed or in mourning) and will strive to improve myself in those respects.

The preceding two paragraphs may not be at odds with Hill's interpretation. They add some rigorism that he may or may not oppose. His discussions of the duty to promote others' happiness do not mention the effects on it of the duty to improve oneself morally nor, more generally, any responsibility to do more than help others from time to time (and be ready to help in any emergency, as long as the risks and costs to oneself are small). Of course we must have the right sorts of maxims, but just what count as the right sorts (and as having a maxim) is not spelled out in a way that suitably modifies the suggestion that, with the parenthetical proviso just given, the wide imperfect duties require only that one "act accordingly, at least sometimes, if he gets a chance."[14]

This brings me to a feature of his interpretation which I would deemphasize, despite the fact that it has firm support from the only

14. Hill, *Dignity*, p. 150.

passage in the *Groundwork* which mentions perfect and imperfect duties. There, while indicating that the distinction will be developed later in "a future *Metaphysics of Morals*," Kant offers for the time being this characterization: a perfect duty is "one which allows no exception in the interests of inclination" (*G* 422n). As Hill writes, this leaves us to "infer that imperfect duties allow some such exception." Hill is cautious here— "some such exception"—but the view he develops is that the wide imperfect duties allow "freedom to choose to do *x* or not on a given occasion *as one pleases*, even though one knows that *x* is the sort of act that falls under the principle, provided that one is ready to perform acts of that sort on some other occasions."[15] This is, I think, slightly mislead-ing. If my maxim were to help others only when I felt like it, my conduct would violate my imperfect duty to make the happiness of others my end. I may not, in keeping with the imperfect duty of promoting others' happiness, allow the fact that something pleases or fails to please me decide the way in which, and the degree to which, I help others.

This does not contradict what Hill says. It is true that I may, on some occasions, omit helping others without having any very good reason for doing so, though (as Hill recognizes and suggests in a footnote) together with the reason 'I didn't feel like it' would have to be the absence of certain factors (e.g., that it was a life-and-death matter and that I could easily have done something to help). The point is that the duty in question carries with it a responsibility considerably greater than that of acting beneficently from time to time (as one pleases, but at least occa-sionally) and not being indifferent to the welfare of others. There are many subsidiary maxims that would be acceptable specifications of the more general maxim, 'Promote the happiness of others'; but 'Do so only when it's easy' or 'Do so only when it's convenient' or 'Do so only when it promises to bring you praise [or, to enhance your career]' would, like 'Do so only when you feel like it', decidedly not be appropriate specifica-tions of the maxim 'Promote the happiness of others'. That this is so indicates both the latitude allowed and the difficulty of saying how far we must go or how hard we must work to promote others' happiness, and it at the same time shows why it is somewhat misleading to characterize their latitude in the way that Hill does.

My primary concern in this chapter has been to consider alternative positions that might be taken as to how much latitude the wide imperfect

15. Ibid., pp. 148 and 155.

duties allow. Having canvassed the more rigorist possibilities and proposed adding a bit of rigorism to Hill's view, I now evaluate another challenge.

4 The challenge to my understanding of the wide imperfect duties which I need now to consider comes from the opposite end of the spectrum: the latitudinarian direction. The claim, advanced by Richard McCarty in a discussion of supererogation and Kantian ethics, is not exactly that Kant's imperfect duties allow more latitude than I have suggested, but that what they require admits of an upper limit.[16] In Chapter 1, I quoted (and affirmed) the following observation from Warner Wick: the imperfect duties "not only allow us considerable leeway in achieving their objectives, but they are indefinite in the further sense that what they demand is also without assignable limits." McCarty reminds us that Kant does not say that imperfect duties admit of no limits, but only that they admit of no *determinate* (or assignable) limits. Although there is no warrant for McCarty's assertion that in denying that they have determinate limits, Kant is "implying that [they] have *indeterminate* limits," the possibility that Kant *does* hold that they have indeterminate limits deserves consideration.[17]

McCarty explains his claim that the imperfect duties have indeterminate limits as follows:

> We cannot say precisely how much one ought to contribute to ends enjoined by duties of virtue. This does not, however, prevent us from recognizing efforts which clearly surpass the limits of those duties. Consequently, determining the exact point at which one's sacrifices on others' behalf surpass the limits of obligation is impossible, just as it is impossible to determine the point at which a balding man becomes bald. Yet some heroic actions on others' behalf are clearly well beyond the reasonable limits of imperfect obligation, just as some men are clearly bald.[18]

His arguments appeal to the fantastic virtue passage and specifically to Kant's rejection of fantastic virtue. They aim to show that since Kant

16. Richard McCarty, "The Limits of Kantian Duty, and Beyond," *American Philosophical Quarterly* 26 (1989): 43–52.

17. Ibid., p. 45. McCarty uses the words 'determinate' and 'indeterminate' because he is working with Gregor's 1964 translation: "it cannot assign determinate limits [bestimmte Grenzen] to the extent of this sacrifice" (Immanuel Kant, *The Doctrine of Virtue*, trans. Mary Gregor (New York: Harper and Row, 1964; reprint, Philadelphia: University of Pennsylvania Press, 1971), 393/53).

18. McCarty, "Limits of Kantian Duty," p. 45.

rejects fantastic virtue (and also denies that wide imperfect duties have determinate limits), he must hold that wide imperfect duties have indeterminate limits. Unfortunately, his reasoning appears to hinge either on an error that I cautioned against above—namely, the error of thinking that the fantastically virtuous person is someone who is too virtuous—or (what amounts to a very similar mistake) on an equivocation concerning '*limits* to moral obligation' (or what it is to take virtue "too far").

One can be said to take virtue too far (to fail to recognize its limits) in two different ways. First, someone might be said to be *too* good. Second, one might be said to take the notion of virtue into territory to which it does not apply if, for example, she thinks a certain activity is virtuous or is vicious when in fact it is morally neutral. Similarly (to explain the equivocation now as an equivocation on the *limits of duty*), an act can be beyond the limits of duty in two quite different ways. It can be morally *indifferent*, as is, Kant thinks, eating meat on Fridays, or it can be *supererogatory*. A morally indifferent act is morally neutral; a supererogatory act is not.

"Unless we recognize reasonable limits to moral obligation," McCarty writes, "Kantian virtue is 'fantastic'."[19] Now this is true in that there are limits to the *reach* of moral obligation. Some things are, Kant holds, morally indifferent, for example, whether to drink beer or wine, and the fantastically virtuous person fails (at least with respect to certain matters) to grasp this.

But McCarty seems to have something else in mind when he says that

19. Ibid., p. 44. The sentences preceding the passage just quoted provide further indication that he is blurring two senses of 'limits to moral obligation' (and two ways in which one might be said to "carry things too far," or "take morality too far"): "The fantastically virtuous person rises daily with moral determination, eats with moral discrimination, organizes *all* activities toward moral destinations, and retires in moral deliberation. . . . It is part of Kantian virtue, however, to develop a sound understanding, to know when duty calls and when it is silent, to gauge the limits of one's obligations with good judgment" (p. 44). The first sentence provides a sketch of the fantastically virtuous person which differs from Kant's picture of fantastic virtue. Kant does not depict the fantastically virtuous person as taking morality too seriously, organizing too many activities toward "moral destinations," or engaging in moral deliberation too often. That McCarty supposes this an accurate represention of Kant's character indicates, I think, that he is blurring the two senses of 'limits to moral obligation'.

Turning now to the second sentence: he certainly is correct to say that it is part of Kantian virtue to know when duty calls and when it is silent, and if "the limits of one's obligations" means the boundaries of morality (as opposed to the boundaries between the morally required and the supererogatory), I agree with the whole sentence. However, given his conclusion ("admitting such limits . . . entails the possibility . . . of acting beyond the call of duty"), it is fairly clear that he means the latter.

we need to recognize reasonable limits to moral obligation. His very next sentence reads, "Admitting such limits, however, entails the possibility of surpassing the limits, of acting beyond the call of duty." Here, then, he clearly means limits in a different sense. From the claim that there are limits to the reach of moral obligation, it does not follow that there is a limit to how much can be demanded of us within the realm of things that are *not* morally indifferent. It is consistent with there being some things that are morally indifferent that we be, for instance, morally obligated to strive as hard as we can to promote the happiness of others.

McCarty may not be guilty of equivocation. Rather, when he says that unless we recognize reasonable limits to moral obligation, Kantian virtue is fantastic, he may mean by 'limits' *not* (primarily) limits to the reach of moral obligation but limits to the degree to which we are to strive to perfect ourselves and to help others. This would clear him of the charge of equivocation; but if this is his meaning, his claim is false and based on a mistake concerning what Kant means by "fantastic virtue." In rejecting fantastic virtue Kant recognizes the realm of the morally indifferent. But he does not, in rejecting fantastic virtue, thereby recognize the possibility of going beyond the limits of duty in the sense of doing something supererogatory.

One might argue that what I have called an equivocation is in fact not an equivocation. There is a connection between the two senses of 'limits' which might be put as follows. If there are no limits to duty—in the sense that nothing is supererogatory—I am morally required constantly to do all I can to promote others' happiness and develop my moral and natural talents; and since there is always something I can do along those lines, that means that there are no moments when I have, morally, the option to do something else. But then that means that nothing is morally indifferent. True, it does not mean that whether to drink beer or wine is itself a moral issue; but if I am to be doing all I can to promote these ends, wouldn't I have to forego both and save the money to give to someone more needy? (Or, one might argue, wouldn't I have to forego both so that I remain sharp and alert, able to spend the next few hours working on my French or Greek or doing something useful for others?)

The problem with this argument lies in the first premise, that is, in the claim that if there are no limits to duty, I am morally required constantly to do all I can to promote others' happiness and develop my talents. As Section 2 indicates, there is more than one view for the rigorist to take. The view taken in the above paragraph is R_2, and insofar as R_2 is coherent enough to be worthy of discussion, it is clear that it would have the effect of squeezing the realm of the morally indifferent to the point of annihilation. But, as explained in Section 1, this is not true of R_1, and brief reflection reveals that it is also not true of R_3. So, this attempt to salvage McCarty's argument fails. The equivocation—or error about fantastic virtue—really is that.

In the absence of any other reason for believing that Kant recognizes indeterminate limits to imperfect duty in McCarty's sense, I conclude that he does not.

5   I have argued in this chapter in support of an interpretation of Kant's imperfect duties which gives primacy and rigor to the duty to improve oneself morally. The account I offer is slightly more rigoristic than Gregor's and Hill's, both because it understands the duty of moral self-perfection to allow less latitude than the other imperfect duties *and* because the rigor of this duty impinges on the duty to promote others' happiness (as explained above in Sec. 3). The results of this chapter buttress the claims in the previous two chapters concerning Kant's rejection of the category of the supererogatory.

However, this chapter may also buttress or perhaps give rise to worries about Kant's ethics. Kant's ethics may seem too stern, particularly in its demands of self-perfection. Recall an observation made toward the end of Section 2. It might seem that my happiness should be a reason for limiting my endeavors to become morally better, and I noted that this is not a view that Kant holds. A critic might comment, in regard to this section, "You've convinced me that Kant's ethics is not minimally moral, and I can understand his reasons for rejecting the supererogatory. But they are not reasons that I accept, insofar as they rely on an assumption that no matter how good we are, we have a duty to strive to be better. This would not be so bad if the duty could be weighed against considerations of one's own happiness. But apparently they cannot, and this is just the sort of thing that seems wrong with Kant's ethics. It demands too much. The problem, I now see, lies in the duty to perfect oneself morally. The duty to promote others' happiness leaves enough latitude that it doesn't get in the way. But the duty of self-perfection really is too intrusive. It doesn't allow one to live one's life."

Here we reach a standoff. This is a disagreement that some will have with Kant's ethics. Whether it allows us to live our own lives depends of course on what we conceive our lives to be. Any morality worth its salt will not allow us to live immoral lives; Kant's goes further than some in not making virtue optional from the standpoint of duty. Kant's ethics is demanding because it does *not* just state a moral minimum but tells us what ends we must have and requires us to take them quite seriously. What to supererogationists is optional from the standpoint of duty, Kant's ethics builds into moral requirements (though of course it does so in a way that allows considerable latitude).

THE next two chapters address objections to acting from duty. But before turning to them, a summary of the last three chapters is in order.

The concern of this entire work is to evaluate objections to the effect that Kant's ethics is too taken up with duty. The objection can be better articulated by dividing it into two criticisms: first, that duty is given far too broad a scope, so broad as to leave no room for the supererogatory and, second, that the motive of duty is accorded far too much value relative to other desirable motives. It is the first objection that has been the concern of Chapters 1–3.

The first question to consider was whether Kant's ethics perhaps does leave room for the supererogatory, or could, with slight modification, make room for it. I argued that it does not, and explained why Kant would resist even partial accommodation of the supererogationist proposals. Among those reasons is that the designation of certain types of acts as beyond duty introduces a "minimalist" approach to duty, and perhaps also to morality. It clashes with Kant's emphasis on embracing certain ends, setting maxims for ourselves, and—rather than taking our limitations as limitations on duty—striving to improve ourselves morally.

The explanation at the same time indicated why Kant does not need a category of the supererogatory: his classification of imperfect duties allows him to recognize duties to adopt an end and, indirectly, to act accordingly—but the imperfect duty does not translate into a duty to perform these deeds, on these occasions. So one is not required to help others on every occasion where help could be given; yet that is not to say that helping others is supererogatory. Finally, I considered arguments put forth by supererogationists in defense of the view that the category of the supererogatory really is needed, and I argued that they are inadequate.

In Chapter 2, I delved further into the questions of the preceding chapter and, in particular, sought a deeper understanding of the supererogationist view(s). My principal aim was to figure out just what objection supererogationists have or would have to the Kantian approach to acts they regard as supererogatory. I found that the disagreement between supererogationists and Kantians can be traced to differences concerning the nature of morality and, in particular, of duty; what sorts of things can be or are our duties; and moral excellence. Kant holds that we have a duty to improve our characters; our character flaws are not to be regarded as givens around which duties must be tailored. In addition, moral excellence on Kant's view is not monotonic; perhaps an assumption that it is monotonic motivates the views that a moral requirement that we become more virtuous would be excessive. Finally, on Kant's view, the practice of living morally, of striving to improve oneself, of setting moral ends for oneself (ends subsidiary to the obligatory ends) is not just a burden to be endured because of the results of people acting morally; rather, it is meaningful in itself and expressive of one's moral agency. This view may not be shared by Kant's critics and seems not to be held by supererogationists.

The present chapter investigated a textual question postponed in the previous chapters: how much latitude do the wide imperfect duties really allow? I concluded that although duties to promote others' happiness and duties to perfect oneself (apart from moral perfection) allow the degree of latitude indicated by Hill, the duty to perfect oneself morally is somewhat stiffer. This corroborated claims in the previous chapters concerning the special role in Kant's ethics of the duty to perfect oneself morally.

I turn now to a related objection to Kant's ethics: the objection that Kant places inordinate value on the motive of duty.

PART II

Introduction
to Part II

◈◈◈

The tasks of Part II are rather different from those of Part I. In Part II I examine the objection that Kant places far too much emphasis on and attaches too much value to acting from duty. This objection is related to that addressed in Part I inasmuch as both oppose Kant's emphasis on duty; but my concern in Part I was the scope of duty, and specifically the worry that Kant's ethics leaves room for nothing of moral merit beyond duty. The objection examined in Part II has received much more attention. But partly because of this, it is more cumbersome to examine. In Part I, it was necessary to chart some uncharted terrain: little has been published on just what those who champion a category of supererogatory acts champion, much less about what is at issue between the Kantian and those who champion the category. The challenge in Part II is different because although the terrain is charted, it is charted misleadingly. Presuppositions, often very difficult to detect, are embedded in the terminology used to formulate the questions. This is the case at several junctures.

This difficulty left me two options. One was to try to chart the territory anew, ignoring what has been done already. The other was to pursue the questions as they have been formulated and see where they take us, while attending to ways in which they mislead and demonstrating, through an examination of where and how they mislead, that the problems in Kant's ethics which they seek to address are less serious than they seem. For the most part, I have taken the second path. I have done so not only because I want to demonstrate the trouble that we get into when we accept the questions usually asked as the correct questions, but also because I want to contribute to the debate that ensues when those questions are asked. That may seem perverse; why should I want to contribute to the debate? The answer is that there is confusion around almost every bend—as well as insight to be gleaned from tracking the confusions. I want to explore these bends, to point out the confusion as well as to note the insights, and this is best done by tracing the paths onto which the usual questions take us. My remarks here apply especially to Chapter 5, a very complex chapter, for whose complexity I apologize in advance. Hopefully this introduction will render it more accessible.

In Chapter 4, I step back from Kant's ethics and try to determine just what is supposed to be objectionable about acting from duty. As noted earlier, part of the problem is that 'acting from duty' conjures up images of blind obedience to an authority or blind conformity to social norms. These are associations with the term 'duty' which bear no connection to the Kantian notion of duty, and I mention them only in passing. I focus instead on figuring out what serious grounds there are for objecting, as many critics do, to placing much value on acting from duty. Just what these grounds are is not very fully explained by critics, who express their criticisms primarily by offering examples of someone who acts from duty in a situation in which it would seem preferable, and maybe even morally preferable, that they act from love or fellow feeling. Mining these examples for clues, Chapter 4 articulates and motivates the objections. It argues that although on some conceptions of acting from duty the objections are serious, they do not impugn acting from duty as such.

The subsequent chapters examine Kant's positions directly. Does he place too much value on acting from duty?

In Chapter 5, I consider whether Kant holds, as many have claimed he does, that an action has moral worth only if it is done from duty alone. It is often thought that Kant is in trouble if he cannot allow that some overdetermined actions have moral worth. I consider both whether he can allow this, and whether we should think that he is in trouble if he cannot allow it. Consideration of these questions requires figuring out just what is meant by overdetermination. This proves to be a complicated matter and an important one, because how 'overdetermination' is to be understood affects what evidence counts for or against the claim that Kant can allow that overdetermined actions may have moral worth. I distinguish overdetermined actions from "hybrid" actions (which clearly could not have moral worth on Kant's view) and argue that much of the textual evidence marshaled to show that Kant cannot allow that overdetermined actions may have moral worth in fact shows only that hybrid actions cannot have moral worth.

Some textual evidence does, however, tell against the hope that he can allow that overdetermined actions might have moral worth. Here I turn from the textual evidence for and against that hope to the hope itself and raise the following question: *Is* it an embarrassment to Kantians if Kant cannot allow that some overdetermined actions have moral worth? Contrary to what most of us have thought, the answer is 'No'. In fact, the very notion of an action being overdetermined makes little sense on a Kantian picture, and when it does make sense, there is little reason to ascribe moral worth to any such actions.

The remainder of Chapter 5 argues that despite initial appearances, the value that Kant attaches to acting from duty attaches primarily not to actions done from duty as a primary motive—to individual actions prompted by the thought, 'This is morally required'—but to governing one's conduct by a commitment to doing what morality asks. (The following paragraph elaborates on this distinction.) This is important because one conclusion of Chapter 4 was that the objections stick only insofar as it is acting from duty as a primary motive that is treated as having special value. They miss their target if the value attaches primarily to governing one's conduct by a commitment to duty (or, as I there put it, to duty operating as a secondary motive). Insofar as it is the latter, not the former, that is of primary value in Kant's ethics, he is not vulnerable to the criticisms examined in Chapter 4.

The discussions into which Chapters 4 and 5 enter are generally couched in terms of motives: acting from the motive of duty, acting from more than one motive, acting from duty as a sufficient motive but not necessarily as the sole motive, and so on. I follow suit, and I also follow Barbara Herman in distinguishing between primary and secondary motives. Duty operates as a primary motive if it is the main impetus to action, the thing that moves me to act. It operates as a secondary motive without functioning at the same time as a primary motive if it constrains my conduct while what prompts me to act is something else, for example, an inclination to please someone. In this case, the primary motive is the inclination. Duty serves as a secondary motive if I am committed to doing whatever duty requires. I use this terminology to explain in Chapter 4 how acting from duty is compatible with inclinations playing a motivational role. It is compatible if what is key to acting from duty is that one's conduct is governed by a commitment to doing what is morally right, but it is not compatible if acting from duty is understood as acting from duty as the (sole) primary motive. In Chapter 5, I again employ the distinction, this time to ask which it is that mainly concerns Kant: (a) acting from duty as a primary motive, or (b) being governed by a commitment to duty. Although Kant seems to place great value on (a), it would be peculiar if he did, since his theory provides no reason for doing so, though it provides excellent reason for emphasizing the importance of the fact that we are *able* to act from duty as a primary motive. But there is no Kantian reason to think that it is morally better if one's action is prompted directly by the motive of duty than if it is prompted by, say, a desire to please another person, as long as the desire is governed by a commitment to duty. In fact, the passages that are thought to show that Kant holds there to be special value in acting from duty as a primary motive actually show only the importance of governing one's conduct by a commitment to duty.

Chapter 5 uncovers assumptions about Kant's ethics—either about what it says or about what it should say—that have hindered our understanding of his theory. These assumptions, which are accepted by most of his sympathizers as well as his critics, include the suppositions that he should allow that overdetermined actions may have moral worth and that a major concern of his is to provide an account of the moral worth of actions. But there is an assumption that I do not question in Chapter 5, namely, that it is appropriate to speak in terms of *motives* when we seek to understand Kant's account of moral motivation. In the second interlude I suggest that this assumption may be false. The language of motives evokes a model of agency quite different from Kant's and thus may mislead. Moreover, it may drive some of the worries about Kant's ethics addressed in Chapters 4 and 5. The second interlude further undermines those worries by showing the extent to which they are motivated by a misconception concerning Kant's theory of agency, a misconception fostered by use of the term 'motive' to formulate questions about Kant's account of moral motivation.

Chapter 6 addresses the flip side of the concern that Kant places too much emphasis on acting from duty, namely, that he places too little value on compassion, fellow feeling, and the like. Even if it is granted that Kant does not place excessive value on acting from duty as a primary motive (to use the terminology I adhere to in Chapters 4 and 5), it might still be felt that he undervalues affection for others. Could he allow, for instance, that someone who abides by the perfect duties and embraces the obligatory ends of self-perfection and the happiness of others (and, of course, acts accordingly) nonetheless is morally deficient if she lacks affection for others or if she is not moved as we think a person should be by the suffering of another? This is the concern of Chapter 6; and as it, happily, lacks the byzantine complexity of Chapter 5 (and, more broadly, of Chapter 4 through the second interlude), no further introduction to it is necessary.

4

Is Acting from Duty
Morally Repugnant?

❖❖❖

1   Kant's readers, both in his time and in our own, have been troubled by the value that he places on acting from duty. There is something disturbing about the idea of acting from duty; to many it seems morally repugnant. But why?

One part of the problem is that our picture of someone who acts from duty may be that of the all-too-obedient soldier, or the good Nazi citizen who overcomes feelings of compassion to turn in the Jews hiding in the neighbor's home and the neighbor who provided refuge. Here the worry is that acting from duty may involve mindless obedience to laws or to a superior's commands.[1] As noted earlier, there is no reason to think that duty on a Kantian picture involves blind obedience and every reason to think that Kant eschewed it.[2] So, although this *could* be a reason for concern, it would not be a reason for concern regarding Kant's ethics.

But there are other reasons for wariness regarding acting from duty.

1. Adolf Eichmann's claim to have lived his entire life according to Kant's moral precepts lends some support to the suspicion that acting from duty often, maybe typically, involves blind obedience to authority. Hannah Arendt discusses Eichmann's claim in her *Eichmann in Jerusalem: A Report on the Banality of Evil* (New York: Penguin Books, rev. and enl. ed., 1994), pp. 135–137.
2. Someone might argue that even if it involves not blind obedience but careful, sincere thought, there is still the danger that the agent will come to morally heinous conclusions. True, there is this danger, but it is not clear what conclusions we should draw from the fact that the danger exists. (That one should not act on one's convictions, no matter how much one has subjected them to scrutiny, since after all they might be wrong? Surely not; but what?) An influential paper that articulates this danger is Jonathan Bennett, "The Conscience of Huckleberry Finn," *Philosophy* 69 (1974): 123–134.

Those who hold that acting from duty is morally undesirable may hold that to act from duty is to act just minimally morally or that acting from duty is alienating. The first objection is that someone who acts from duty does not really care about others, but fulfills his duties toward them in order to meet a minimum requirement. The second objection is more complex and harder to make explicit: here the worry is that action done from duty expresses and perhaps nurtures the wrong sorts of attitudes toward others. The bulk of the chapter focuses on the second charge. The first objection requires far less discussion, because Chapters 1 and 2 covered much of what needs to be said. I will discuss it at the end of the chapter.

2   I begin with the charge that acting from duty is alienating. The idea, roughly, is that acting in a certain way and, more specifically, from a certain type of motivation, betrays (and perhaps further entrenches) attitudes toward others and toward one's relationships which are, morally and otherwise, regrettable. To get a better sense of the objection, I will analyze a well-known example by Michael Stocker.[3] My hope is to determine what it is that makes the conduct depicted in the example disturbing and to use the findings to decide whether acting from duty is as such alienating or whether only certain modes of acting from duty are objectionable in this way.

Stocker's example is that of someone hospitalized who receives a visit from a friend, Smith:

3. Michael Stocker, "The Schizophrenia of Modern Ethical Theories," *Journal of Philosophy* 73 (1976): 453–466. In a more recent article, "Friendship and Duty: Some Difficult Relations," in *Identity, Character, and Morality: Essays in Moral Psychology*, ed. Owen Flanagan and Amélie Oksenberg Rorty (Cambridge: MIT Press, 1990), Stocker claims that I erred in thinking that "Schizophrenia" argued for (to quote Stocker) "a general repugnance in acting *from* duty, and more particularly for an incompatibility between friendship and acting *from* duty." He was concerned there, he says, with "friendship and acting *for* duty." (The quote is from p. 221 of the 1990 article.) He does not explain the difference, but presumably if acting for duty means something different from acting from duty it would have to mean acting solely for the purpose of doing one's duty. If that is what it means, acting for duty differs from acting from duty in that the latter, but not the former, is compatible with having some aim—such as to save the child who has just fallen into the swimming pool—in addition to the more general aim of doing one's duty.

It would be odd, though, if "Schizophrenia" sought to show the repugnance of acting for duty, thus understood; for who (or which "modern ethical theory") defends or advocates acting for duty? I took his article to be arguing against a view that some people really do take, a view that is indeed important to modern ethical theory. I will proceed in this chapter accordingly, taking the claims in his 1976 article to be pertinent to acting from duty, even if he did not intend them to be.

You are very bored and restless and at loose ends when Smith comes in once again. You are now convinced more than ever that he is a fine fellow and a real friend—taking so much time to cheer you up, traveling all the way across town, and so on. You are so effusive with your praise and thanks that he protests that he always tries to do what he thinks is his duty, what he thinks will be best. You at first think he is engaging in a polite form of self-deprecation, relieving the moral burden. But the more you two speak, the more clear it becomes that he was telling the literal truth: that it is not essentially because of you that he came to see you, not because you are friends, but because he thought it his duty, perhaps as a fellow Christian or Communist or whatever, or simply because he knows of no one more in need of cheering up and no one easier to cheer up.[4]

Clearly there is something disturbing about Stocker's example. None of us would want to be treated by a friend the way Smith's friend is treated by Smith; moreover, we can see that there is something morally objectionable about Smith's conduct. But what?

There are a number of different ways in which (perhaps without knowing it) we may be filling in Stocker's sketch of Smith. We need to consider them separately in order to determine just what is disturbing about Smith's conduct and whether or not it impugns acting from duty.

The image that we have of Smith is something like this: he does not want to visit his friend, but believing it to be his duty to visit her, he forces himself to do so. The main feature of this picture of Smith that contributes to the overall repugnance of his conduct is his disinclination to see his friend. He may also strike some of us as sanctimonious; if he does, that contributes to our negative judgment. I will say little about sanctimoniousness and will concentrate on determining the relevance of disinclination to the moral repugnance of acting from duty. To do so it will be necessary to examine a number of different cases.

Consider first the case in which Smith is disinclined to visit the hospitalized friend—whom I'll call Thompson—and yet visits her because he believes it is his duty to visit fellow X's and she is, he believes, a fellow X. 'X' could be replaced by 'Christian', 'Communist', 'Republican', and so on.[5] This case will be contrasted with those in which Smith thinks it

---

4. Stocker, "Schizophrenia," p. 462.

5. The type and size of the group that gets covered by 'and so on' would make some difference to how one would feel about Smith's visiting him or her from a sense that he ought to pay a call on hospitalized fellow X's, but I ignore that here.

his duty to visit her *as a friend.* Suppose that in Stocker's story Thompson
thinks that Smith is coming to see her as a friend and then realizes, with
a jolt, that it is not friendship but a sense of (community and) special
obligation to other Christians (or whatever) that brings him to her
hospital room. She will feel alienated if she thinks he is not coming to see
her, but rather to see the member of his church who is in the hospital. All
the worse if he misleadingly acts as if he is coming as a friend when he is
not. Even if he does not mislead, and she is clear from the outset that he
is visiting her as a fellow Christian, the situation may still be alienating
if she does not strongly identify herself as a Christian (and all the more
so if he had no reason to suppose that she did). And even if she *does,* the
situation may still be alienating if it signals to her that whereas she
thought they were friends, he apparently sees them simply as co-members
of a group—for example, as members of the same church.

All the above are details that we may more or less clearly have in our
various pictures of Smith, and any of them accounts for at least some of
what bothers us about Smith's conduct. But none of them is tied specifically to acting from duty. To see this, just note that what goes wrong
would equally go wrong if Smith visited her simply from an inclination
to visit a fellow Christian.

Once these features are pushed to one side, there is, I think, nothing
objectionable in Smith's visiting Thompson because he thought it his
duty as a fellow *X.* Thompson thought he was visiting her as a friend, but
in fact he came in quite a different capacity; and this itself may be
alienating if she regarded him as a friend. Moreover, he was wrong to
pretend to come qua friend, if indeed he did pretend this, and it was
thoughtless of him to visit her as a fellow *X* if he had reason to think that
she did not have a sense of community with *X*'s. But barring these
problems, there would be nothing expressive of or conducive to alienation or otherwise objectionable about one fellow Christian or Communist visiting another because he thought it right to do so.

3   Stocker's example becomes more compelling if we think of Smith
as visiting Thompson because he thinks it is his duty *as a friend* to do so.
This situation is interestingly different insofar as friendship, unlike a
sense of community with fellow *X*'s, does not sit easily with not wanting
to visit one's friend (or fellow *X*) and opting to do so out of duty.
Stocker's belief appears to be that insofar as one is motivated on a
particular occasion to do something for a friend out of duty, one is not

acting as a true friend. The point has considerable plausibility. The fact that the agent acted from duty seems to suggest (as in Stocker's example) that he is not much of a friend—or at least not much of a friend to the person in question.

We should note that much of the compellingness of Stocker's belief draws from the conception of the motive of duty as excluding inclination to do what one regards as one's duty. This conception needs to be questioned. But to that later. Let us first examine whether visiting a friend from duty (or for that matter helping or trying to comfort a friend from duty) without the inclination to do so is somehow objectionable. More specifically, let us see whether acts of friendship, if done from duty, lose their status as acts of friendship.

Depending on how one interprets Stocker's example (and how one pictures other instances of friendly acts done from duty), there are a number of reasons one might have for supposing that this is the case. One might picture Smith visiting Thompson grudgingly or resentfully. Thus understood, his conduct is morally objectionable on two counts. First, his attitude may show through, making the visit rather unpleasant for Thompson. If this is the case, then the problem lies primarily not with Smith's motives, but with what he did. He acted contrary to duty. His duty was not to make an appearance in Thompson's room, but to do her some good by visiting her—cheer her up, divert her, alleviate her boredom, let her see that at least one of her friends is thinking of her and is concerned about her. Of course, if he fails to cheer her up because she is too depressed, this would not impugn his conduct, but it is another matter if he conveys hostility toward her for having occasioned, as he sees it, the moral demand that he visit her, when he would much prefer to be elsewhere. The important point here is that the flaw in his conduct lies not in his acting from duty, but failing to do his duty (and perhaps also failing to understand what his duty is).

Visiting a friend grudgingly or resentfully is objectionable on a second count. Thompson may be unaware of Smith's resentment and may find his visit enjoyable, even gratifying. Yet there is something amiss in Smith's conduct if he harbors resentment toward Thompson, or even annoyance that takes no particular object. He ought not have such feelings, and although that is not to say that he must be in control of whether or not he has those feelings and is at fault for having them, his conduct is morally deficient. Part of what one morally ought to do is cultivate certain attitudes and dispositions, for example, sympathy rather than resentment or repulsion for the ailing and a cheerful readiness to help and to find ways in which one can help.

If Smith's deficiency is that he lacks such attitudes and dispositions and feels resentful, then whether or not he successfully masks it, the problem does not indict acting from duty as such. It shows that there is something wrong with acting from a false conception of one's duty, a conception that overlooks the importance of the attitudes and feelings one has when one performs certain acts, especially those that are intended to express affection or concern. Thus although it does not indict acting from duty as such, it points to certain parameters within which satisfactory ways of acting from duty must be located. It highlights the fact that any ethical theory that dismissed such feelings as irrelevant as long as "outwardly" the agent did her duty (narrowly construed) and did it from the sense that she ought to, would be unacceptable.

So far, then, the problems we have uncovered in Smith's conduct do not signify any flaws in acting from duty as such. The same can be said of a number of other worrisome attitudes one might attribute to the man Stocker describes. One might, for instance, suspect that if Smith is disinclined to visit Thompson and goes solely from duty, he may persistently think of his visit under the description of *what, morally, I ought to do* (or *what it is right to do*). Here one might be worried that Smith will be thinking throughout the visit about the moral character of his conduct or, worse yet, reveling in his own goodness. And this, one may suspect, will render him cold, cut off from others, alienated from people by his preoccupation with morality.[6]

One's response to this, at least initially (cf. Sec. 4 below) is that if throughout the visit he focuses his attention on his own goodness, then his flaw is again that he is not conducting himself as he ought, that is, not really doing his duty. This is the problem; there is no reason to pin it on acting from duty. And so once again, no conclusions concerning the merits or hazards of acting from duty can be drawn. For there is no reason to suppose that if one acts from duty, one must be preoccupied with morality.

One might object to Smith's conduct on different grounds. One might imagine that since Smith is visiting Thompson out of duty and against his predominant inclinations, this must be the way he always is with the

6. See Susan Wolf, "The Failure of Autonomy," Ph.D. diss. (Princeton University, 1978), p. 52.

people he thinks of and speaks of as his friends. The inference is not warranted. It may be that Smith enjoys the company of his friends and generally does not need to push himself to spend time with them; it is only because he is ill at ease about visiting Thompson just before her surgery and is generally uncomfortable in hospitals that he needs the prodding of moral considerations to counteract his disinclination. But although the inference is not warranted, the objection is nonetheless instructive. For though there is no reason to think that someone who acts from duty on an occasion such as the one described always needs the motive of duty to impel him to seek out his friends, it is worth noting that if one *were* so dependent on the motive of duty, this would be a flaw in one's character. A person is morally deficient if she is so motivationally depleted that, for actions to which most of us would be moved by sympathy, fellow feeling, or affection for a particular person (the list is not exhaustive), the only sufficient motive she has is her belief that the action is morally called for.[7] (In Chap. 6, I will ask whether this is a charge that applies to Kant's ethics: is the Kantian agent morally deficient in this way?)

To sum up the foregoing: we have considered a number of different explanations of what it is that we find morally repugnant about Smith's conduct in Stocker's example. In each case the explanation could be exploited to point to ways of conceiving of acting from duty which, typically because of misconceptions of what one's duty is, are of dubious merit. The explanations did not, however, provide any reason for thinking that acting from duty is by its very nature alienating or otherwise morally repugnant.

4 It might be objected that I have not yet done justice to Stocker's worries. What if the problems we have detected are more deep-seated than I indicated?

Earlier I mentioned that one may suspect that if Smith is disinclined to visit Thompson and does so solely from duty, he'll be reveling throughout the visit in his own goodness. The reply I suggested is that if he does this, he is not doing his duty. So the problem is not that he acts from duty. But perhaps his concern to do whatever he morally ought to do gets in the way of fulfilling certain duties. Perhaps it leads him to think

7. In both this and the previous sentence I mean by 'motive' what later in this chapter is called a "primary" motive.

persistently of his visit under the description of *what it is right to do*. Or again, recall the last way of picturing Smith mentioned in Section 3: one might infer from the example that it is generally true of Smith that when he visits his friends, he does so from duty and without wanting to see them. Although the inference, as I said, is not warranted, it might be argued that a commitment to doing whatever one morally ought to do— to doing one's duty—gets in the way of acting from friendlier, warmer motives.

Perhaps, in other words, the whole problem is that Smith is alienated from others by virtue of his commitment to doing whatever he morally ought to do. If so, the objectionable features enumerated above are mere symptoms of the real difficulty. The real difficulty, as Stocker sees it, is that insofar as one acts from duty, one is unable "to realize the great goods of love, friendship, affection, fellow-feeling, and community," for these goods "essentially contain certain motives and essentially preclude certain others," among those precluded being the motive to do what one believes one morally ought to do.[8]

If this is right, then the answer I have suggested will not suffice. It will not do to say that the problem lies not with acting from duty but with failing to do one's duty, if in fact there are certain duties that one cannot fulfill (or certain goods that one cannot realize) if one acts from duty.

The objection expresses either or both of the following worries:

> *Worry* 1: Insofar as one acts from duty, this shows there to be something awry in one's "natural affections." It shows one to lack, or to have to an insufficient degree, certain motives and dispositions which are crucial to realizing the great goods of love and friendship. A truly good person does not need the motive of duty. Anyone who needs it, or at least anyone who needs it often, must be lacking in affection for others.

> *Worry* 2: Whatever fellow feeling one has, and whatever other feelings and motives one has that are essential to love and friendship, are undermined—"driven under"—insofar as one acts from duty. Two things happen. One ignores the direct concern one feels for the other, focusing instead on the *duty* one has to help him or her. The deep concern one has for the other and the bond between the two people are treated as if they are insignificant; what matters is that *here is a duty*. Second, insofar as one strives to make duty the

8. Stocker, "Schizophrenia," p. 461 and pp. 461–462.

motive of one's action, one regards affect in its various forms as either a rival to the motive of duty—a rival in the competition as to which will motivate one to do the required act—and thus as a hindrance to *acting from duty*, or a contrary motive—a motive inclining one in an opposing direction—and thus as a hindrance to *acting in accordance with duty*. In each instance the natural affections are denigrated.

5   I begin with Worry 1. An obvious response, though not my response, is to say "True; if one needs the motive of duty all the time, there is something missing in his character. Such a person is evidently quite cold and heartless, and thus incapable of loving others or being much of a friend. And this is no slight defect. But the problem arises only if he *too often* needs the motive of duty to supply sufficient motivation to phone or visit or write or give a present to a friend or relative. It is no blemish on his character if he needs the promptings of duty at times, for example, to visit a friend in a hospital or a prison, or to spend an afternoon babysitting a friend's two-year-old twins. After all, friendship does not require that on any occasion, nothing appeals to one more than being with, or doing a favor for, that particular friend. So there is no conflict between Smith's visiting his friend from duty and being a true friend to Thompson, assuming that ordinarily he seeks her out without needing the promptings of duty."

This answer is partly right—it is right about friendship, and what friendship does not require. But it concedes too much. In particular it concedes the implicit assumption (and indeed a widely held, rarely questioned assumption) that acting from duty is of value only as a sort of backup or insurance policy: when something else fails, the sense of duty serves as a substitute. P. H. Nowell–Smith once put the view as follows: "The sense of duty is a useful device for helping men to do what a really good man would do without a sense of duty."[9] Acting from duty is second best; if we were better people, we would have no need for a sense

9. P. H. Nowell Smith, *Ethics* (London: Penguin Books, 1954), p. 259. John Hardwig takes a similar but more sweeping position in his "In Search of an Ethics of Personal Relationships," in *Person to Person*, ed. George Graham and Hugh LaFollette (Philadelphia: Temple University Press, 1989). Hardwig writes: "Nor am I claiming that actions motivated by a sense of duty or obligation, by altruism or self-sacrifice, by benevolence, pity, charity, sympathy, and so on *never* have a place in personal relationships. They may be appropriate in unusual circumstances. But such motives and actions are a fall-back mechanism which I compare to the safety net beneath a high wire act" (p. 76).

of duty and would act from such motives as fellow feeling or a desire to help.

Those who accept the assumption err, I believe, in supposing that motives of friendship, fellow feeling, and so on, *ideally should* always serve the function of prompting us to do what we morally ought to do. What they do not notice is that sometimes there is a gap between the goodness of a desire and the rightness or wrongness of the act to which it inclines us. The goodness of the desire does not ensure that if we act as it directs, we act as we should. This is particularly clear in instances in which one's special tie to a particular person is in conflict with duties of general beneficence. In some instances it is clearly good that one is pulled toward giving all of his attention to one particular person—we would not think better of him if his affective responses were less "partial," and might well think the less of him—and yet because of certain features of the situation, it would not be right to act accordingly. Imagine someone whose child or dearest friend is hurt but clearly not in mortal danger, or very frightened and in need of reassurance (e.g., in a car accident); at the same time someone else, with no claims on his affections, is in need of emergency medical help. Imagine too that there is no one else at the scene who can fetch help, or otherwise render assistance. Although it would certainly not be wrong—far from it!—to feel like giving all of one's attention to one's badly shaken, frightened child, it would be wrong not to attend first to the other person. But here I am anticipating a discussion to come later in the chapter (of an example made famous by Bernard Williams).

The general point is that at times the very good motives of very good people need to be tempered lest they act wrongly. Consider a different sort of example. As a parent you may be too protective. Fortunately, you temper your desire to shield your child from harm. It is not the case that ideally you would not be *tempted* to shield her from harm, or that ideally you would desire to, but only to the proper degree and not to a point at which the desire needs to be tempered.

There is a related problem in the response to Worry 1 sketched above. The assumption that acting from duty is of value only as a sort of backup is flawed not only for the reason given, namely, that it is a mistake to think that if we were better people, we would have no need for a sense of duty, but also because it wrongly supposes that the sense of duty is nothing more than a substitute for the proper motive. It construes the sense of duty as a backup motive: as a safeguard that somehow kicks in when the normally functioning motive (such as love for a particular person) is weak or absent.[10] Whether this is a coherent way of thinking is not clear to me, for reasons to be explained shortly. But in any case it is not the way we would expect someone who places great stock in acting from duty to understand it. Those who attribute importance to acting from duty see the sense of duty to play a *regulative* role. Worry 1 ignores this regulative role.

One way to understand the regulative role is to consider what it would mean for the sense of duty to operate merely as a backup motive. Suppose it did function as a backup. How would it work? For it to function as a backup, the agent would need to know when to "engage" it. The sense of duty does not suddenly "click on" when it is needed. It is not as if we are wired so that, without reflection, we just know, 'Here is a duty which I am not inclined to fulfill' and knowing this, simply employ the assistance of the motive of duty. Something, some sense of what is right and some concern to act accordingly is needed if the agent is to notice that here is something she really ought to do, and is to be prompted, even in the face of conflicting inclinations, to act accordingly. What is needed is something that heightens one's awareness of moral considerations, makes one morally sensitive, that is, attuned to moral nuances that are easy to miss and alert to moral considerations that should be attended to. What is needed is something that expresses and reinvigorates one's commitment to acting morally, to being a good person.

Two points emerge from this discussion (in addition to the point that it is a mistake to think that ideally we would act from such motives as fellow feeling and love for a particular person and would have no need for a sense of duty).

10. In a famous passage, David Hume seems to think of it in this way (though it is not clear that this is, all told, his view; see my "Morality as a Back-Up System: Hume's View?" *Hume Studies* 16 [1988]: 25–52). "But may not the sense of morality or duty produce an action, without any other motive? I answer, It may . . . When any virtuous motive or principle is common in human nature, a person, who feels his heart devoid of that motive, may hate himself upon that account, and may perform the action without the motive, from a certain sense of duty, in order to acquire by practice, that virtuous principle, or at least, to disguise to himself, as much as possible, his want of it" (Hume, *A Treatise of Human Nature*, ed. L. A. Selby-Bigge; 2d ed. with text revised and variant readings by P. H. Nidditch [Oxford: Clarendon Press, 1978], 479). It is interesting that even in this passage, famous for its "dummy motive" picture of the sense of duty, the sense of duty seems to be playing a slightly larger, regulative role: one aims to acquire by practice the virtuous principle that is wanting.

First, the notion that the motive of duty can be simply a backup for other motives barely makes sense. It could function as a backup only if it (or something working closely with it) also prompted us to be attentive to moral considerations, to reflect on what is right, to question, in moral terms, some of our government's policies, and so on. It makes sense to speak of the sense of duty as operating not *merely* to prompt us to do our duty (in the face of opposing desires), but also to draw our attention to moral considerations, to prompt us to reflect on ourselves and our lives. How it does this becomes clearer if we think of acting from duty as acting from a commitment to act morally. (See Sec. 6 and n. 22, below.) Part of being committed to something or someone is reflecting on the object of that commitment and one's relation to the object.

As the parenthetical "or something working closely with it" in the previous paragraph indicates, it would not be accurate to say that the very same thing must *both* come into play at the moment when added motivation is needed to bring one to do one's duty *and* supply the motivation needed to see (be on the alert for, and often reflect on) what one's duty is. Arguably, the sense of duty could fulfill the first, and something else (but what?) could perform the second function. Such a division of labor would be possible, I think, but also highly artificial. In any case, such a division of labor would be necessary if one were to try to make sense of the sense of duty operating as a backup motive without also playing a grander function. If the sense of duty is not to be assigned a regulative role, something else has to be.

The second point is this. Even if there is a way to make sense of the idea that the motive of duty serves merely as a backup motive, it is nonetheless clear that this is not the only way of understanding acting from duty. And it is silly to suppose that those who attribute importance to acting from duty understand it in that way. They see it, rather, as playing a role that is both motivational and regulative, or to put it differently: a role that is motivational with respect not only to specific actions but also to proper attending, proper ordering of one's ends, and appropriate moral reflection.

What I called the "obvious" answer to Worry 1 is based on the assumption that acting from duty must be understood as acting from a backup motive. For the reasons indicated, this assumption should be rejected, and the "obvious" answer should not be our answer. Our answer, rather, is simply that the worry is ill-grounded. It is grounded on the dubious assumption that the motive of duty serves as a backup and that its sole value lies in that function.

6 My claim has been that the sense of duty comes into play not simply as a motive for some individual actions, but also as something that guides and regulates one's conduct. There are really two related points here—two parts of a proposal as to how we should think of the motive of duty. The first is that it has a regulative function as well as a function of prompting certain actions. The second, presupposed by the first, is that the motive of duty does not come into play only episodically. It does not concern only individual actions, but also conduct over long stretches of time. It concerns how one lives, and in that broad sense, what one does. (The "obvious" answer failed to consider this possibility, and assumed that the motive of duty enters the scene solely as a motive for individual acts.)

To underscore the point that the sense of duty serves to regulate one's conduct, it will be helpful to introduce a distinction. The distinction, which I borrow with some modification from Barbara Herman, is between primary and secondary motives.[11] As Herman presents it, a primary motive supplies the agent with the motivation to do the act in question, whereas a secondary motive provides limiting conditions on what may be done. Accordingly, the sense of duty can function in two different ways. First, my sense of duty may prompt me to refrain from doing something that I recognize to be wrong but am tempted to do, for example, lie to save face. Here my sense of duty operates as a primary motive. Second, it may, in effect, ratify my plan. Imagine that I want to help someone—for example, a student who is having trouble with an assignment—and do so in the conviction that I should help him (or, that I do not act wrongly in helping him). In this case, my sense of duty functions as a secondary motive. It tells me that I may or that I should act as I wish. In different circumstances—suppose the assignment was such that students were not to get outside help of any sort—it would tell me that I should not so act.

Three clarifications. First, it bears emphasis that the secondary motive serves a regulative function. I do not govern my conduct by a sense of duty if it just turns out by chance that my conduct meets the limiting condition; as described above, I actively *govern* my conduct by my commitment to acting morally. Second (and here I may differ from Herman), as I understand the distinction between primary and secondary

11. Barbara Herman, "On the Value of Acting from the Motive of Duty," *Philosophical Review* 90 (1981): 359–382; reprinted in revised form as chap. 1 of her *The Practice of Moral Judgment* (Cambridge: Harvard University Press, 1993).

motives, a motive may initially operate as a secondary motive but then, if it conflicts with another motive, assume the role of a primary motive. Hence the distinction, as I see it, is not really between types of motives, but rather between functions that the motives assume. Third, and here I almost certainly part company with Herman, I think of a secondary motive as informing the agent not merely that the proposed conduct is or is not permissible but also that the proposed action is of a sort that is morally required, even though the particular action is not morally required. In other words, it "speaks" not only to permissibility but also to an action's falling under a principle of imperfect duty.

For my purposes, the distinction, clumsy though it is, is helpful in two respects.[12] First, it highlights the regulatory function of the motive of duty. Second, it enables us to recognize differences among those who value acting from duty as to what it is that they value. Some will see great value in acting from duty as a primary motive. Others will hold that it is in its function as a secondary motive, a secondary motive that can assume the role of a primary motive when necessary, that the motive of duty is of value. These views are not inconsistent; one may say that both are of value. The disagreement is this: some will deny any special value in acting from duty as a primary motive, while others will affirm it. If what is of particular value is acting from duty as a primary motive, the concerns voiced in Worry 2 have some foothold. But if, as I believe, what really matters is the sense of duty in its regulative function—together with its capacity to serve as a primary motive if the agent does *x* because morality requires it and despite his inclination to do otherwise—Worry 2 is easily defused. (Worry 2, recall, is that whatever feelings and motives one has that are essential to friendship are undermined insofar as one acts from duty.)

Consider the latter position—that what matters is the sense of duty in its regulative function—and its bearing on Worry 2. When duty functions as a secondary motive, other motives not only may enter in; they must. Something other than the fact that the act I am about to perform is morally permissible or recommended must have attracted me to it (unless it is the only permissible or recommended action open to me; but in that

12. Its clumsiness is due to the underlying clumsiness of speaking in terms of motives while expressing a Kantian view of moral agency. The problem is that the picture suggested by the term 'motive' is a mechanistic one, and to correct for this, we try to inject a Kantian regulative role by distinguishing secondary motives from primary motives. See the end of Sec. 6 of this chapter and the second interlude.

case the action is morally required). So the motive of duty, in its function as a secondary motive, operates together with other motives. In that sense, at least, it is not in conflict with them. It does not "drive them under." But does it somehow undermine them?

The motive of duty is not generally in competition with affective motives since (on the view under discussion) no premium is placed on the action being done from duty as a primary motive. What matters is that the action is in accord with duty and that *it is no accident that it is*: it accords with duty because the agent governs her conduct by a commitment to doing what is right. But in so governing her conduct she does not denigrate her affective motives and sentiments. She does not try to ignore them or regard them as irrelevant—after all, why should they not bear on what she ought to do? (If she is feeling hostile toward or impatient with a friend, perhaps it would be best *not* to seek him out just now.) Nor is she obsessed with thoughts about duty or constantly wondering what her duty really is. One can govern one's conduct by a commitment without it absorbing all or most of one's thoughts.

Perhaps because we tend to think of the motive of duty as simply engaging individual actions rather than as governing one's conduct as a whole, we also imagine the agent who is committed to doing what is right to be thinking before each action about whether the proposed action is morally permissible. But this would be a waste of time and counterproductive (to put it mildly). There are right times and there are wrong times for reflecting on the moral status of various forms of conduct, and the period immediately prior to action will frequently be one of the wrong times. To the extent that we can even imagine what it would be to evaluate the rightness or wrongness of every action just before engaging in it, it would be as inappropriate for a responsible moral agent to do so as it would for a responsible driver to think about the correctness or incorrectness of applying the brakes or quickly turning the steering wheel before performing each such action.[13] A responsible moral agent should

13. The analogy between morally responsible agents and responsible drivers is drawn by W. D. Falk in "Morality, Form, and Content," in his *Ought, Reasons, and Morality* (Ithaca: Cornell University Press, 1986), p. 241. It is important to note that although the analogy is useful in that it brings out the fact that one can have certain principles in one's mind—be they moral or principles of driving—and be influenced by them without consciously thinking of them, the analogy breaks down at another point: whereas there is such a thing as having the rules and techniques of driving "down pat" there is no comparable stage in morality. My point is not that few of us reach such a stage, but rather that moral principles must be regarded as always open to revision. It is possible that someone could

take an active interest in a wide range of moral questions—questions about her relationships with others, about her character, about particular courses of action she is pursuing, about her ends and the relative value she places on them, about the policies of her government, and so on. None of this says—nor do I think it is fruitful to try to say—how often she should reflect on these things. What is important is that these thoughts be action-guiding: she should be committed to changing herself so as to be, for example, more sensitive to how her biting wit undermines others (and willing to forfeit an opportunity to exhibit her wit if the witty remark will be hurtful to the listener); or less isolated in her own affairs, and more aware of social injustices and prepared to contribute to ameliorating them.

The second worry assumes that to act from duty is to act from duty as a primary motive. But if it is duty as a secondary motive that is crucial, there is no disharmony between duty and motives of fellow feeling, friendship, or love—except, of course, when the latter motives would prompt one to act wrongly. An agent who governs her conduct by a commitment to doing what is right does not, contrary to Worry 2, strive to make duty the primary motive of her actions. So there is no reason to expect that she ignores the direct concern she feels for her friend and instead focuses on the fact that it is her duty to do x (x being what she also wants to do) for the friend. Duty takes precedence only if a conflict arises between what morality requires and what her friend wants.

In itself, acting from duty as a primary motive is not objectionable in the ways expressed in the objection. Acting from duty does not denigrate affective motives. In acting from duty we will often be affirming some inclinations while counteracting others. My inclinations may conflict, and if they do, some may be contrary to duty while others accord with it. The problems brought out by Worry 2 arise for a theory only if it places too much value on acting from duty as a primary motive. (They are even worse if the theory holds that the more one acts from duty as a primary motive, the better one is, or the better one's conduct is.) But if what matters (and if what the theory emphasizes) is that one govern one's conduct by a commitment to doing what is right and be prepared so to act even in the face of strong opposing desire(s), the difficulties do not take hold. For the aim is not to upstage affective motives and replace

accept moral principles that are absolutely correct, leaving no room for improvement, but it is impossible that anyone (with the possible exception of a deity) could *know* that they were correct.

them with the motive of duty but only to be ready to give the latter priority in case of a conflict.

In summary, if it is in its role as a secondary motive (which includes the capacity to assume the function of a primary motive) that the motive of duty is valued, Worry 2 does not take hold. If it is valued instead in its role as a primary motive, and particularly if this means that the more one acts from duty as a primary motive, the better, then the objection does apply, and is serious.

7   This addresses the objection that Sections 5 and 6 set out to address. Two further comments are in order.

First, I have been suggesting that we can value the motive of duty without placing special value on acting from duty as a primary motive. One advantage is that we avoid the problems raised in Worry 2. Yet another is that it steers clear of some familiar, awkward questions that confront those who defend acting from duty. It is sometimes asked, 'Should one always act from duty? Even when eating lunch? Taking a bike ride? Greeting one's parents? Hugging one's children? If not always, when? How often and in what sort of circumstances?'. It is not that the questions are utterly unanswerable, or that the only available answer is the lame 'Sometimes, and only when what is involved is a duty—sometimes people should keep promises from a sense of duty, but it is fine sometimes to keep the promise because one wants to do what one is bound by the promise to do'. This answer fails to explain or even hint at what it is about acting from duty that is supposed to be of value. It gives no indication as to what, if anything, is special and desirable about acting from duty. It is almost as if it is a sort of offering, or an offering of evidence of one's goodness: act from duty sometimes, so that you will thereby show that you take duty seriously.

An alternative answer to the questions is that one ought to act from duty only when other motives are insufficient to prompt one to do one's duty. This is the view we discussed above: the view that acting from duty is of value only as a backup. This answer at least takes a stand on what the value of acting from duty is, and it gives some clue as to when acting from duty is in order. But it is inadequate for the reasons given above. First, for the sense of duty even to function as a backup, one would need to know when to "engage" it; and, as explained earlier, one knows this, and wants to engage it, only insofar as the sense of duty plays a regulative role. Second, there is good reason to doubt that other motives ideally would always prompt us to act as we should, for the relation between the goodness of motives and the rightness of actions is such that the goodness of a motive does not guarantee that the actions to which it inclines us are right.

The problem is not primarily with the answers to the questions. It lies with the picture of acting from duty from which the troublesome questions emerge. The questions arise insofar as we understand acting from duty as acting from *duty as a primary motive*. The role of the motive of duty described above—as guiding and regulating our conduct—is that of duty operating principally as a secondary motive. As such, it attaches primarily not to individual actions but to *conduct*, to how one lives, and only derivatively to isolated actions. It serves generally as a limiting condition and at the same time as an impetus to think about one's conduct, to appraise one's goals, to be conscious of oneself as a self-determining being, and sometimes to give one the strength one needs to do what one sees one really should do.

Second, someone might question whether duty as a secondary motive really is a motive and whether acting from duty, when this is understood as acting from duty as a secondary motive, really is acting from duty. There certainly is room for doubt on each point. With respect to the former: I think calling it a motive is warranted, given the continuity between it and duty as a primary motive, and given the role it plays, in its function as a secondary motive, of prompting us to reflect on our conduct and in maintaining or heightening our moral sensitivity. What about calling this *acting from duty*? The basis for so speaking is that even in its function as a secondary motive, the sense of duty plays a motivational role, as was just noted. The awkwardness in calling it 'acting from duty' is that we usually use this term in connection with individual actions. 'Acting from' suggests individual acts, performed from particular motives; the notion of "acting from" a secondary motive flies in the face of that, suggesting instead conduct guided by a commitment. The problem lies largely with our vocabulary of motivation, which seems to favor isolated actions.

The problem has another source, closely related to the first: the term 'motive' suggests a force that moves one to act, and yet the Kantian picture of agency is *not* one of agents being moved, but rather of agents acting for reasons or (to put it as Kant does) on maxims. The awkwardness of the distinction between primary and secondary motives is ultimately due to the clumsiness of expressing a Kantian picture of motivation in the un-Kantian terminology of *motives*. The terminology of motives is well-suited to an empiricist picture of agency, but not to the Kantian picture, and yet the idea of acting from duty, as I am developing it, is a Kantian one. As developed in this chapter, it is only loosely Kantian, but even so it strains against the empiricist framework suggested by the term 'motive'. The need for the primary/secondary distinction arose because the term 'motive' does not fit the Kantian picture of motivation. To improve the fit, we introduced a regulative element by distinguishing between primary and secondary motives. No wonder it seems strained. The distinction introduces Kantian elements that do not fit the empiricist picture that is suggested by the term 'motive'.

Because the issues I take up are almost always discussed in terms of motives, I follow suit, attempting to address the criticisms in their own terms. In the second interlude, I suggest that many objections to Kant's emphasis on acting from duty are fueled by a false picture of Kant's view of agency, a picture suggested by the usual terminology of motives. In the meantime I continue to maneuver within the framework of that terminology, noting, as they arise, problems due to the clumsiness of speaking in terms of motives.

8   The preceding sections help to make the case that a commitment to doing whatever one morally ought to do does not generally alienate one from others. It neither makes one unable to care for or about other people nor makes the concern or affection that one has for others less deep or less genuine. Nor is it an expression or symptom of alienation.

This is so because the motive of duty, understood as a secondary motive that can take on the function of a primary motive, operates together with sympathetic concern, deep attachment to another person, and so on. By 'together' I do not mean merely 'alongside'; the motives will typically be interwoven. This is probably clear from the foregoing, so I will just briefly indicate ways in which the motives are interwoven. First, one's awareness of how one ought to conduct oneself will be enriched by one's affective responses to those to whom one is close, to fiction, and to the plight of victims of war, famine, and injustice, even when one does not know the victims and even when they live in distant lands. Second, since any materially adequate sense of duty will recognize that one has duties to be concerned about the welfare of others and that one has special duties as a friend, among one's duties will be those of cultivating certain attitudes and dispositions. Third, and most important for present purposes, one's sense of duty will serve to undergird affective motives. Affective motives need to be grounded on a moral commitment. This is not primarily because we are fickle, but because we have more than one (legitimate) pursuit. We care about our friends and relatives and want to help them in times of crisis; we also need to relax quietly at home and enjoy some solitude. We care about the suffering of strangers in distant lands beset by famine or civil war; it is also easy to forget about faraway suffering amid the pressing demands of work and home. Duty does not barge in as a force hostile to our interests and inclinations; it aligns with some and against others and, if construed broadly enough, provides a vantage point for reflecting on the proper ordering of (at times) competing concerns. There is no ground for regarding acting from duty as symptomatic of or conducive to alienation.[14]

9   Thus understood, conduct governed by a sense of duty seems to be unobjectionable. But that there is ample room for disagreement is clear from commentary by Susan Wolf and Bernard Williams on an example from Charles Fried.[15] Indeed, Wolf remarks that the example, as Williams develops it, is particularly apt in that, unlike Stocker's, it reveals the flaws in acting from friendship or love that is governed or mediated by one's sense of duty—not just the flaws in acting from duty as a primary motive. The example describes a situation in which a man in a position to save one of two persons in equal peril chooses to save his wife. Fried explains that it is permissible for him to choose his wife rather than make the choice by a flip of a coin, because "the occurrence of the accident may itself stand as a sufficient randomizing event to meet the dictates of fairness." Insisting that "surely this is a justification on behalf of the rescuer, that the person he chose to rescue was his wife," Williams objects to the "idea that moral principle can legitimate his preference." "This construction," he elaborates in an oft-cited passage, "provides the agent with one thought too many: it might have been hoped by some (for instance, by his wife) that his motivating thought, fully spelled out, would be the thought that it was his wife, not that it was his wife and that in situations of this kind it is permissible to save one's

14. But see Susan Wolf's "Morality and Partiality," *Philosophical Perspectives* 6 (1992): 243–259. "To ask what one may do, and what one has to do, is to express a reluctance to help or to respect the wills of others" (p. 258).

15. Charles Fried, *An Anatomy of Values* (Cambridge: Cambridge University Press, 1980), p. 27.

wife."[16] Echoing Williams, Wolf adds, "Ideally, it seems, when one acts on behalf of a loved one, one acts plainly and simply *for his sake*. One's motivating thought, fully spelled out, is something like 'It's good for George'."[17]

The objection to the idea that the man should be thinking about fairness in such a situation can be dismissed, since we have seen that one's action can be governed by a belief that one is acting fairly without it being the case that one thinks about fairness at the time of action.[18] But what about the claim that the agent should act "plainly and simply" for his wife's sake? Here the point goes beyond the suggestion that he should not be thinking at that particular time about fairness.

Would it be preferable if the action of the man in Williams's example were motivated simply by love for his wife, that is, if it were not governed by a belief that what he does is morally permissible? I think not, and the reason why can be gleaned if we revise the example slightly and imagine that his wife is badly shaken up, in terrible pain, but, unlike the stranger, not in any life-threatening danger. Assuming that there is hope of saving the stranger's life but very little time, it would be wrong of the husband to devote his attention to his wife before attending to the stranger. It is difficult to turn away from the anguished cries of someone whom one loves dearly in order to administer mouth-to-mouth resuscitation to a stranger; we expect that the man has to push himself to tend to the stranger. But far from supporting Wolf's and Williams's claims, this underscores the need for the motive of duty. Moreover, it shows that the sense of duty is not needed merely as a backup, to prompt us to do what we would "naturally" do if our affections were as they should be; for we are imagining that the man's affections and affective responses *are* as they should be. We would not admire him more if he easily turned his back on his wife and directed his energies to reviving the stranger; indeed we would (without a special story) think the less of him. If his affective network were such that he just naturally and spontaneously tended to the more seriously injured person, seeing the two people simply as people in need, we would not be especially impressed. (We do not share the Stoic

16. Bernard Williams, "Persons, Character, and Morality," in his *Moral Luck: Philosophical Papers 1973–1980* (Cambridge: Cambridge University Press, 1981), p. 18.

17. Wolf, "Failure," p. 50.

18. The belief that a Kantian agent would be thinking about duty or rightness or fairness in such a situation is, however, a fairly common one. See, for example, Joel J. Kuppermann, *Character* (New York: Oxford University Press, 1991), p. 69.

view that one should think of one's loved ones just as some mortals, and respond to their deaths as one would respond to the report that someone one only distantly knows has died.)[19] Yet though we expect people to be deeply moved by the misfortunes of those close to them, and moved much less by those of strangers, we do not think it desirable that they always act in accordance with such feelings. We do not want the husband to do as his "best desires" bid; we think it preferable—morally preferable—that he aid the person whose life is in jeopardy.[20]

The revised example brings out the need for the motive of duty—a need not conditional on any imperfection in the agent's character. In addition, it may put the original example in a somewhat different light. Even when we act on behalf of a loved one, we should not act blindly. We may act plainly and simply for the other's sake (as Wolf put it) *provided* that this does not mean that we should (or may) be oblivious to everything else. Our conduct should be informed by other considerations as well, even if we are not thinking about moral principles at the time. Moral considerations should have a certain salience for us.

What about the argument that it might have been hoped by some (e.g., by his wife) that the thought that it was she would have been sufficient motivation for him? Several comments are in order here. First, the mere fact that she might have hoped this is in itself of no relevance. Many of us are insecure about the strength of our loved ones' affection for us: it might worry us that our spouse was not so overwhelmed by the sight of us in excruciating pain as to lack the presence of mind needed to see that the stranger was in greater need. The spouse in the example as I revised it might be pained because she did not receive comfort or reassurance right away. She may realize that her husband was right to save (or try to save) the person whose life was imperiled before comforting her; but her

---

19. Epictetus writes in sec. 26 of the *Handbook*:

It is possible to learn the will of nature from the things in which we do not differ from each other. For example, when someone else's little slave boy breaks his cup we are ready to say, "It's one of those things that just happen." Certainly, then, when your own cup is broken you should be just the way you were when the other person's was broken. Transfer the same idea to larger matters. Someone else's child is dead, or his wife. There is no one would not say, "It's the lot of a human being." But when one's own dies, immediately it is, "Alas! Poor me!" But we should have remembered how we feel when we hear of the same thing about others. (Trans. Nicholas P. White [Indianapolis: Hackett, 1983], pp. 18–19)

20. Part of the preceding paragraph is taken from my "Morality as a Back-Up System: Hume's View?"

pain may persist. If this is the situation, Williams's point is again of no relevance.

It is true of both his example and my variation on it that there *might* be cause for worry. It is possible that the husband saw his wife's suffering just as *someone's suffering*, or the prospect of her death just as the prospect of *someone's* tragic death. But we would need to know more about the husband to determine this. As the example stands, there is no reason to expect this. In any case, there is no reason why this would have to be part of the example.

Of course his wife would have reason to be dismayed if it had not pained him to hear her moans and to be unable to comfort her while tending to the more severe case. There would be cause for worry if his sympathetic responses were naturally directly proportional to the severity of the case: equal anguish in Williams's example for his spouse and the stranger; in my example, greater for the stranger than for his wife. But it is one thing to claim that there is something wrong if a person's spontaneous affective responses are not such and such in circumstances C; it is another matter to say that there is something wrong, in circumstances C, with putting one's affective responses through a filter rather than acting on them with no thought of what it is right to do or what one ought to do.

Now it must be admitted that the conduct of the man in Fried's example is questionable. The man has curious moral intuitions if he thinks that in the absence of "a sufficient randomizing event" he might be morally required to toss a coin to determine whom to aid. In the absence of reasons that weigh in favor of helping the stranger rather than his wife, the fact that she is this person whom he dearly loves and to whom he stands in a special relationship is reason enough to choose her.[21] Of course, the fact that he has bizarre moral intuitions in no way implicates acting from duty, since there is no reason to think that people who act from duty necessarily or even generally have his intuitions, or other bizarre intuitions.

Our scrutiny of Williams's and Stocker's examples discloses nothing that impugns acting from duty as such. It is true that there are instances in which someone may feel alienated or rejected if a friend puts some moral consideration above his needs or wishes, but to the extent that this

21. But this is not to say that no other thoughts or beliefs should influence his action. The agent does well to be alert to the possibility that there are reasons that weigh in favor of helping the stranger.

is an instance where acting from duty is alienating, it hardly seems to support the claim that acting from duty is morally repugnant.[22]

10   At the beginning of the chapter I indicated two charges concerning acting from duty that I would discuss. The one that has been the subject of most of this chapter is that acting from duty alienates one from others. I now turn to the other charge, the claim that to act from duty is to act just minimally morally. My response to this charge draws both on the discussion of imperfect duties in previous chapters and on preceding sections of the present chapter.

The criticism is hinted at by something in Stocker's example not noted above. Stocker writes: "It is not essentially because of you that he came to see you . . . but because he thought it his duty, perhaps as a fellow Christian or communist or whatever, *or simply because he knows of no one more in need of cheering up and no one easier to cheer up.*" The underscored suggestion conjures up another set of images that we may have of Smith: he looks for the person most in need of cheering up and tries to help him or her (without any regard to the person's connection to

___

22. This is a good place to correct a misunderstanding of my view, a misunderstanding that makes my view seem weaker (i.e., more "moderate") than it in fact is. In his "Egoists, Consequentialists, and Their Friends," William Wilcox attributes to me (and to Peter Railton) the following line of response to the objection that "a commitment to impersonal morality would interfere with individuals' commitments to their personal projects and to their friends":

> One's commitment to impersonal morality does not have to interfere with one's day-to-day life to the extent Williams and Stocker suggest, because moral motivation can be understood as something that is in a sense 'held in reserve', making itself felt only in circumstances in which the agent is about to depart from the moral life. In one's ordinary dealings when nothing morally serious is at stake, one's enthusiasm for projects or affection for friends is allowed to express itself directly in action unmediated by moral considerations. (*Philosophy and Public Affairs* 16 [1987]: 73)

My concern here is not with his reply to the line of response just quoted—though I think that whatever its success with respect to Railton's position, it fails to address mine because it relies on an assumption of Railton's which I do not accept: that morality involves maximizing some impersonal value. I want only to indicate that the view attributed to me— the view spelled out in the indented quote above—is different from and weaker than my actual view. It would be accurate if I held that one's conduct is governed by the sense of duty just so long as she meets a counterfactual condition; but as indicated above, this would not suffice. The agent has to be *committed* to doing what is right.

How is this commitment to be understood? We should first observe that a "perfect record" in doing one's duty is not only not sufficient to acting from duty but also not necessary. A certain amount of backsliding is consistent with having this commitment; one can correctly be said to act from duty even if one occasionally fails to do what one sees one should do. But the commitment will have other manifestations besides conformity to one's sense of duty, most notably, reflection on how one ought to live, readiness to revise one's

him and his chances of being helpful to him); he looks for the neediest person, of those who are easy to cheer up; he looks for the person who best satisfies both conditions, setting the measure in such a way as to ensure that the person is both very needy and very easy to cheer up. But I'll ignore these intricacies. I am interested in Stocker's inclusion of "no one easier to cheer up." It brings to light something else that we associate with a concern to do one's duty: we are sometimes suspicious that a person with such a concern really aims just to be morally "in the clear": to do what he *must* do to be off the hook, above moral censure (and perhaps also to feel entitled to criticize others)—but no more. He aims to be minimally moral: he aims simply to do his duty.

In what way does this give rise to an objection to acting from duty? The idea is that if acting from duty is just acting from a concern to do the minimum, no more, then it does not deserve to be praised and encouraged. Better to encourage more generous motives. Or, one might put it this way: to teach children, as Kant advocates, to aim to do their duty (and moreover, to do it from duty) is to lead them to set their sights too low.

The objection is a serious one if directed toward those who favor acting from duty *and* adhere to a narrow, legalistic notion of duty, such as Urmson's (discussed above in Chap. 2). Those who think of duties as delineating a cutoff, a moral threshold below which one must not fall, are open to the charge of what we might call "minimal moralism" if they champion guiding and governing one's conduct by a commitment to doing one's duty.[23] Because of their narrow notion of duty, this will not

---

moral beliefs and one's plans and aims in light of one's reflections, and willingness to entertain evidence that tells against one's moral beliefs. In addition, one who acts from duty will reflect on her conduct and not be left cold by thoughts about how she acted—nor will she feel only the retrospective emotions (e.g., regret, unlike remorse) which enable one to evade moral responsibility for the conduct in question. And, of course, the agent will sometimes evince *resolve* to act as she sees she ought to act.

The sense in which one acts from this commitment, even in instances in which she gives no thought to the ethical nature of her conduct before proceeding with the intended action, is roughly as follows: a very rich explanation of any nontrivial choice or action, e.g., the sort of explanation that a novelist might give, would make reference to some of the manifestations listed above.

23. I say 'minimal moralism' despite the fact that one might interpret it to mean that the person in question is being as nonmoralistic as possible, and why fault that? That is not the meaning, though; what I mean is that the person understands morality far too narrowly. The term 'minimal morality' sounds better but does not work because those who are open to the minimal morality objection are the agents who follow a minimal morality. We need

encourage moral reflection, sensitivity, or readiness either to help others on an individual basis or to join in projects to improve the world in bigger ways (to improve the quality of our air and water, to oppose torture and imperialistic domination of the poorest nations, etc.).

I will argue (briefly, because the point will quickly become obvious) that if duty is understood broadly, in the way advocated in Chapters 1 and 2, the problem does not take hold. Before doing so, I want to clarify the objection.

It may help to separate two ways the objection might be construed. One claim would be that the person who is very concerned to do his duty is just trying to do all that is necessary to be "off the hook" in the sense of being fairly safe from social ostracism. Think here of the man who tries to change his sexist ways, but only so as not to seem sexist. He cleans up his language, from time to time "helps" his wife with the housework (which he sees as *her* housework) or prepares supper. He does so to avoid being thought of as sexist—or at least to have some replies at hand which he hopes will be adequate to disarm anyone who raises questions about his attitudes concerning sexual equality. His attitudes do not change, nor does a good deal of his behavior; but at least to those who do not know him well, he does not seem sexist.

A second claim would again be that the person who is very concerned to do his duty is just trying to do what is necessary to get off the hook—but this time, a truly moral hook. He is concerned to do what is necessary to avoid being immoral—but only what is necessary. He aims to do just what he has to do and no more (rather like the student who wants to do exactly what is needed to get a certain grade and no more). He wants a line drawn, just as Urmson does, between the morally required and the supererogatory; and for whatever reasons, he firmly intends to do all that is required *and no more*.

It is the second version of the objection that concerns me. Of course, the motivation described by the second claim may contain that described by the first: in the second, the person may be motivated by a desire to avoid social ostracism. But the motivation of the latter person goes further: he really wants to be minimally moral, not just to be so perceived.

---

a different name for the objection that applies to those who *conceive* of morality too narrowly—those whose views appear to promote (albeit unintentionally) minimal morality. Hence 'minimal moralism'.

The worry is certainly well-founded if 'duty' is understood as demarcating a moral minimum, for then a concern to do one's duty amounts to a concern to do what morally one must do. Acting from duty, on that understanding of 'duty', just *is* acting minimally morally. With that understanding, a theorist would have reason at the very least to downplay the idea of acting from duty and to emphasize moral ideals (unless, perhaps, she held the views classified as "moral decentism" in the first interlude).

But duty on a Kantian conception does not demarcate a moral minimum. In effect, moral ideals are built into it. This is because of the open-endedness of imperfect duties, and in particular because of the duty of self-perfection. There simply is no 'minimally moral' conduct within the rubric of Kant's ethics unless one understands 'minimally moral' to refer to the perfect duties: there it might be said (with, however, some distortion) that one acts minimally morally if one fulfills only one's perfect duties.[24] But since one acts unacceptably if one rejects or ignores the obligatory ends of one's own perfection and the happiness of others, the allegedly minimally moral conduct would be morally deficient, thus not minimally moral.

But a worry may linger. It is all very well, someone will say, to point out that acting from duty does not cover only perfect duties, since duty encompasses more than perfect duties; but what is not clear is how one could act from duty in fulfilling imperfect duties. After all, the objection continues, duty either prompts us to do what we are strictly required to do or affirms us in doing what we propose to do. How, on this picture, could duty play any larger a motivational role with regard to acts that fall under principles of imperfect duty than it does with regard to merely permissible acts? How, in other words, could it play any role beyond that of indicating that helping a particular person in a particular set of circumstances is not morally prohibited, thus affirming a plan to help him?

If it cannot, then the minimal morality allegation sticks: Kant's ethics does not dodge it. For the complaint is that to act from duty is to act only from a commitment to doing what is morally required. If the reply is 'No, the commitment is to imperfect duties as well as perfect duties', and thus is not only to doing those actions which are strictly required, the

24. I say 'with some distortion' because, as has been noted, the perfect duties in certain circumstances may require tremendous sacrifice.

rejoinder is 'Tell us how the commitment to imperfect duties translates into action'.

The objection may seem serious at first, for it seems that it is only with respect to perfect duties that the motive of duty serves to "filter out" anything impermissible that we propose to do. But the picture on which the objection is based omits an important fact: the Categorical Imperative tests maxims, not proposed actions. It filters out impermissible maxims. And although it is generally the case that imperfect duties do not require or forbid specific actions, they do require some maxims and forbid others. So there is something impermissible to be filtered out even when only imperfect duties are at issue: maxims of neglecting obligatory ends. This point is crucial to understanding how the motive of duty functions with respect to all Kantian duties.

In its role as a secondary motive, the motive of duty operates in roughly the same way with respect to imperfect duties as it does with respect to perfect duties. In each case it filters out impermissible maxims. There *is* one difference, but it is not a difference that tells in favor of the objection. There is a positive role for the motive of duty to play with respect to imperfect duties for which there is no exact counterpart concerning perfect duties. Suppose that I want to help my sister in a time of crisis but am also tempted to keep my life simpler by maintaining a safe distance from her woes. The consideration that I ought to help her (where this does not mean that helping her is strictly required) weighs in: it is an important consideration that may, together with my affective concern, decide me to set aside my concern not to become too emotionally involved in the situation. (Or, it may prod me to figure out a way to help without becoming very emotionally involved and without keeping me from my other commitments.) Part of what it is to govern my conduct by a sense of duty is that I give a greal deal of weight in thoughts about my conduct, indeed my life, to matters that fall under the headings of the obligatory ends. (This is not to say either that such considerations trump all other considerations—after all, I am not required to help whenever possible—or, at the other extreme, that the consideration that one should help on occasions like this is just one among many considerations, all on an equal footing. The consideration is weighty, but not decisive; and given the latitude in imperfect duties, this is about all that can be said.)

In light of what I said in Chapters 1 and 2 in connection with the charge of minimal morality discussed there, it is clear that the worry that one who acts from duty will be acting just minimally morally is without substance if the notion of duty in question is Kant's. Given what duty encompasses on Kant's view, a commitment to doing one's duty will have to be a commitment to doing much more than a minimum (even though it will not be a commitment to doing the maximum possible).

THIS completes our consideration of objections to acting from duty. The objections have been helpful in pointing to how acting from duty is to be understood so as not to run afoul of the problems that, in examining the objections, we have uncovered. I turn now to a topic that the preceding paragraphs anticipate: Kant on acting from duty.

5

Kant on Acting from Duty

❖❖❖

1   Kant's claim that only actions done from the motive of duty have moral worth prompts the perennial question: What about actions done from both duty and inclination, that is, overdetermined actions? Suppose I help my friend both because I want to and because I know that morally I should. Does my action have moral worth? It seems, on the face of it, that it should; it would be odd if helping my friend had moral worth only if I did it *because* I morally ought to, and not if I did it because I wanted to *and* because it was something that I morally ought to do.

What position does Kant take with respect to overdetermined actions? This proves to be a complicated question, not only because it is difficult to get a clear reading of the texts, but also because of the question itself. It is not clear exactly what an overdetermined action *is*. The question will have to be refined before much headway can be made.

There is another difficulty. It is not clear that the question is a good one to ask. If it is not, this is a discovery of some import, since the question shapes much discussion and evaluation of Kant's ethics. In the course of discussing it, I will be suggesting that the emphasis in classrooms and in Kant scholarship on this question has led to a somewhat distorted picture of Kant's concerns.

If the question misleads, why do I pursue it at all? I do so in part because I want to show how it *has* misled. More fully, the reason is this: I aim ultimately to undermine an objection to Kant's ethics—the objection that he places too much value on the motive of duty)—and the objection is typically pursued via questions about overdetermination.

Although I could challenge the objection by claiming that this way of thinking about Kant's views is not the best way and by suggesting a different way, I think that a thorough and fair evaluation of the objection requires trying out the usual way of looking at Kant. One advantage to this approach is that it provides an opportunity for showing how much more complex the interpretive questions are than is usually supposed. Distinctions such as that drawn in Section 3, below, between hybrid actions and overdetermined actions, are necessary for evaluating how much support key passages provide for the theses in question (as Sec. 5 shows). There is, nonetheless, a danger in trying out the usual way of looking at Kant. In pursuing the questions of overdetermination, I risk distorting his aims and concerns. To obviate that danger, I will occasionally interrupt the discussion to point out aspects of his view that are eclipsed by the usual approach.

2   Although the question—What position does Kant take with respect to overdetermined actions?—needs refinement, some headway can be made before fine-tuning it if we first address an easier question. The easier question is this: Does Kant hold that it is a necessary condition of an action's having moral worth that one does not want to perform it, or at least has no desire to perform it? If the answer is 'Yes', we won't have to discuss the harder question, because the answer to it will be a simple 'No'. Unfortunately for simplicity, the answer to the easier question turns out to be 'No'.

The ground for suspicion that Kant holds that an action has moral worth only if we have no inclination to perform it is that Kant's examples of morally worthy actions in the first section of the *Groundwork* are in each case examples of actions to which the agent either lacks positive inclination or has counterinclinations. Addressing Schiller's famous criticism of Kant, H. J. Paton has pointed out that the fact that in each example the agent is not inclined to perform the action in question does not show that a lack of inclination is crucial to acting from duty (and thus to an act's having moral worth); moreover, there is a straightforward explanation for this feature of Kant's examples. Kant is putting forth examples in which it is as evident as it could be that the person must be acting from duty. To do this, he describes the action in a way that brings out starkly the fact that the action lacks any other incentive. In Paton's words, Kant is employing a "method of isolation" in which he isolates the motive of duty from other motives in order to focus on instances where it is clear that the person must be acting from duty.[1]

Despite hints from critics that Paton's interpretation is contrived, there is textual support for his reading. The way Kant sets up the examples strongly suggests that his object is to throw into relief the motive of duty and to contrast two sharply different kinds of motivation, inclination and duty.

Kant speaks first of people of "so sympathetic a temper that, without any further motive of vanity or self-interest, they find an inner pleasure in spreading happiness around them," and asserts that actions "of this kind" have "no genuinely moral worth" since their maxims lack moral content (G 398). He then asks us to imagine that the mind of such a person "were overclouded by sorrows of his own which extinguished all sympathy with the fate of others," thus emphasizing that the motives available to him earlier are now no longer available to him. We are asked to "suppose that, when no longer moved by any inclination, he tears himself out of this deadly insensibility and does the action without any inclination from duty alone; then for the first time his action has its genuine moral worth" (G 398).[2] The example is set up so as to bring to the fore the point that unless the person acts from duty, his action lacks moral worth—no matter how good the action and how amiable the inclination. (It also aims to convince us that we *have* this motive of duty and that it can be effective even when we lack any cooperating inclination.)

Critics charge, however, that "for the first time," in the sentence just quoted, makes it plain that Kant is saying that the man's action lacks moral worth unless he has no inclination to it. The only way around it, they claim, is to take the liberty of inserting into the proposition "the qualification that it is the first time we can *know* that an action has moral worth."[3] But as Barbara Herman points out, it matters that Kant is not

1. H. J. Paton, *The Categorical Imperative: A Study in Kant's Moral Philosophy* (London: Hutchinson's University Library, 1947), p. 47. See also Lewis White Beck's introduction to his translation of Kant's *Grundlegung*, and Barbara Herman, "On the Value of Acting from the Motive of Duty," *Philosophical Review* 90 (1981): 359–382.

2. Here and elsewhere I alter Paton's translation, translating *aus Pflicht* as 'from duty,' rather than 'for the sake of duty.'

3. Judith Baker, "Do One's Motives Have to Be Pure?" in *Philosophical Grounds of Rationality*, ed. Richard Grandy and Richard Warner (London: Oxford University Press, 1986), p. 460. See also Richard G. Henson, "What Kant Might Have Said: Moral Worth and the Overdetermination of Dutiful Action," *Philosophical Review* 88 (1979): 39–54.

speaking at the end of his example of a *different person* from the one described earlier in the example. He is not comparing two people, one who acts from inclination, and another who lacks inclination and acts from duty. He is saying of someone who formerly acted on others' behalf from inclination and not from duty that only now, when the inclination to act on their behalf is not available, does his action of aiding them have moral worth. Herman explains: "Of *him* it is . . . said: only when the inclination to help others is not available does *his* helping action have moral worth. For of him it was true that when he acted with inclination he did not also act from the motive of duty."[4]

In sum, Kant's "for the first time" does not signify that only when one acts *without inclination* does the person's action have moral worth. He is saying of someone who, when he acts with inclination, *does not act from duty*, that only when he lacks the inclination to help others does his action of helping have moral worth; for only then does *he* act from duty.

The presentation of this example is similar to that of the man with gout who lacks the inclination to happiness and seeks to further his happiness from duty: "for the first time his conduct has a real moral worth" (*G* 399). In neither case does he say, 'Only in a case like his does an action have moral worth'; but rather, 'Only now does his conduct have moral worth', contrasting it to the agent's previous conduct. So the critics are wrong to claim that if we are to reject the 'if inclinations, no moral worth' interpretation, we have to insert the qualification that only now *can we know* that an action has moral worth.[5]

Baker is addressing an interpretation that holds that on Kant's view an action can have moral worth even if the agent's decision to so act is influenced by an inclination (not merely that it can have moral worth if the agent has an inclination to perform it). Since her remarks about 'for the first time' apply to the weaker interpretation, which I defend, just as much (and in exactly the same way) as they do to the stronger interpretation, I think it is fair to discuss her claims in this context.

4. Herman, "On the Value," p. 378. A revised version of this paper appears in Herman's *The Practice of Moral Judgment* (Cambridge: Harvard University Press, 1993). Unfortunately, her book appeared as I was completing my manuscript, too late for me to take it into account beyond checking the passages that I have cited from her article to see whether she revised or omitted any of them in revising the article for her book. None was omitted, and the only quotation that was altered is the one just cited. The second sentence of it was revised as follows: "For of him it was true that when he had the inclination he did not act from the motive of duty" (pp. 18–19).

5. Baker claims that Herman's reading "does not seem adequate for the text." "For, without any break, Kant follows the example of the man struck with misfortune by the example of a man poorly endowed by nature with fellow-feeling. And of this creature Kant

Two further bits of textual evidence come from the *Critique of Practical Reason*. Kant likens the philosopher who arranges an "experiment" to "distinguish the moral (pure) determining ground from the empirical," to the chemist (92). And he writes that "the purity of the moral principle ... can be clearly shown only by removing from the incentive of the action everything which men might count as a part of happiness" (156).

But the most decisive evidence that he does not hold absence of inclination to be a necessary component of acting from duty, and thus of an action's having moral worth, can be found in the beginning of his discussion of moral worth in the *Groundwork*. He says that it is far more difficult to tell that an action has been done from duty if the agent has an immediate inclination to the action than if the agent has reasons of self-interest for performing the action. "This difference is far more difficult to perceive when the action accords with duty and the subject has in addition an *immediate* inclination to the action" (397).[6] If absence of inclination were necessary for the action to qualify as an action done from duty, it would *not* be difficult at all to tell whether an action to which the agent had an inclination was done from duty. It would be clear that it was *not* done from duty. The fact that Kant says that it is more difficult in such cases shows that he allows the possibility that actions to which the agent is inclined may be done from duty and thus may have moral worth.

3   I take it to be settled that Kant does *not* hold that absence of an inclination to *x* is a necessary condition for *x*'s having moral worth.[7] Does this mean that Kant allows that overdetermined actions can have

---

says that he has the opportunity to give himself 'a far higher worth', by acting not from any inclinations, but from duty alone" ("Do One's Motives," p. 461). The passage Baker cites tells against Herman's reading only if we take Kant to be saying that the man has an opportunity that someone who has fellow feeling lacks (namely, an opportunity to give himself a 'higher worth'). But this would be a very strange view for Kant to take. It cannot be that the very having of fellow feeling debars one from acting from duty. For that would clash with Kant's views on freedom: no matter what our inclinations, we are always capable of acting from duty. A much more Kantian reading of the passage is simply that in acting from duty, the man gives himself a higher worth than does the person who never acts from duty. The latter *could* act from duty, but doesn't; and so despite the former's lack of fellow feeling, he can give himself a higher worth than the latter *in fact* does.

6. I have substituted 'difference' for 'distinction' as a translation of *Unterschied*. Thanks to Mario von der Ruhr for pointing out that 'difference' is a more apt translation.

7. Baker ("Do One's Motives," p. 460) cites a passage from the *Groundwork* which she takes to show decisively that on Kant's view, one cannot "be influenced by an inclination

moral worth? Before answering this question, it is important to distinguish overdetermined actions from actions with which they might be (and often are) confused. By 'overdetermined actions' I mean actions that are prompted by more than one motive (for simplicity, and because the simplification does no harm, I'll assume two motives), where either motive by itself would have sufficed. By 'prompted by more than one motive' I mean that each motive contributes, as a primary motive, to the person's so acting. The overdetermined actions of relevance to this discussion are actions from duty together with some inclination.

This explanation of overdetermined actions needs refinement, which will be offered shortly. But it suffices to enable us to distinguish overdetermined actions, so understood, from actions where neither motive is by itself sufficient. To distinguish such actions from overdetermined acts, I'll refer to them as 'hybrid actions'. The difference between overdetermined actions and hybrid actions is that in the latter cases, the two motives join together to produce what neither alone would produce; by contrast, in the case of overdetermined actions, each motive alone would suffice to prompt the act.[8] (Of course, there are also actions that fall in between: actions prompted by more than one motive, where one of the motives is sufficient but the other is not. But it would only complicate matters unduly to give them, too, a name.)

I return to the question posed two paragraphs back: Assuming that Kant does not hold that absence of inclination to do *x* is a necessary condition for doing *x* to have moral worth, does this entail that overdetermined actions may have moral worth? The answer is *No*. Nor does it entail that hybrid actions (or the unnamed actions that fall between hybrid actions and overdetermined actions) can have moral worth. The reason, in each instance, is fairly simple: overdetermined actions (and likewise, hybrid actions and the unnamed actions) are done from both duty and another motive. Both motives *contribute* to the action in question. All that I argued above is that the fact that the agent

---

to determine to do an action which has moral worth" (p. 459). The translation she cites is Beck's and reads as follows: "an act done from duty wholly excludes the influence of inclination." Paton's translation is: "an act done from duty has to set aside altogether the influence of inclinations." Paton's translation seems to me more apt, since the German is "ganz absondern." But on either reading, this quote would not bear on the interpretation that I am defending, since I claim only that morally worthy actions do not exclude inclination, not that they do not exclude the influence of inclination. (See the remainder of Sec. 3 for more on this distinction.)

8. To put it roughly. I will refine this characterization of overdetermined acts in Sec. 5.

is inclined to do a certain action does not entail that the agent does not do the action from duty, and thus that the action lacks moral worth. But arguably, at least, the agent may have the inclination *without its contributing to her action*, that is, without it serving as a primary motive on a particular occasion. She may act solely from duty, even while being inclined to the action in question.

If this is right—if having an inclination to x does not entail that if one does x, one does it (partly) from that inclination—then to show that Kant does not hold that absence of inclination is necessary for an action to have moral worth is not yet to show that overdetermined actions may have moral worth. *Is* it right?

Certainly it is Kant's view. It is part of our freedom that we do not have to act from an inclination just because we have that inclination. I think that it is, moreover, a compelling view. The following example illustrates the possibility of having an inclination to x and doing x without acting from that inclination. Kevin agrees to pay Karen a set sum for painting his living room. She paints it as planned and does an excellent job, and he pays her the sum agreed on. Why does he pay her? Because he agreed to (and because, barring unusual circumstances, e.g., that the painter spills paint all over one's furnishings, one should pay people one hires in accordance with the prior agreement). He also is happy to do so, since she did such a good job. But his "inclination" to pay her does not contribute to his action of paying her. He pays her the set sum not because he wants to, or because he wants to *and* because she did such a good job, but because that was the agreement.[9]

4   So the question of overdetermination and of hybrid actions remains undecided. *Presence* of inclination is consistent with the action's being done from duty, and thus having moral worth. But can the action qualify as an action done from duty if it is done *from* inclination as well as from duty?

We need to consider hybrid actions and overdetermined actions separately. Consider hybrid actions first. This is the easier case. That hybrid

9. This paragraph overlaps my "Freedom, Frailty, and Impurity," *Inquiry* 36 (1993): 431–441, a discussion of some issues in Henry Allison, *Kant's Theory of Freedom* (New York: Cambridge University Press, 1990). In that article I raise a problem concerning the notion that one can choose not to act from a particular inclination. Henry Allison replies in the same issue. Since publishing that article I discovered that Lewis White Beck raises the same problem in his "Sir David Ross on Duty and Purpose in Kant," *Philosophy and Phenomenological Research* 16 (1955): 98-107.

actions cannot have moral worth is clear from numerous passages in which Kant says that the motive of duty must be a sufficient motive. If the motive of duty requires the assistance of cooperating inclinations, the action lacks moral worth. Here is one of the passages that make this plain: "What is essential in the moral worth of actions is that the moral law should directly determine the will. If the determination of the will occurs in accordance with the moral law but only by means of a feeling of any kind whatsoever, which must be presupposed in order that the law may become a determining ground of the will, and if the action thus occurs not for the sake of the law, it has legality but not morality" (*PrR* 71).

There is a danger, when we focus on the questions of over-determination, that we will miss Kant's central claims. So it is worth straying off our path to observe that many of the passages that support the point just made—that the motive of duty must be sufficient by itself if an action is to have moral worth—have as their main point something slightly different, namely, that we should not seek out other incentives to help us to do what we see to be morally required. This is similar enough to the point about moral worth that one might not take notice of it as a different point. But it is different: it concerns what we, as agents, are to do, and not how our actions are (retrospectively) to be evaluated. The difference is important. It reflects something that is often overlooked: Kant's pragmatic concern in discussing moral motivation is not primarily with evaluating acts retrospectively as morally worthy or lacking in moral worth, but with the cultivation of character and, more specifically, the cultivation of a good will. He is concerned with both the cultivation of one's own character and the cultivation of character in children.[10]

It is easy in discussions of moral worth to overlook this, since there is little in the *Groundwork* explicitly about the cultivation of a good will (and most discussions of Kant's account of the moral worth of actions focus, understandably enough, on the *Groundwork*). The concern that we not cultivate an impure will in ourselves is evident in the second *Critique* and in the *Doctrine of Virtue* but is especially prominent in the

---

10. It should be borne in mind that we are not, on Kant's view, to be cultivating the characters of other adults. It is not our business to try to improve other adults' characters; as noted earlier, our imperfect duty to perfect ourselves does not involve a duty to perfect others. (Of course this does not preclude helping a friend, at his request, to improve himself. But the project should be one of *self*-improvement, one in which Joe asks Steve to help him improve himself, not one in which Joe asks Steve to improve Joe.)

Religion. "Impurity," which Kant says arises from "the propensity for mixing unmoral with moral motivating causes," is the middle of three levels or degrees in the capacity for evil. It falls in between "frailty" (weakness of will) and wickedness. He describes the intermediate degree as follows:

> the impurity . . . of the human heart consists in this, that although the maxim is indeed good in respect of its object (the intended observance of the law) and perhaps even strong enough for practice, it is yet not purely moral; that is, it has not, as it should have, adopted the law *alone* as its *all-sufficient* incentive: instead, it usually (perhaps, every time) stands in need of other incentives beyond this, in determining the will^w [*Willkür*] to do what duty demands; in other words, actions called for by duty are done not purely from duty. (R 29–30/25)[11]

Kant's concern is notably not that despite our best efforts, our otherwise moral motivation is sullied by the intrusion of a cooperating inclination, but rather that we deliberately seek out other incentives rather than adopt the moral law alone as an "all-sufficient incentive." Seeking out other incentives is wrong. It is not just that the action that ensues lacks moral worth—a matter, interestingly, that Kant does not bring up in the *Religion* at all—but that we are, in seeking out other incentives to make it easier to do what we morally ought to do, cultivating an impure will. As Kant implies, it is worse to cultivate an impure will than to lapse occasionally. Impurity is the second level or degree in the capacity for evil; frailty is only the first.

Impurity, furthermore, is a short step away from full-blown wickedness, which consists in subordinating the moral incentive to a nonmoral incentive.[12] Kant depicts the fall from impurity to wickedness in an imaginative retelling of the story of the Fall:

> The moral law became known to mankind, as it must to any being not pure but tempted by desires, in the form of a *prohibition* (Genesis II, 16–17). Now instead of straightway following this law as an adequate incentive (the only incentive which is unconditionally good and regarding which there is no further doubt), man looked about for other incentives (Genesis III, 6), such as can be good only conditionally (namely, so far as they

11. I have altered the translation, translating *aus Pflicht* not as 'for duty's sake', as Greene and Hudson do, but as 'from duty'. I also inserted *Willkür* as a reminder that 'will^w' is the translators' way of distinguishing *Willkür* from *Wille*, which they translate as 'will'.

12. See Roger Sullivan's discussion in his *Immanuel Kant's Moral Theory* (Cambridge: Cambridge University Press, 1989), chap. 9.

involve no infringement of the law). He then made it his maxim—if one
thinks of his action as consciously springing from freedom—to follow the
law of duty, not as duty, but, if need be, with regard to other aims.
Thereupon he began to call in question the severity of the commandment
which excludes the influence of all other incentives; then by sophistry he
reduced obedience to the law to the merely conditional character of a
means (subject to the principle of self-love); and finally he adopted into his
maxim of conduct the ascendancy of the sensuous impulse over the incentive which springs from the law—and thus occurred sin (Genesis III, 6).
(R 42/37)

Once I regard the motive of duty as less than a fully sufficient incentive
(or even as potentially sufficient, but as not fully compelling unless it
coincides with my own interest or with some inclination), I call into
question the supremacy of morality. Once I search for cooperating
inclinations, I will scarcely be able to maintain the belief that moral
considerations always trump any competing considerations. For insofar
as I adopt a policy of seeking assistance from the inclinations, I in effect
allow that moral considerations are not fully compelling, motivationally;
but if they are not fully compelling motivationally, presumably they are
not fully compelling, period. I will end up asking myself, "It's obligatory,
and that carries some weight; but what other reasons are there for
doing it?"

This is not simply a slippery slope argument. The claim is not merely
that if I search for cooperating inclinations, I'll soon slip further and end
up regarding moral considerations as just some considerations among
others. Rather, the idea is that it makes little sense to hold the position
that is implicit in the very activity of searching for other incentives, unless
one holds that moral considerations are not decisive.[13]

We now return from the detour (the need for which was signaled in the

---

13. It is not incoherent; I could hold, for example, that moral considerations are
decisive, but that I am morally weak and am not always strongly swayed by moral
considerations, even though I should be. Since I want to do what I morally ought to do but
think that I am likely to fail if I try to act from duty, I bring myself to do my duty by finding
something appealing about the action in question, or by "bribing" myself (e.g., I indulge in
an expensive dinner by way of rewarding myself for being honest). One could take this
view, but not without rejecting Kant's view of us as free.

For this reason, I think that Baker's "reconstructive" proposal is misguided insofar as it
purports to be Kantian. She asserts that "one may be deemed to act from the sense of duty
as a single, albeit complexly structured, motive, if one judges that a given action is one's
duty, thinks that this thought provides one with sufficient reason to perform the action, but
finding oneself insufficiently motivated to actually do it, searches out ways of motivating
oneself" ("Do One's Motives," p. 470).

first section of this chapter). We saw, just before the detour, that hybrid actions cannot have moral worth. The question to address now is: Can overdetermined actions have moral worth?

5   The difference between hybrid actions and overdetermined actions is, recall, that in hybrid actions the motives join together to produce what neither alone would produce; whereas in overdetermined actions, each motive alone would suffice to prompt the action. Or so I put it before. But there is a problem in the characterization of overdetermined actions that we need now to address.[14]

If an overdetermined action is one prompted by both the motive of duty and an inclination, where either alone would suffice, just what is meant by saying that inclination alone would suffice? Is it that inclination would suffice, even if the agent saw the act to be wrong? If that is what is meant, then clearly such actions cannot have moral worth. In fact, the description is not even coherent. To say that inclination would suffice even if the agent saw the action to be wrong would be to say that in the event of a conflict between duty and inclination, inclination would win. But then what would it mean to say that duty suffices? Only that as long as there is no conflict between duty and inclination, duty will be a "sufficient motive": it will "win" as long as there is no contest. Clearly, to understand 'inclination alone would suffice' in this way robs the motive of duty of any sufficiency worth having.

If the notion that overdetermined actions can have moral worth is to have any plausibility, we need to refine 'overdetermined' to clarify what is meant by saying that either motive alone would suffice. We can do so by appending that we mean by 'inclination alone would suffice' not inclination pure and simple, but *inclination governed by duty as a secondary motive*. With this problem addressed, we can now characterize overdetermined actions as follows.

If my action is overdetermined, this means:

> (1) that as long as I did not believe the action to be wrong, my inclination to do it would suffice to motivate me to perform the action (and would not need to be supplemented by additional motives, such as that this will pay off in the future, or that this is morally good to do, albeit not required); and

14. There is another problem, too, which Barbara Herman has pointed out. See n. 36, below.

(2) that in the absence of cooperating inclinations the motive of duty would suffice; and

(3) that the action is determined by both motives (duty in its function as a primary motive, and inclination) operating separately, not by a happy marriage of the two (i.e., not through acquiring force by buttressing each other).[15]

(Readers who are trying to track the successive formulations of 'overdetermined' should note that despite the fact that this final one divides into three parts and thus has a very different look than the previous one, the only substantive difference is in [1].)

With this explanation of 'overdetermined' complete, let us delve further into Kant's stand on overdetermined actions. We have seen that duty must be a sufficient motive, and that the fact that a person is *inclined* to perform the action does not debar it from having moral worth. But, as noted earlier, Kant *may* hold, consistent with holding that the mere presence of an inclination does not preclude moral worth, that an action is precluded from having moral worth if an inclination serves as a *motive* to the action. This position may seem to be suggested by the following passages:

(A) The essential point in all determination of the will through the moral law is this: as a free will, and thus not only without co-operating with sensuous impulses but even rejecting all of them and checking all inclinations so far as they could be antagonistic to the law, it is determined merely by the law. (*PrR* 72)

(B) The majesty of duty has nothing to do with the enjoyment of life . . . and however much one wishes to mix them together, in order to offer the mixture to the sick as though it were a medicine, they nevertheless soon separate of themselves; but, if they do not separate, the moral ingredient has no effect at all. (*PrR* 89)

15. A different way of addressing the problem would be to revise the question, so that instead of asking whether overdetermined acts can have moral worth, one would ask whether acts moved by duty and inclination, *where duty alone would suffice but inclination alone would not suffice*, can have moral worth. These are like overdetermined acts, but also rather like hybrid acts; we might call them 'half-overdetermined', though that confuses since there would have to be two types of half-overdetermined acts: those to which inclination alone would suffice, while duty would not, and those just described, where duty alone would suffice while inclination would not. It will be simpler to set aside this alternative approach to the problem and stick with the more straightforward one of understanding inclinations, in the explanation of overdetermined acts, to be inclinations-governed-by-secondary-motives.

(C) All admixture of incentives which derive from one's own happiness are a hindrance to the influence of the moral law on the human heart. (*PrR* 156)

The section of the *Doctrine of Virtue* entitled "On Man's Duty to Himself to Increase His Moral Perfection" is also relevant:

(D) This perfection consists subjectively in the *purity* . . . of one's disposition to duty, namely, in the law being by itself alone the incentive, even without the admixture of aims derived from sensibility, and in actions being done not only in conformity with duty but also *from duty*. (*MM* 446)

Who knows himself well enough to say, when he feels the incentive to fulfill his duty, whether it proceeds entirely from the representation of the law or whether there are not many other sensible impulses contributing to it that look to one's advantage (or to avoiding what is detrimental) and that, in other circumstances, could just as well serve vice? (*MM* 447)

Some of these passages lend little support to the view that Kant holds that overdetermined acts cannot have moral worth. Although (D) could be read as supporting it, given what he says in *Religion* about purity, "purity" in (D) probably contrasts not with there being a second motive, which separately contributes to the action, but rather with the assistance ("admixture") of another motive.[16] If so, it is evidence only for the claim, which is not at issue, that hybrid actions cannot, on Kant's view, have moral worth. One could argue that (B) also concerns the commingling of the motive of duty with other motives (and it more specifically cautions against cultivating an impure will). Although (C) *could* be read either way, since an 'admixture' *might* be two motives that separately influence an action, more likely it is, as it seems to be in (B), cooperating motives. If the latter reading is accepted, (C), like (B) and (D), would not speak to the question of overdetermination as I have defined it. (Recall that we already established that hybrid actions, i.e., actions that are determined by the motive of duty in cooperation with other motives, cannot have moral worth.)

This reading of (C), (D), and perhaps (B) is debatable, however. Moreover, it is harder to avoid reading (A) as ruling out the possibility of an overdetermined act having moral worth.

16. I discuss the first part of (D) in Sec. 12.1 of this chapter.

6   At this stage many interpreters would search for a way to explain (A) as, given its context, not so clearly saying what it seems to be saying. This might indeed be feasible. But rather than grope for a different way of reading it, I want to pose this question: *Should we be bothered if Kant does exclude the possibility that overdetermined actions could have moral worth?* It is usually assumed that this exclusion is an embarrassment for Kant (if not also that the slightly weaker claims discussed earlier are likewise an embarrassment). But in her "Do One's Motives Have to Be Pure?" Judith Baker provides reasons for questioning the assumption that what Kant seems to say here is something that he should not have said. Indeed, her essay raises the possibility that what many readers think Kant should have said is barely coherent. It does so by prompting the following question: Can an action even *be* overdetermined, by duty and an inclination, in the sense explained? Consider the following from Baker's article:

> An individual thinks that standards of fair grading require him to give a student a certain grade, which in this case is a good one. Liking the student or liking to give good grades, one feels, cannot be an additional motive which helps the agent in determining the grade if he is to be credited with acting from a sense of fairness. It looks as if the requirements of fairness are what must exclusively determine the action, if it is done from a sense of fairness, and that additional motives are not compatible with the idea of what fairness requires.[17]

The general point is this. Suppose I believe that something is required of me, and act accordingly. If I act from the thought that it is required, it does not make sense to say that I may at the same time be acting from other motives.

Now a teacher could give the student a good grade because she liked the student and wanted to give him a high grade. Consistent with this, the teacher might acknowledge, "In fact, the paper is very good—so I'd have given him a high grade even if I hadn't liked him." But it is still true that she did not act from fairness if she gave him a high grade because she liked him. To act from fairness, she would have had to give him the high grade that he deserved because he deserved it, because the standards of fairness required it, and not for any additional reason.

The general point can be illustrated by examples that do not exhibit a

---

17. Baker, "Do One's Motives," p. 466.

moral motive, as well as by examples such as the one just cited. In fact the following example, also from Baker's article, more clearly than the last is an instance of a putatively overdetermined action. Someone might argue that the motives in the last example cooperate, rather than contribute separately, and thus that it would not really be a case of overdetermination. That is questionable, but in any case it is clear that the next example is a would-be case of overdetermination (though not a case involving a specifically moral motive). "A student is committed to being a philosophy major. . . . He finds that a given course is required by the department. Suppose it is also a course which has some appeal for the student. It does not seem intelligible to say that the student takes the course both because it is required and because it is appealing." Is there some way to render it intelligible? Only, I think, if we illicitly imagine the requirement to be, in the student's eyes, something less than a strict requirement. It is crucial to the example that the student is committed to being a philosophy major. If he were ready to consider switching majors if courses were required that did not sound interesting to him, the example would not work. Similarly, if an agent regarded moral requirements as requirements that she ought to fulfill unless they clash with something that she badly wants to do, she could not be said to act from duty when she acts from the thought that a certain course of action is morally required. As Baker says, requirements "are not decisive if they are not taken to be unconditional."[18] But when they are taken to be unconditional, they are decisive.[19] If the student is committed to being a philosophy major, then if he takes a given course because it is required, the fact that he also wants to take the course does not enter in as another motive. (Of course, if he has a choice as to when to take the required course, the appeal that it has for him may affect the decision of *when* to take it.)[20]

The claim would be challenged by someone who did not believe that

18. Baker, "Do One's Motives," pp. 466–467; p. 467.

19. It might be claimed that there can be two conflicting unconditional requirements, e.g., 'Be polite' and 'Be honest' (and thus that not all unconditional requirements are decisive). But at least one of them has to be conditional if they can conflict. Perhaps it is really 'Be honest unless that requires being impolite', 'Be polite unless that means being dishonest', or 'Be honest unless that requires hurting someone's feelings', etc.

20. Her other examples, which I have not cited, show less than these do. They show that the additional motive cannot be *needed*, a claim that is less startling and more immediately obvious than that the additional motive cannot operate together with the motive of duty (operating as a primary motive).

one must take moral requirements to be decisive. If they are just one among several considerations, then one could act from a blend of duty and inclination. But if one accepts the view, as Kant does, that to see something to be a moral requirement is to see it as decisive, then Baker's point is right on target.[21]

Baker's examples and discussion thus yield a surprise: claims such as "all admixture of incentives which derive from one's own happiness are a hindrance to the influence of the moral law on the human heart" (*PrR* 156) are not the embarrassment to Kant and Kantians that most of us have taken them to be.[22] Many writers have tried to show that Kant can recognize as morally worthy actions done from both duty and inclination, as long as the motive of duty sufficed, that is, did not rely on the assistance of inclination. They argue that Kant simply did not discuss such cases.[23] Our discussion and Baker's suggest that this effort on Kant's behalf is misguided. Overdetermined actions involving duty and inclination do not merely lack moral worth; they are not intelligible (on the construal of 'overdetermined' indicated above, in Sec. 5, according to which the motive of duty is itself sufficient). That is not to say, of course, that duty and inclination cannot "mix," but only that they cannot mix in *this* way: they cannot overdetermine actions in the way described.

7   Why, then, were we troubled in the first place about Kant's emphasis on the purity of the moral motive and his claim that it is (at best) a mistake to try to mix the moral motive with other motives? Part of the explanation is that we were thinking of a certain kind of case: not the type that we see in Baker's examples, but cases of *helping another from*

21. Now, a committed philosophy major could take the course because he wants to. It is not the case that if he is a committed philosophy major he has to take the course because it is required. We can imagine that he takes it because he wants to, and that it is also true that if he did not want to take it, he would take it anyway because it is required. But that does not make his action overdetermined. He is taking it because he wants to, because the course appeals to him; in other circumstances he would take it for a different reason—because it is required. But he does not take it for *both reasons at once*.

22. See also *PrR* 89. As will emerge shortly, I think that the view expressed in these passages *is* problematic, if it is to be the whole story on the motive of duty. For, as indicated in the previous chapter and developed below, I think that the motives of duty and inclination can "mix." But if in these and similar passages Kant is thinking of the motive of duty only in one capacity, specifically, where it serves as a primary motive to acts which are (which the agent sees to be) strictly required, then, for reasons brought out by Baker, the claim makes perfect sense.

23. See, for example, Paton, *The Categorical Imperative*.

duty. There it does seem peculiar to say that an action of helping another is better if done from duty alone than if done from duty together with inclination. Moreover, it is hard to find anything unintelligible about an overdetermined action in that instance. Why can't one help a child with the book she is reading both because he wants to and because he thinks that he should?

Baker's examples differ in a telling way from cases of helping others: the actions in Baker's examples are, as individual actions, strictly required; actions of helping others are generally not. Actions of helping come under the heading of imperfect duties, and thus are obligatory only in a highly attenuated sense: it is required that one help others, but not at every opportunity, or as much as possible.

The relevance of this difference will be immediately apparent. If a particular action of helping another is not morally obligatory, what could be meant by saying that one performed the action from duty alone? To perform the action from duty alone is to act from duty as a primary motive (and as the sole primary motive). Yet duty can operate as a primary motive only to prompt one to do something that is itself required (or to prompt one to refrain from doing something that is forbidden). The upshot is clear: if the particular action of helping another is not morally required, it cannot be done from duty as a primary motive.[24]

24. I have oversimplified. It is not strictly speaking true to say that one cannot act from duty alone unless the action is strictly required, for two reasons. First, one can act from duty alone if one *mistakenly believes* that the action is strictly required. (There are three possibilities: the action that one mistakenly believes to be strictly required might fall under a principle of an imperfect duty, be a merely permissible action, or be morally impermissible.)

Second, *arguably* one could act from duty alone in helping another if one had a maxim or policy such as: Help whenever asked, but only then, and only if you can do so without thereby failing to help someone whom you already promised to help. It is not clear that actions with this as their underlying policy should count as actions done from duty. The end has not been specified, and it is not clear what it is, and thus what the full maxim is. The refusal ever to offer unsolicited help—the refusal, for instance, to offer badly needed help to a lost child too frightened to request aid—leaves us unsure whether the acts of helping which fall under the principle that the agent has adopted are in fact done from duty rather than, say, a desire to comply with moral requirements.

So let us consider now a different policy, one that does not entail a refusal to help in circumstances not covered by the policy. For instance: 'Always help when you can do so without danger or great inconvenience to yourself, and without violating a perfect duty'. The problem that beset the previous policy is now avoided because here nothing is said about what to do in other circumstances where one could help. What should we say about this case? Should helping another in a situation that the policy covers ever count as acting from duty? If so, then, contrary to what I have claimed, one *can* act from duty alone in some situations in which the action is not strictly required.

More generally: insofar as we are not required to help this person rather than that person, or on this occasion rather than another, my choice to help this person will be based on considerations other than, or in addition to, duty. For both helping and refraining from helping are likely to be permissible.

Does this mean that such actions *can* be overdetermined? Not at all. It means that they cannot be and that the reasons why they cannot be are different than in the case of strictly required actions. The latter can be done from the motive of duty as a primary motive, but actions that are not strictly required cannot be. Since they cannot, they cannot be overdetermined.

No wonder it seems peculiar to say that an action of helping another is better if done from duty alone than from duty together with inclination. For, except in cases where a particular action of helping another is morally mandatory, acts of helping cannot be done from duty (as a primary motive). (For the same reason, they cannot have moral worth.)[25]

This is a tricky case. Initially the answer seems to be 'Yes': helping another in a situation covered by the policy could indeed count as acting from duty. But the following consideration suggests that the answer should be negative. One could always revise one's policy, with the result that the action that now falls under the policy would not fall under it. That suggests that we should not count it as acting from duty, since duty always involves constraint, and here the constraint is conditional on one's having a particular policy that one is at liberty to change.

If, however, we do allow that helping actions covered by the policy can count as actions from duty (duty as a primary motive), the picture has to be as follows: the agent's policy treats some actions that, were it not for her policy, would simply fall under the heading of an imperfect duty, as if they were required by perfect duty. If we take this line, what is the bearing on my claim that helping actions cannot be done from duty (duty as a primary motive)? It (like the first point in this note) indicates the need for qualification: actions cannot be done from duty unless they are either strictly required (by perfect duty) or treated by the agent as strictly required.

Thanks to Walter Schaller for pointing out the need to address this matter.

25. There is a problem for my claim. Although the claim is unavoidable—a logical point, really—it seems not to square with Kant's text. At *Groundwork* 398 Kant gives an example of helping others from duty. How can sense be made of this? How can one help others from duty, if the act is not morally required? Two possibilities: First, the act could be one of those instances of helping others where no one else is around to provide the aid, and where the aid needed is so easy to give, yet so vital to the recipient, that there is no minimally decent reason for not providing it. There it is reasonable to say that the act is mandatory (and thus could be done from duty as a primary motive). Kant does not ever say that some acts of helping others are mandatory, but it is plausible to suppose that he would grant that.

A second and more interesting approach is to say that what is obligatory is adopting a maxim of aiding others, and this can of course be done from duty. Imagine someone who does, from duty, adopt a maxim of aiding others. Imagine too that this person lacks any

Can any sense be made, then, of the example of helping a child with a book that she is reading both because one wants to help her and because one thinks that one should? Certainly. The description of the action is in no way incoherent; it merely does not (at least not without further detail) describe an overdetermined action. The person—let's call him Pablo and imagine that it is his niece who needs help with reading—thinks that it is right to do such things. He thinks that it is right not merely in the weak sense that it is permissible, but in the strong sense that one ought to do such things. It is right to help others, and this is an occasion for helping others. One need not, morally, help others at every possible opportunity, however, and Pablo realizes this. So the fact that this is an occasion for helping someone does not by itself decide him to help. His desire to help her (and to help her in this activity) enters in, too. Thus both motives contribute to the action. The motive of duty alone does not suffice to decide him to act. It cannot, since the action is not (and is not regarded by him as) morally required.

It might, however, in a slightly different case. Imagine someone else, Paolo, whose own child needs help with her reading. Paolo comes to realize that his daughter has difficulty reading, or that she shows far too little enthusiasm for reading. In that case he might, even if he does not enjoy helping her read, resolve to help her read and believe that he has a duty to do so.[26] In such a scenario he could help her from duty. But that

---

inclination to help others. He realizes that he will perform no such acts unless he fixes on certain ones (or certain types) and, with resolve, performs them. Arguably, the acts that he sets out to do accordingly will have moral worth. This reading finds some support in the texts, inasmuch as Kant's examples are of people who do not merely lack any inclination to help now, or to help soon, but are very strongly disposed *never* to help others. Thus, when they help another, they do so solely because they have judged it to be their duty to help and have somehow, but not because of any inclination to help, decided to help *now*. In a sense, then, they help from duty because they adopted a maxim of helping others from duty.

26. He might reasonably judge, however, that because he does not enjoy helping her read, he should find someone else who enjoys reading with children—an older child in the neighborhood, perhaps—and invite or hire him or her to help his daughter read. I mention this in order to acknowledge and endorse the view that one is sometimes less able to do S if one does not enjoy doing it. Just when this is the case, and how disabled one is in situations where it does apply, are points on which there can certainly be reasonable disagreement. (I am reminded of a colleague who expressed annoyance when a letter of recommendation stated that the job candidate loves teaching. "Why is that supposed to matter?" my colleague asked. "Apparently it's supposed to be evidence that the candidate teaches well, but why think that?") In any case, there is no reason why a Kantian cannot allow that a lack of enjoyment of S may make one less able to do S effectively.

is a different case from that of Pablo, since Paolo, unlike Pablo, believes that it is morally incumbent on him to help.

The general point is this: an action that is not itself morally required, even if it is of a type that is required by an imperfect duty, cannot have moral worth, for it cannot be done from duty as a primary motive. Duty can of course enter into the motivation, but not in a way that can bestow moral worth on the action.

8   To recapitulate points from the last several pages: actions cannot, on a Kantian view, even *be* overdetermined, in the sense of 'overdetermined' explained above. If one recognizes moral requirements to be decisive, one cannot act both from the sense that it is morally required to do x and because one wants to do x. If one does it because it is morally required, other considerations, for example, that one will enjoy it or that it will help or please a friend, do not then serve as actuating motives. This does not mean that they have to be seen as entirely irrelevant; one may be pleased upon noting that what one must do, morally, will bring great happiness to a loved one, just as the philosophy major may be pleased to discover that the one required course he has yet to take is a course that had been highly recommended to him by a friend and that he intended to take anyway. But if one does these things because they are required, one cannot at the same time be doing them for a different reason, as well.

Why, then, has so much attention been lavished on the question of whether Kant can allow that overdetermined actions have moral worth? Why all the concern, if actions cannot even be overdetermined by the moral motive and some other motive? One possibility is that there is another sense of 'overdetermined' in which actions *can* be overdetermined. A critic might claim that if my construal of 'overdetermined' yields the result that overdetermined actions (overdetermined by the motive of duty and some other motive) are not intelligible, that just shows that there is something wrong with my construal. If the critic can offer a different construal that *is* intelligible, we could then ask whether overdetermined actions should ever be seen as having moral worth.

But to that presently. First, I summarize and expand on the answer suggested thus far to the question of why we were troubled in the first place about Kant's emphasis on the purity of the moral motive and, more specifically, to the question, Why all the attention to the question of whether Kant can allow that overdetermined actions have moral worth?

The points brought out in Sections 6 and 7 in answer to the latter question emerge from the observation that in discussions of Kant's position on moral worth, examples of overdetermined actions that should be seen as morally worthy are almost always of a particular sort: actions of helping another, where one wants to help, sees it to be morally required, and acts from both the desire to help and the motive of duty.[27] It is troubling to think that a helping action should have moral worth only if done from duty alone, and not if done from a desire to help together with the motive of duty. But in fact helping actions generally cannot be performed from the motive of duty at all (as a primary motive), and so the "fact" that seems troubling is not a fact at all. The comparison—between helping actions done from duty and desire, and helping actions done from duty alone—is based on a confusion. Like all actions that fall under the principles of imperfect duties, actions of helping another are required as a class, but individual instances are very rarely required. So, except in those instances where they are required, one cannot act from duty (as a sufficient primary motive) to help another. This fact is almost always overlooked in discussions of moral worth and overdetermined actions. Since in most cases of helping another, one cannot act from duty as a primary motive, such actions generally cannot be overdetermined. They can be overdetermined only in instances in which duty can serve as a primary motive, which is to say, only in instances in which the action is strictly required (rather than being merely an instance of a type of action that we are required to perform but are not required to perform at every opportunity).

One might retort that it is those (admittedly atypical) cases where the helping action is morally required that concern people who are troubled by what seems to be Kant's stand on moral worth. Consider the case of the father who helps his young daughter with her reading and does so from duty, recognizing that she does not read well, already has come to dislike reading, and is unlikely ever to read well unless he regularly spends time reading with her. (Let's imagine that he is a single parent and that there is no one else who will give her the help that she needs unless he does.) Someone might argue that his action surely has no less moral worth if he acts from duty and from the desire to help her than if he acts

---

27. By contrast, Richard Henson cites lecturing from both duty and inclination as an example of an overdetermined action. See Henson, "What Kant Might Have Said," pp. 42–43.

from duty alone. But if the foregoing is correct, he cannot act both from duty and from the desire to help, for to act from duty is (on a Kantian view) to act from the belief that the action in question is morally required *and that this decides the matter*. If this decides the matter, other considerations do not enter in as motives. Of course one may act from duty and also desire to help, but the latter does not function as a motive if one acts from duty.[28]

9   In the previous section I asked why so much attention has been lavished on the question of whether Kant can allow that overdetermined actions have moral worth if actions cannot even be overdetermined by the moral motive and some other motive. One possibility is that there is some other sense of 'overdetermined' in which actions *can* be overdetermined. Someone might claim that my construal of 'overdetermined' is idiosyncratic, and is thus a shaky ground for the surprising results that I reached. I don't believe that it is idiosyncratic, though it is unusual in that I have gone to some length (and subjected readers to considerable tedium) to refine it and distinguish overdetermined actions from a close relative (the "hybrid" action). Readers who share my view that it is not idiosyncratic might wish to skip ahead to Section 10.

Probably the best way to address any possible worry that it is idiosyncratic is to explain how I arrived at my construal. In any case, a few words about its genesis will serve as a summary. After that, in the interest of thoroughness I'll consider whether there might be an alternative

28. In correspondence Richard Henson has raised the following worry: "That Paolo's helping his daughter is morally required 'decides the matter', you say, and that means that other considerations 'do not enter in' as motives. Yes, I think that decides the matter—but perhaps only on condition that the matter has not already been decided. What if he loves his child and loves reading and teaches her in a spirit of joy and gratitude for her companionship, and someone congratulates him on being a dutiful father—and he says, 'Ah, yes, I guess that was a duty, wasn't it?'" This is a good articulation of a common concern about Kant's emphasis on acting from duty: the really virtuous person, it is suggested, would never have occasion to think of helping his child as a duty, since he or she would delight in doing so. We need to know more about Paolo, as described by Henson, to know just what to say. There is no indication that Paolo is attuned to the moral dimensions of his conduct. Is he aware that he should help his child even if it ceases to be fun? After all, no matter how virtuous he is, his child, like all children, will sometimes be testy and impatient. No matter how virtuous he is, turmoil at work or health problems or marital problems (all of which happen to the virtuous as well as the vicious) might turn his attention away from reading with his child. So although it is wonderful if he loves reading with his child and engages in it without any thought that morally he should, still it is important that he be aware that her needs make a normative claim on him.

construal of overdetermination according to which Kant can or should accord moral worth to overdetermined actions.

My discussion was prompted by the view, held by many readers of Kant, that if actions done from duty have moral worth, actions done from both duty and inclination should be eligible for moral worth, too. Referring to actions of the latter type as 'overdetermined actions', friendly critics challenge Kant scholars to show that Kant can allow that some overdetermined actions have moral worth. (Whether they would be morally worthy would depend on the inclination involved.) Overdetermined actions, on this picture, are determined by both duty and some inclination. This suggests that either—duty or inclination— would suffice to determine the action in the absence of the other. Not quite, as it turns out; inclination alone would not determine it if the agent saw the action to be wrong. This called for a refinement in the characterization of an overdetermined action, and the result, as explained in Section 5, was this: If my action is overdetermined, this means (1) that as long as I did not believe the action to be wrong, my inclination to perform it would suffice to motivate me to perform the action; (2) that in the absence of cooperating inclinations the motive of duty would suffice; and (3) that the action is determined by both motives operating separately, not by a happy marriage of the two.

In what other way might 'overdetermined' be construed? One possibility would be to understand by 'overdetermined action' what I called a 'hybrid action', namely, an action prompted by more than one motive, where neither was sufficient by itself to prompt one to action, but jointly the motives sufficed and moved the agent to act accordingly. This is not likely to be anyone's proposed way to think of overdetermination since it fails to capture the notion that some sort of "overkill" is involved, that is, that there was more than enough to determine the agent to act. In any case, it is clear what Kant would say about according moral worth to such actions: it is out of the question. Such actions clearly cannot, on a Kantian view, have moral worth since they violate the requirement that the action be done from duty as a sufficient motive. (See Sec. 4, above.) So, even if this were thought a reasonable way to understand 'overdetermined', it would not give us anything more to talk about: thus understood, there is no room for controversy over what Kant's view is (or what, on Kantian grounds, it should be) regarding "overdetermined" actions.

Another possibility would be to understand 'overdetermined' to mean that the agent had more than one motive available to her: she acted from duty but also wanted so to act and would have so acted even if she had not seen the action to be morally required, *or* she acted from inclination but would have acted from duty had she lacked the inclination. In other words, the action is overdetermined not in that both motives contributed to and in that sense determined the action, but in that the action would have taken place anyway, even if one of the motives had not been present, as long as the other motive was.[29]

Overdetermined actions, thus understood, divide into two types: (1) those that were done from duty yet are such that they would have been done from inclination if (and here it is hard to spell out the condition) they had not been (seen by the agent as) morally required, and (2) those done from inclination, but which would have been done anyway, from duty, had (again it is not entirely clear what the condition is) the agent lacked the inclination. Even without improving on the statement of the condition, we can see what Kant's view of the first type of action would be. Actions of the first type do have moral worth, since the agent does them from duty. What she would have done had she not seen them to be morally required (or, had they not been morally required) is immaterial.[30] Actions of the second type would seem, on Kant's view, not to have moral worth, since they were not done from duty (but see Sec. 11 for an indication that this is not entirely certain).

For those who want to understand 'overdetermined' this way, the only interesting questions concern actions of the second type. The first question concerns the condition that the agent would have so acted anyway, from duty, *had she lacked the inclination.* Is the idea (a) that when she acted from inclination, the action was not morally required, but had it been—and had she lacked the inclination—she would have done it anyway, from duty? Or is it (b) that it was morally required, but she did not see that it was? Or is it (c) that it was morally required, and she saw that, but acted from inclination? The last would be odd, on a Kantian view, for if she saw the action to be morally required, would she not perform the action for that reason—assuming that she takes morality seriously?

29. This way of understanding overdetermined actions is riddled with complexity, only some of which I indicate here. For more, see Herman, "On the Value."

30. Actually, it might not be immaterial if in the counterfactual scenario some other action was morally required. See Paul Benson, "Moral Worth," *Philosophical Studies* 51 (1987): 365–382, for a defense of the claim that what one would have done in such scenarios is indeed relevant.

(See Sec. 6.) If the idea is (b), there would be little temptation to credit her action with moral worth, since she failed to see that the action was morally required. Only in the case of (a) would there be any temptation to credit her action with moral worth, and there, presumably, only if the action came under the heading of an imperfect duty. That, I think, is the interesting case, and if one wants to construe 'overdetermined' in this way and ask whether Kant could credit overdetermined actions with moral worth, the question would best be asked with regard to such instances (e.g., a case of helping another, where the action is not morally required, and one does it from duty but would have so acted without the inclination had it been morally required). In fact I think there are good reasons for holding that if actions done from duty as a primary motive have moral worth, so should some actions from inclination (depending on the inclination), provided that duty there operates as a secondary motive.[31] But rather than convincing me that therefore the latter, too, should be accorded moral worth, they lead me to question the very idea of assigning moral worth to certain actions. To this shortly, in Section 11.

To summarize this section: there is an alternative construal of 'overdetermined' which allows one to say that Kant can recognize overdetermined actions, but there is little room for debate over Kant's stand concerning the moral worth of such actions. If done from duty they have moral worth; if done from inclination, they do not. Still, one might argue that on Kantian grounds some of the actions done from inclination should be accorded moral worth. We will consider this in Section 11.

   10   Before considering cases where the agent acted from inclination but would have performed the action from duty had it been morally required, I want to consider an argument put forth by Henning Jensen concerning overdetermined actions. Jensen argues that Kant holds, or at least is committed to holding, that overdetermined actions may have moral worth. Indeed, according to Jensen, Kant must hold that "we are morally obliged to strive to perform dutiful actions which are overdetermined by being done from duty and from some cooperating nonmoral motive." It is Kant's account of indirect duties, Jensen contends, that implies that morally worthy actions may be overdetermined,

31. See Benson, "Moral Worth."

and that such overdetermination is "actually desirable."[32] The first step in the argument (and the only one that I will address) is to show that Kant recognizes overdetermined actions; more precisely, that he has to recognize them, given his notion of indirect duties.

Jensen seems to be using 'overdetermined' as I do (though as I note below, he may not be). So if he can show that Kant has to recognize overdetermined actions (even apart from the further claim that Kant has to hold that some of them are morally worthy) this would pose a serious challenge to my view.

Consider the indirect duty to cultivate sympathetic feelings. The "notion of an indirect duty to cultivate affections such as love or sympathetic feelings," Jensen writes, "implies that there will be occasions in which dutiful actions will be overdetermined by being done from the motive of duty and from some other nonmoral motive or motives." Why is this? Jensen is assuming that the role of the sympathetic feelings is to "help us to do our duty from the motive of duty by opposing those motives which tempt us to transgress our duties and by supporting the motive of duty in such a way that it stands a better chance of being predominant." More generally, he is assuming that the role of the sympathetic feelings is a motivational one and, specifically, that their role is to help us to act *from duty*. He asserts that Kant "cannot maintain without contradiction both that we have indirect duties of the kind under consideration and that dutiful actions may only be done from the single motive of duty. The very existence of such indirect duties as the duty to cultivate sympathetic feelings requires that there must also be dutiful actions which are sometimes overdetermined by being done from duty and some other nonmoral motive."[33]

I think that Jensen is mistaken in his assumption that the role of the sympathetic feelings has to be that of cooperating motives. Kant says that "nature has implanted in us" sympathetic feelings "so that we may do what the representation of duty alone would not accomplish" (*MM* 457), and this certainly lends itself to the interpretation that the sympathetic feelings serve as motives that join in and bolster the motive of duty; but there are other possible interpretations. Our sympathetic impulses might

32. Henning Jensen, "Kant on Overdetermination, Indirect Duties, and Moral Worth," in *Proceedings: Sixth International Kant Congress*, edited by G. Funke and Th. M. Seebohm (Washington, D.C.: Center for Advanced Research in Phenomenology; University Press of America, 1989), p. 167 and p. 161.

33. Ibid., p. 167; p. 166; p. 166.

provide us with a sensitivity that we would not otherwise have, a sensitivity needed for us to be able to perceive certain situations as (for instance) ones in which we can help. If they play this role, there is no reason to assume that they are to function as cooperating impulses that buttress the motive of duty.

There are yet other possibilities. Sympathetic feelings might play a motivational role without serving to buttress the motive of duty. Their function might indeed be to motivate us, but not together with duty as a primary motive; rather, they might operate alone, with the motive of duty serving only as a limiting motive.

The textual support for Jensen's reading, I suggest, equally supports some alternative readings. We will examine the relevant passages in Chapter 6. For now I note that there is reason to be glad that there are plausible alternative readings. Jensen's reading attributes to Kant a view that is in serious tension with Kant's emphasis on purity. As explained earlier, a key claim in Kant's practical philosophy is that we are not to seek out nonmoral incentives for doing what we see to be morally required. Duty, as a motive, does not need help. If an action is morally required, we are capable of performing it for the reason that it is morally required. We are not to seek out other reasons for doing it. To do so would be to cultivate an impure will. Yet if Jensen is right, this is just what Kant would be saying that we have a duty to do when he says that we have an indirect duty to cultivate sympathetic feelings.

The problem can be looked at in another way. What Jensen calls "overdetermined" may in fact be a form of what I called "hybrid" actions: actions done from duty and some other motive, where duty alone does not suffice. Duty needs the help of the other motive. As explained earlier, such actions cannot possibly have moral worth, since duty does not serve as their "all-sufficient" motive.

In any event, it is clear that Jensen has not shown that the "very existence of such indirect duties as the duty to cultivate sympathetic feelings requires that there must also be dutiful actions which are sometimes overdetermined by being done from duty and some other nonmoral motive."[34] Whether they require this depends on why it is that we are supposed to cultivate them and what purpose they are to serve. It will not do to assume that they are supposed to serve the purpose of helping the motive of duty as cooperating motives.

34. Henning Jensen, p. 166.

11 Throughout this chapter I have been challenging the framework through which Kant's claims about acting from duty are typically viewed, arguing that the usual objections employ a blurry notion of overdetermination which, once clarified, turns out not to raise the difficult questions for Kant that it is thought to raise. (Jensen's arguments are different. They claim that Kant can recognize overdetermined actions and regard them as eligible for moral worth, but they rest on a questionable understanding of the role that Kant expects sympathetic feelings to play.) Unless overdetermined actions are understood as actions for which more than one motive was available to the agent (though only one motive determined the action), I find no basis for the claim that Kant should have held that overdetermined actions can have moral worth. Setting aside arguments suggested by that construal of 'overdetermined', I think it safe to conclude that objections to Kant's emphasis on the motive of duty that arise from concerns about overdetermination are groundless.

But this does not lay to rest my own doubts concerning Kant's positions on acting from duty and moral worth. Granted all the moves to defend Kant which I have made in the preceding sections of this chapter, the question of moral worth remains. *Why should moral worth be assigned only to those actions that are done from duty as a primary motive?* What is so special about acting from duty as a primary motive? What value does it have that acting from some other primary motive, guided by duty as a secondary motive, invariably lacks? Why should an action of, say, keeping a promise from duty, or refraining from making a false promise (again, from duty) have moral worth while an action of helping another, an action guided but not determined by one's sense of duty, lacks moral worth?

One way to meet the problem is to see if Kant might, contrary to usual views, be plausibly read as holding that actions may have moral worth even if they are not done from duty as a primary motive. Or, if that reading is not plausible, one might argue that this is a view that Kant *should* have held. This is Paul Benson's position (and, although he does not develop it by reference to the notion of an overdetermined action, it is the sort of argument that would be suggested by the alternative construal of 'overdetermined' noted above at the end of Sec. 9).[35]

35. Benson, "Moral Worth," p. 380. Benson leaves unstated, until the end of his article, whether he believes that the view he develops was, or might plausibly be said to be, Kant's actual view. But he then clarifies that although it is "faithful enough to the intentions Kant's

Benson develops and motivates his interpretation through a critique of Herman's "On the Value of Acting from the Motive of Duty." Herman's nonaccidental rightness condition is (among Kantians) uncontroversial: for an action to have moral worth, it must be nonaccidentally right. So is the moral concern condition: the reasons for which the action is done "must include concern" for its "moral rightness." But just how are these conditions to be understood? It is here that Herman and Benson disagree. Benson proposes that we understand "nonaccidentally right action" as follows: "an agent's performance of a right action is nonaccidentally right just when the agent's will is such that she would have performed a different action (no matter what the circumstances) had that latter action been morally required of the agent." On Herman's view, this requires too much. She relies, as Benson points out, on the following side constraint on conditions of moral worth: "The failure of the agent to do the right thing in circumstances different than the actual ones does not show that the agent's actual action lacks moral worth."[36] On Herman's view, an action has moral worth just in case it was done from duty as a primary motive. It does not matter whether the agent would have failed to act as morality required in different circumstances.

They disagree on the moral concern condition, as well. On Herman's view, the moral concern condition entails that the action must be done from duty as a primary motive. Benson claims that this is not necessary. The conditions for moral worth are met as long as the action is governed by a commitment to acting as morality requires. As he puts it, "The agent's moral concern must support counterfactual obedience to moral demands, but it can do this without functioning as the sole determining

---

work reveals to warrant saying that it is a natural extension of Kant's statements about moral worth," he cannot claim that it is Kant's actual view (p. 380).

36. Ibid., p. 367; p. 376; p. 369. Herman forwards the side constraint as part of her argument against a sufficiency account of moral worth, according to which an act has moral worth if and only if it was done from duty as a sufficient motive. (Such an account would allow that overdetermined acts can have moral worth.) Herman points out that it is not clear what 'sufficient' means here. Is it enough if the motive of duty suffices by itself without the aid of any inclination? Or must it be sufficient even in the face of opposing inclination? The first and weaker reading is too weak, she says; Benson agrees, as do I. But the second reading, she claims, is too strong, for "moral worth is not equivalent to moral virtue" (p. 369). Hence her side constraint. For discussion of Herman's argument see, in addition to Benson's article, Karl Ameriks, "Kant on the Good Will," in *Grundlegung zur Metaphysik der Sitten: Ein kooperativer Kommentar*, ed. Otfried Höffe (Frankfurt: Vittorio Klostermann, 1989).

reason for action. The moral motive could function as a higher-order constraint on lower-order, nonmoral motives, allowing them to issue into appropriate action when they align with duty, blocking their efficacy when they would inhibit dutiful action."[37]

In short, on Benson's view the putative morally worthy action must in one respect pass a much tougher test than Herman requires: the agent's will must be such that she would have done whatever was morally required, even if the circumstances were different. But the test is also weaker in another respect: the action need not have been done from duty as a primary motive.

Although Herman has not published a reply to Benson, her remarks in support of the side constraint on conditions of moral worth give us some idea of how she would reply. Moral worth is not equivalent to moral virtue; it is "*actions* and not agents that are credited with moral worth." This is not quite accurate; Kant ascribes moral worth to both actions and persons. (See Sec. 12, below.) In a footnote Herman anticipates doubt.

> This may not seem so clear, for moral worth of an action is said to be in its maxim (G 399): the expression (in rule form) of an agent's volition (what the agent is moved to do and for what reason). Thus there is a sense in which moral worth *is* about agents—it is about their willings. The point of saying that it is actions that are credited with moral worth is to highlight the relationship between *an* action and *its* motive (via the action's maxim), which is where moral worth resides (and not in the permanent structure of an agent's motives: that is the matter of virtue . . .).[38]

I am not clear on why Herman thinks that moral worth resides in the relationship between an action and its motive, but in any case we can see in her footnote a plausible ground for objecting to Benson's account: Benson's account seriously undermines the distinction between moral worth and virtue. One might question whether he is really offering an account of the moral worth of actions. As his gloss on "nonaccidentally right action," quoted above, indicates, the moral worth of any individual action is derivative from the goodness of the agent's will.

Related to this is another possible objection. On his account, actions done from a desire for profit or in a quest for glory or professional recognition qualify as morally worthy as long as they are governed by duty, meeting the nonaccidental rightness condition. This is troubling.

37. Benson, "Moral Worth," p. 377.
38. Herman, "On the Value," p. 371; p. 371.

Whatever temptation we have to treat actions done from fellow feeling but governed by duty as no less morally worthy than actions done directly from duty, we are still not likely to regard actions done from a quest for glory, yet governed by duty, as just as morally worthy. But in fact on his view all actions that are governed by duty will be morally worthy. They need only meet his nonaccidental rightness condition. This is closely connected to the previous objection, since it is a consequence of the fact that although officially assigned by his account to individual actions, moral worth is really based on the agent's conduct as a whole and, more specifically, on her commitment to doing what morality requires.

Although these are problems insofar as Benson is offering an account of the moral worth of actions (and that is indeed what he is doing), they can also be viewed differently: as considerations that steer us away from wanting an account of the moral worth of actions, as distinct from an account of virtue or of a good will. They raise the question of what, indeed, we are asking in asking under what conditions an action has moral worth. They prompt a related question, too: Is there any ground for attributing special value to actions done from duty as a primary motive that is not equally a reason for attributing it to actions done from duty as a secondary motive? If not, perhaps what is of value is not certain actions, but conduct governed by a commitment to acting as morality requires.

(All of this makes great sense when we quit talking of motives and talk as we should of maxims. What is important is having certain maxims, maxims that subordinate to morality all other considerations. And that is just to say that what matters is governing one's conduct by a commitment to acting as morality requires. But this anticipates the second interlude.)

Benson's account is not altogether plausible either as an account of the moral worth of actions that Kant should have held or as a statement of what Kant did hold. But his critique of Herman's account is astute (with one exception: the Dr. Jones example), and the considerations that motivate his account are instructive. In particular, they show that Herman provides no reason for attributing special value (call it moral worth or call it something else) to acting from duty as a primary motive that is not equally a reason for attributing the same value to acting from duty as a secondary motive, and they strongly suggest that no such reason exists.

12 Benson's reconstructive account of moral worth held some promise of providing an argument for viewing some "overdetermined" actions—if construed not as I proposed to understand "overdetermined action," but rather as suggested at the end of Section 9—as actions that Kant should have considered morally worthy. But in fact it does not succeed or, at best, succeeds only at the cost of providing no basis for according moral worth to actions done from fellow feeling and governed by duty without according it to actions done from a desire for glory and governed by duty. That concludes that matter: I see no reasonably plausible way to construe 'overdetermined' that provides a basis for saying that Kant should have allowed that some overdetermined actions can have moral worth.

But my worries, expressed at the beginning of Section 11, acquire more force in the light of Benson's discussion. His discussion brings to the fore that when we ask whether an action has moral worth, we are really asking something about the agent's character (specifically, whether she is committed to doing whatever is morally right). To ask whether an action has moral worth seems at best a roundabout way of asking questions about the agent's character. It seems misdirected to ask of individual actions whether they have moral worth, and it is hard to see why Kant should have wanted to provide an account of the moral worth of individual actions.

Moreover, careful study of the many passages in which Kant discusses acting from duty yields the observation that only in the *Groundwork* and the second *Critique* does he speak in that context about the moral worth of actions. This together with other observations raises the possibility that the importance of his discussion of moral worth has been overblown by readers and the aims misunderstood. I will explore that possibility together with the related question: To what extent *does* Kant place special value on duty as a primary motive?

In the remainder of this chapter, I examine various passages in which Kant discusses acting from duty and try to discern what his concerns are, what value he attaches to acting from duty, and whether it is specifically duty as a primary motive on which he is placing importance. There is no doubt that Kant values governing one's conduct by a commitment to morality, that is, that he values duty operating as a secondary motive. The question is whether he places greater value on duty as a primary motive—whether there is something especially good, on his view, about acting from duty as a primary motive. It is generally assumed that there is, and his discussion of moral worth in the *Groundwork* certainly provides a basis for the assumption. My hope is to show that the assumption is false. I am selecting passages that seem most to support the view that I am challenging.

12.1   Almost no one needs to be reminded that moral worth is mentioned repeatedly in the first section of the *Groundwork*. It is easy to think that the point of talking about acting from duty is to supply a test for determining whether an action has moral worth. Elsewhere the point seems entirely different—and more worthwhile.

Consider the following passage from *The Doctrine of Virtue*. Under the heading "On Man's Duty to Himself to Increase His Moral Perfection," Kant writes, "*First*, this perfection consists subjectively in the *purity* (*puritas moralis*) of one's disposition to duty, namely, in the law being by itself alone the incentive, even without the admixture of aims derived from sensibility, and in actions being done not only in conformity with duty but also *from duty*. Here the command is 'be holy'" (*MM* 446). In light of the claims about moral worth and acting from duty in the *Groundwork*, one might read this passage as saying that we have a duty to act from the motive (primary motive) of duty. Since the heading tells us that this is a duty to increase our moral perfection, the duty would thus be understood to require that we act from the motive of duty as often as possible (or, at least that we endeavor ever to increase the frequency with which we act from duty)—whatever that would mean.[39] But the reading does not fit the passage. Kant's concern here is clearly with disposition or attitude (*Gesinnung*): we are to strive to have a pure disposition. We are to strive to be holy. The concern here is not with action, but with having a pure will. The command is not to act from duty as a primary motive, but to cultivate a pure will.

What this entails is spelled out more fully in the *Religion*. It is also briefly explicated in the introduction to the *Doctrine of Virtue*: "Man has a duty to carry the cultivation of his *will* up to the purest virtuous disposition, in which the *law* becomes also the incentive to his actions that conform with duty and he obeys the law from duty. This disposition is inner morally practical perfection" (*MM* 387). What is purity? From the section of *Religion* cited earlier (Sec. 4, above) we know that the

---

39. Would it mean that we should put ourselves under an obligation wherever possible (by making promises, for instance) so as to have more occasions to act from duty?

"human heart" is impure just in case "it has not, as it should have, adopted the law *alone* as its *all-sufficient* incentive" (*R 30/25*). We infer that the heart—and I think it is safe to say the *will*—is pure just in case it adopts the law alone as its all-sufficient incentive. This is borne out both by the quote above and in the second *Critique* where, in the Methodology, Kant repeatedly uses 'pure' or 'purity' to indicate that the agent embraces duty as an all-sufficient motive.

Kant's point in the passages from the *Doctrine of Virtue* is that it is not enough that we act in accordance with the law; we must have a pure *Pflichtgesinnung*. Since he often makes this point by saying that it is not enough that our actions conform to duty, for they should also be done from duty, it is easy to think that he is saying that we ought (as much as possible) to act from duty as a primary motive. But the inference is not warranted. Purity in no way requires that one act from duty as a primary motive. It only requires that one be ready to. It requires that one subordinate all competing interests to duty.

Here is another way to put the point (with reference to *MM* 387, cited above). Each individual action need not be done from duty (as a primary motive) for it to be the case that one "obeys the law from duty." For one may adopt a general, overarching maxim from duty and be committed to acting accordingly.

Indeed it is just the adoption of such an overarching maxim that is needed if we are to be good. Kant explains in *Religion* that "the restoration of the original predisposition to good in us is . . . but the establishment of the *purity* of this law as the supreme ground of all our maxims, whereby it . . . must be adopted, in its entire purity, as an incentive *adequate* in itself for the determination of the will^w" (42/37). Again: "Only when a man has adopted into his maxim the incentive implanted in him of allegiance to the moral law is he to be called a good man" (45n/ 40n).

12.2   The passages we have examined do not support the claim that Kant holds that we have a duty to act (often) from duty as a primary motive. Is there any other evidence that he holds this view or a similar view, for example, that the best of us do so act or that virtue requires it? A natural place to search for support is in his remarks about virtue in the *Doctrine of Virtue*. But we find no evidence there that the virtuous person (often) acts from duty as a primary motive, rather than from other primary motives governed by duty as a secondary motive. Kant characterizes virtue as "the moral strength of a *man's* will in fulfilling his *duty*, a moral *constraint* through his own lawgiving reason, insofar as this constitutes itself an authority *executing* the law" (*MM* 405). There is no suggestion here that the virtuous person acts from duty as a primary motive. "Two things are required for inner freedom: being one's own *master* in a given case (*animus sui compos*), that is, subduing one's affects, and *ruling* oneself (*imperium in semetipsum*), that is, *governing* one's passions. In these two states one's *character* (*indoles*) is noble (*erecta*); in the opposite case it is mean (*indoles abiecta, serva*)" (*MM* 407).

In fact, the evidence tells in favor of my position. Virtue concerns matters that are handled by duty operating as a secondary motive just as well as by duty operating as a primary motive. His main concern is not particular actions and their primary motives, but self-control, self-mastery, self-governance.

> Since virtue is based on inner freedom, it contains a positive command to a man, namely to bring all his capacities and inclinations under his (reason's) control and so to rule over himself, which goes beyond forbidding him to let himself be governed by his feelings and inclinations (the duty of *apathy*); for unless reason holds the reins of government in its own hands, man's feelings and inclinations play the master over him. (*MM* 408)

It is apparent that Kant does not hold, at least in the *Doctrine of Virtue*, that we have a duty to act from duty as a primary motive, or that virtue consists in doing this, or that we are better if we so act. That is a good thing, since it is not clear what such a claim would mean. Consider, for instance, the claim that virtue consists in acting from duty as a primary motive. Virtue is not additive: we do not sum up the number of instances of certain types of actions (or calculate the proportion of all of the individual's acts to date, or that year, which were done from duty) to assess how virtuous the person is. And the point is not merely that we do not employ such a procedure. Virtue is not the sum of actions motivated in such and such a way. It is not the sum of anything actional; indeed, it is not additive at all.

What passages in other works might be read as supporting the view that I am challenging? *Religion* contains virtually no such passages. A possible exception, however, is this:

> There is no difference . . . as regards conformity of conduct to the moral law, between a man of good morals (*bene moratus*) and a morally good

man (*moraliter bonus*)—at least there ought to be no difference, save that the conduct of the one has not always, perhaps has never, the law as its sole and supreme incentive while the conduct of the other has it *always*. (R 30/25)

On a careless reading one might come away with the idea that when Kant says the law is the sole and supreme incentive, he means that it is the primary motive. But this cannot be his meaning, for the claim is that the conduct of the good man *always* has law as its sole incentive. Yet it is impossible that one could always act from duty as a primary motive. One cannot perform only morally required acts. Whenever one performs morally indifferent actions, duty cannot be one's primary motive. (And Kant of course explicitly recognizes in the fantastic virtue passage that there are morally indifferent actions.) He cannot be saying, then, that the morally good man acts always from duty as a primary motive. The passage makes sense only if the good man is understood as someone whose conduct is always governed by a commitment to acting morally, to putting morality before all else—in short, someone whose conduct is always governed by duty as a secondary motive. This tallies with his use of "supreme." To say that it is the supreme incentive suggests that there may be other incentives, incentives that are subordinated to it.

12.3   *The Doctrine of Virtue* and *Religion within the Limits of Reason Alone* give us no reason to think that there is, on Kant's view, some special value in the motive of duty operating as a primary motive which does not also, and to the same degree, accrue to duty as a secondary motive. Indeed, they support the hypothesis that Kant does not hold that view. But if he does not hold it, why does he say in the *Groundwork* that only actions done from duty—and here he does seem to mean duty as a primary motive—have moral worth?

To answer this, we need to recall Kant's aims and strategy in the first chapter of the *Groundwork*. He introduces the notion of duty for the first time at 397 and does so in order to elucidate the concept of a good will. (The concept of duty "includes that of a good will, exposed, however, to certain subjective limitations and obstacles." These, "far from hiding a good will or disguising it, rather bring it out by contrast and make it shine forth more brightly.") He examines actions from duty, contrasting them to actions from self-interest and actions from immediate inclination, with the aim of determining the principle that guides the agent. The aim here is a grand one: "to seek out and establish *the supreme principle of morality*" (G 392). In chapter I, he seeks it out; in chapter III, he tries to establish it. His chapter I determines what, if there is such a thing, this supreme principle of morality is; chapter III seeks to show that it is not just a "chimerical concept." His method in chapter I, though he does not make it explicit, is one that most people associate with Aristotle, not with Kant: he takes as his starting point the good person—or, more exactly, the good will—and from that he tries to determine what right conduct is. Of course Kant's approach is not empirical. He does not look at the most admired or respected people in his midst, see how they act, and declare it right conduct; nor is it, as Aristotle's approach is, a variant thereof. Rather, he analyzes the good will, characterizing it as one that does what is right because it is right, in order to determine the principle that guides the good will; this principle, then, will be the principle that makes right action right and that is to guide our conduct.

To see where Kant's discussion of moral worth fits into this analysis, we need to look at the analysis in more detail. What grounds, Kant asks, does the person of good will have for doing what is right? The answer is that such a person does what is right because it is right. It is these actions that have moral worth, reflecting the agent's moral worth. The worth of the actions is due not to the purpose to be attained, but solely to the maxim itself.

> An action done from duty has its moral worth, *not in the purpose* to be attained by it, but in the maxim in accordance with which it is decided upon; it depends therefore not on the realization of the object of the action, but solely on the *principle* of *volition* in accordance with which, irrespective of all objects of the faculty of desire, the action has been performed. (G 400)

What can determine the will when an action is done from duty?

> Now an action done from duty has to set aside altogether the influence of inclination, and along with inclination every object of the will; so there is nothing left able to determine the will except objectively the *law* and subjectively *pure reverence* for this practical law, and therefore the maxim of obeying this law even to the detriment of all my inclinations. (G 400–401)

In short, the law. What kind of law? It will have to be a curious sort of law: one with as little content as possible.

But what kind of law can this be the thought of which, even without regard to the results expected from it, has to determine the will if this is to be called good absolutely and without qualification? Since I have robbed the will of every inducement that might arise for it as a consequence of obeying any particular law, nothing is left but the conformity of actions to universal law as such, and this alone must serve the will as its principle. That is to say, I ought never to act except in such a way *that I can also will that my maxim should become a universal law.* (G 402)

It will have to be the Categorical Imperative.

This explains how the discussion of moral worth figures in the general strategy of his chapter I. But why does Kant discuss moral worth at such length? Why the focus, for several paragraphs, on actions done from duty? The answer is that this is the best way Kant sees to elucidate the concept of a good will. The good will is manifested in actions done from duty. To understand the good will, we look at the actions in which it is expressed and see how they differ from similar actions. Actions that conform to duty can be performed from duty, from inclination, or from self-interest. Those done from self-interest are different from the others in that they are not performed for their own sakes. An action done from inclination and one done from duty have the same purpose. But their maxims differentiate them. Only the maxims of actions done from duty have moral content. The difference can be spelled out this way: although the purposes are the same, the grounds on which the agents adopted the purposes are different. Christine Korsgaard illustrates the point as follows: "The sympathetic person sees helping as something pleasant, and that is why he makes it his end. The morally worthy person sees helping as something called for, or necessary, and this is what motivates him to make it his end."[40] Kant highlights the difference between actions done from duty and other actions in order to introduce the idea of the Categorical Imperative. He has to motivate the idea of a principle that guides without borrowing anything from inclination; to this end, he examines actions done purely from duty.

This explains why he needs, in chapter I, to stress the difference between actions done from duty and other actions and to claim that actions done from duty have a value that others lack. It also provides an answer to the following question: If it is the motive of duty in its wider

40. Christine M. Korsgaard, "Kant's Analysis of Obligation: The Argument of *Foundations I*," *Monist* 72 (July 1989): 324. I am indebted throughout Sec. 12.3 to Korsgaard; I have learned a lot from this excellent article.

role, not just duty as a primary motive that is so important, why does Kant, in *Groundwork* I, only give examples of actions done from duty as a primary motive? The best way to show that an agent is committed to doing what is right—that her conduct is governed by duty, as a secondary motive—is to sketch a scenario in which her commitment is visible. And it is visible when there is a conflict between inclination and what she sees to be right, that is, when the motive of duty has to function as a primary motive. So, that the examples are of duty operating as a primary motive can be explained by the fact that Kant is offering examples in which it is as clear as it possibly can be that the agent is *not* acting purely from inclination. Rather than presenting an example in which someone acts from inclination, constrained by duty, where we cannot tell that her conduct is thus constrained, he presents examples in which constraint is apparent.

I have tried to show in this section that although the first chapter of the *Groundwork* seems initially to constitute strong evidence for the claim that Kant does see special value in acting from duty as a primary motive which does not accrue to duty operating as a secondary motive, in fact the evidence is at best equivocal. The evidence looks very strong indeed when the relevant passages are read out of context, as if the point of the discussion were simply to offer an account of the moral worth of actions. It would be odd to understand the discussion that way, even ignoring the aims and structure of *Groundwork* I; one oddity that would have to be explained is that just when Kant seems to be presenting an account of the moral worth of actions he shifts—indeed, in the middle of an example—from talking about actions to talking about the moral worth of the agent's character. (See 398–399.) Another oddity is that after that discussion Kant rarely speaks of actions as morally worthy or lacking in moral worth and never in a way that suggests that he is offering or has offered an account of the moral worth of actions. In any case it is apparent from the structure of *Groundwork* I that Kant's discussion of acting from duty serves primarily not to develop an account of the moral worth of actions but rather to provide a crucial step in the analysis of the good will, motivating the first formulation of the Categorical Imperative. The emphasis on duty as a primary motive is easily explained, in the manner indicated above, in the light of Kant's aims in *Groundwork* I.

12.4   There are, however, passages in the *Critique of Practical Reason* which speak of the moral worth of actions and thereby lend some support to the idea that Kant does hold that actions done from duty as a primary motive have some special value (and that duty operating as a primary motive has special value). But here again it is noteworthy that he moves casually from talk of moral worth of actions to talk of moral worth of agents. There is no reason to think that he is especially concerned with the moral worth of *actions*. More revealing, though, are the aims of the discussions in which mention of moral worth occurs. The second *Critique* emphasizes the link between acting from duty and our awareness of our freedom. In judging that we can do something simply because we know that we ought to, we recognize that we are free. It is striking that the link is not specifically between acting from duty as a *primary* motive and our awareness of our freedom. Kant presents examples in which someone is to say whether he *could* (for example) refuse, though the refusal means his certain death, to make a false deposition against an innocent person whom the ruler wished to condemn to death under a plausible pretext (*PrR* 30; quoted above in Chap. 2). What the person is supposed to recognize can be cast either in terms of primary or secondary motives, and is best expressed by saying that he sees that he can adopt the motive of duty as his all-sufficient motive.

The Methodology elaborates on this freedom, and one's discovery of it:

> The second exercise . . . lies in calling to notice the purity of will by a vivid exhibition of the moral disposition in examples. . . . By this, the pupil's attention is held to the consciousness of his freedom. . . . The heart is freed from a burden which has secretly pressed upon it; it is lightened when in instances of pure moral resolutions there is revealed to man, who previously has not correctly known it, a faculty of inner freedom to release himself from the impetuous importunity of the inclinations, to such an extent that not even the dearest of them has an influence on a resolution for which he now makes use of his reason. (*PrR* 160–161)

Kant links this to the worth of agents:

> As soon as this machinery, these leading strings, have had some effect, the pure moral motive must be brought to mind. This is not only because it is the sole ground of character (a consistent practical habit of mind according to unchangeable maxims) but also because, in teaching a man to feel his own worth, it gives his mind a power, unexpected even by himself, to pull himself loose from all sensuous attachments (so far as they would fain dominate him). (*PrR* 152)

A little later he speaks of the "worth which a man can and must give himself in his own eyes through the consciousness of not having transgressed his duty" (*PrR* 155).

Here, as in Kant's other works, it seems clear that what has value is not that one acts from the motive of duty but that one has the *power* to do so and, more important, is *committed*, because it is right, to putting what is right before all else. What matters is, in Kant's words, the "subjection of the heart to duty" (*PrR* 155n).

None of this is to deny that it is unfortunate that Kant introduces the notion of moral worth as he does. It certainly invites the view that he attributes a special value to actions done from duty as a primary motive. It would have been better if he had not spoken as he does of the moral worth of actions. Because the distinction that concerns him is that between legality and morality—between following merely the letter of the law and following the spirit of the law—and since there is worth in the latter that is lacking in the former, he writes as if there is special worth in acting from duty as a primary motive. There *is*, if the comparison is to acting merely in accordance with the law, but not if the comparison is to acting from certain other primary motives, but governed by duty. Even Herman, who reads Kant as offering an account of the moral worth of actions which accords moral worth only to actions done from duty as a primary motive, observes: "The good will is as much present in the settled and sure commitment to beneficence as it is in the helping action done from . . . duty."[41]

If I should turn out to be wrong in my claim that Kant does not attribute special value to actions done from duty as a primary motive, nonetheless this crucial point remains: he *has no need* to do so. The maxim of an action governed by duty as a secondary motive has moral content, just as the maxim of an action done from duty as a primary motive does.

My principal aim in this chapter has been to defend Kant against the objection that he places too much value on acting from duty. As explained in the preceding chapter, I see nothing wrong in placing considerable value on being guided by a commitment to do what is morally right. But I think that it is a mistake to place much value on acting from

---

41. Barbara Herman, "Integrity and Impartiality," *Monist* 66 (April 1983): 239; reprinted with revision in *Practice*.

duty as a primary motive. I sought to show that although in many passages Kant does seem to attribute special value to duty as a primary motive, this is generally an illusion. Moreover, the reasons he gives for valuing the motive of duty provide no basis for according greater value to duty as a primary motive than to duty as a secondary motive.

One way that I defended Kant was to undermine the widespread assumption that Kant is in trouble if he cannot allow that overdetermined actions may have moral worth. I did so by questioning whether the notion of an action overdetermined by duty and inclination even makes sense on a Kantian view. This is important in its own right, and it also forms a part of my defense of Kant against the charge that he ascribes too much value to acting from duty. The same is true of another piece of my argument: I claimed that Kant's remarks about moral worth in chapter I of the *Groundwork* are read out of context, as if the whole point were to develop an account of the moral worth of actions. The supposition that this is one of his central aims steers many off course as they read Kant. They fail to see that he is far more concerned, in his practical philosophy, that we cultivate a pure will than that we perform morally worthy acts. This ties in with another point: he is far more concerned with character and conduct over a long period of time than with the moral worth or lack thereof of isolated actions.

In developing my argument, I have left unchallenged an assumption which motivates and serves as a foundation for the view that Kant places too much value on acting from duty. The second interlude uncovers that assumption. The assumption is that it is appropriate, or at least harmless, to speak in terms of motives when we seek to understand Kant's account of moral motivation. The second interlude suggests that the terminology evokes a model of agency quite different from Kant's, an empiricist model on which motives cause us to act. This is important, because the objections to Kant's ethics that have been the focus of Part II make much more sense if one wrongly supposes Kant to have an empiricist picture of agency. Indeed, when corrected so as to reflect Kant's view of agency, the objections lose much of their initial plausibility.

Interlude

1   In Chapter 5, I faced a dilemma: Should I pursue criticisms and interpretive questions regarding Kant's ethics if they mislead? Should I follow the lead of critics and investigate their questions, or should I dismiss them and discuss the issues in Kantian terms, asking the questions that put the issues in proper focus?

This dilemma I already noted, along with my solution: I opted to address the questions rather than dismiss them as ill-conceived and to warn along the way of ways in which they may mislead. But I faced another dilemma, as well. Should I follow common usage and couch my discussion in Chapters 4 and 5 in terms of motives? Or, recognizing that the term 'motive' may evoke the wrong picture of agency—wrong given that it is Kant's view of moral motivation that concerns us—should I eschew all talk of motives and limit myself to more appropriate terminology, such as 'maxim' and 'ground'? The same reasons that led me to pursue the standard questions rather than couch the issues in a more Kantian manner dissuaded me from dropping the term 'motive' in favor of Kantian terms. My aim is to come to grips with the criticisms, evaluating them fairly and in a manner that will have a serious chance of convincing those who are wary of Kantian ethics. I do not write solely for other Kantians. So it would be unwise to couch my discussion in Kantian terms. Ideally I would couch it in neutral terms, but if there are no neutral terms in this context, I would rather employ the terms of the critics than the Kantian terms, taking care to guard against misunderstandings to which the terms lend themselves.

Whereas I noted in Chapter 5 ways in which the question of overdetermination misleads, I have not paused (except briefly at a couple of points) to observe how talk of motives misleads. This interlude serves to do just that.

2   What is wrong with speaking of acting from the motive of duty? Why is it misleading to say that Kant attributes moral worth to actions done from the motive of duty and denies moral worth to actions done from other motives? The problem is that the term 'motive' suggests causation, as if the motive of duty or a desire to help another were a force within us that causes us to act accordingly. According to this picture, one does x because one is moved or prompted or impelled to do x. If one is moved both to do x and not to do x, the stronger, more forceful motive wins out. We are caused to act, on this picture, by an inner force—a motive.

This is a familiar picture of agency from the empiricist tradition. Kant's theory of agency is very different. Our actions are not the result of a desire or some other incentive that impels us. An incentive can move us to act only if we let it. Kant makes this apparent in the passage from the *Critique of Practical Reason* where he says that if someone claims that his lust is irresistible, ask him "whether he would not control his passion if, in front of his house where he has this opportunity, a gallows were erected on which he would be hanged immediately after gratifying his lust" (*PrR* 30). We are not (except perhaps in pathological cases, where agency is severely impaired) overcome by desires. When we think we are, what is really happening is that we have chosen to regard the desire as a force beyond our control (or for some other reason not to be reckoned with). Kant states his positive view in *Religion*. Underscoring the "great importance to morality" of his claim, he says that "freedom of the will^w is of a wholly unique nature in that an incentive can determine the will^w to an action *only so far as the individual has incorporated it into his maxim* (has made it the general rule in accordance with which he will conduct himself)" (*R* 24/19).[1]

Unfortunately, the terms in which discussions of moral motivation are usually couched make it difficult to avoid tacitly assuming a roughly empiricist picture of agency. The very questions typically addressed, as in Chapters 4 and 5, already lean us in a non-Kantian direction since they

---

1. In his *Kant's Theory of Freedom* (Cambridge: Cambridge University Press, 1990), Henry Allison brings out just how important this thesis, which he calls the "incorporation thesis," is to Kant's ethics.

have us thinking about the motives from which agents act. Use of the term 'motive' has become so standard that many who are sympathetic to Kant, indeed many Kant scholars, use it without noticing that it suggests a very non-Kantian picture. We ask, "Which motive did she act from?" as if the way to understand why someone acted as she did is to point to something that impelled her so to act. We speak of conflicting motives and ask which motive was the strongest. That this way of talking is very un-Kantian is all the harder to see given the not uncommon translations of *aus Pflicht* as 'from the motive of duty'.[2] (That anyone would so translate *aus Pflicht* is an indication of how pervasive the empiricist view is.)

Indeed, since 'acting from duty' and 'acting from the motive of duty' are used interchangeably, even when we use the phrase 'acting from duty' we are, if not aware of the problem, apt to picture individual actions issuing from motives. So it is important not merely to clean up our terminology, but to be alert to misconceptions that we may harbor as a result of thinking in terms of motives. I mentioned that we are apt to picture individual actions issuing from motives. Here the point is not only that we see actions as issuing from motives, but also that our attention is focused on isolated actions. The more appropriate Kantian focus is on conduct, viewed over a stretch of time and guided by reasons. Maxims, unlike motives, have no closer tie to individual actions than to courses of conduct; in fact, maxims connect more naturally to courses of conduct than to individual actions. Thus thinking in terms of motives may contribute to the misconception that Kant's focus is on individual actions.

3   With an appreciation of the distance between Kant's theory of agency and the view suggested by talk of acting from this or that motive, we are now in a better position to understand a problem noted in Chapter 4. There I defended acting from duty in part by arguing that one can act from duty without acting from duty as a primary motive. What immediately prompts one to act is, say, a desire to visit an uncle in a nursing home, while at the same time one is guided by the conception that it is right so to act. Here one acts from duty, but duty operates as a

2. In his translation of *Grundlegung*, Paton sometimes translates *aus Pflicht* as 'from duty', sometimes as 'from the motive of duty', and sometimes even 'for the sake of duty'. See G 397–399. The error can also be found in Greene and Hudson's translation of *Religion*. See, e.g., R 29–30/25.

secondary motive. But the distinction is a clumsy one, because it is odd to suggest that something can be a motive without moving one or that one can act "from" something if that something does not impel one to act. We can now see the source of the problem: 'motive' does indeed suggest that the agent is moved, yet on Kant's picture of agency the agent is not moved. So the difficulty is one of trying to capture a Kantian notion of acting from duty without suggesting that the agent acts from an inner "force," and it is difficult to capture this while employing the standard terminology of 'motive'. The primary/secondary distinction is needed precisely because of the poor fit between the standard terminology and the Kantian view. It attempts to introduce the regulatory aspect of acting from duty within the confining framework imposed by the terminology. But insofar as 'motive' suggests a quasi-mechanical picture, the strain of the Kantian ideas against the empiricist framework only becomes more apparent, and so the idea of a secondary motive jars. (It jars, too, because it tries to shift our focus from isolated actions to conduct, and yet as long as we think in terms of motives, we resist that shift.) Thus the objection raised in Chapter 4 turns out to uncover a problem, though not the one it purported to uncover. The real problem is not the distinction between primary and secondary motives, but the misfit between the term 'motive' and Kant's theory of agency.

What other bearing does the gap between Kant's theory of agency and the picture of agency suggested by the terminology of motives have on the issues addressed in Chapters 4 and 5?

Recall first a specific view of acting from duty discussed in Chapter 4 (Sec. 5), according to which the sense of duty is a backup, a substitute for more admirable and amiable motives such as a desire to help another person. Ideally one would not need ever to act from duty, on this view. This notion finds its home in a picture of agency on which agents act from inner pushes or urges or tugs or drives. It is out of place on a view on which agents must affirm the urge or push if it is to determine them to act accordingly, and on which the sense of duty has a regulative function rather than merely impelling or prompting.

The more general point is this: if one has the latter picture of agency in mind, it is very easy to misunderstand entirely what it is that Kantians value about acting from duty. If acting from duty is viewed as acting from a motive that pushes us in a quasi-mechanical way, it is no wonder that the notion that it is important that one act from duty would be held to be quite odd. How very strange it must seem, to those who so view acting from duty, that Kantians place such value on it! Its value lies in its regulative role, and that is overlooked altogether by those who think of the motive of duty as simply something that pushes us to act as duty requires.

We can take the point further. It is likely that the widespread view that Kant places too much value on acting from duty and too little value on acting from—as we say—other motives is based in no small part on the empiricist picture of agency. Consider the very general worry that Kant expresses too much esteem for the person who acts from duty without being inclined to perform the action in question and too little for the person who performs the same action from fellow feeling and not from duty. The worry is very understandable if we imagine that the person who acts from duty is pushed by the motive of duty and that the other person is pushed by fellow feeling. If we think that the options are to be prompted by fellow feeling or to be prompted by a concern to do our duty, the person in whom fellow feeling is a very powerful force may well seem preferable, indeed, morally preferable, to someone in whom the motive of duty is a very powerful force. The former sort of person sounds congenial, warmhearted, a good soul; the latter sounds a bit dangerous, calling to mind people who mindlessly do things because Duty commands. I remarked earlier that there is no reason to suppose that someone who acts from duty would do so mindlessly, but we can now see a reason of sorts for that supposition. If we assume an empiricist picture of agency, our image of someone who acts from duty will be of a person driven by a concern (perhaps 'obsession' is more apt) to do her or his duty. No wonder acting from duty tends to be valued more by nonempiricists than by empiricists!

I have been suggesting that the objections to acting from duty that are the subject of Part II owe a lot of their motivation to confusion about Kant's conception of agency. But they may owe more than just their motivation to it. It is difficult even to articulate the objections to Kant's ethics that we have been examining once we correct for the confusion about agency and recognize that on Kant's view we act on maxims, not from motives. Consider the objection that Kant places too much value on acting from duty. What does it mean? It cannot mean that he places too much value on acting from one urge—duty—rather than from other urges or desires; the idea, rather, must be that he places too much value on our maxim being of a certain character. What sort of character? The *Groundwork* provides part of the answer: the maxim must have moral content (G 398). That is not the whole answer; a maxim could have moral content together with other content that superseded or placed a condition on it. Kant explains in *Religion* that "man . . . naturally adopts *both* [the law and the incentives of his sensuous nature] into his maxim" (R 36/31). The "distinction between a good man and one who is evil cannot lie in the incentives which they adopt into their maxims (not in the content of the maxim), but rather must depend upon *subordination* (the form of the maxim), i.e., *which of the two incentives he makes the condition of the other*" (R 36/31). So, the objection that Kant places too much value on our maxim being of a certain character would have to be understood as follows: he places too much value on subordinating to the incentive of duty all other incentives.

An interesting result emerges. When the criticism that Kant places too much value on acting from duty is corrected for the confusion regarding his theory of agency, what survives is an objection to the position that moral considerations override all other considerations. It is an objection not to valuing one motive more than another but to valuing a commitment to morality. If recast in terms of motives, it can be spelled out as follows: it is an objection to acting from duty as a secondary motive.

As I indicated in the opening of this interlude, I chose to couch my discussions of Kant on moral motivation in the standard terminology rather than use the Kantian terminology that is much better suited to explain Kant's views. This interlude underscores what a major concession that decision was to Kant's critics. The standard objections that I have been examining in Part II lend much of their initial credibility to a confusion about Kant's theory of agency. They trade on the notion that Kant is concerned that we act from one motive rather than another, where motives are vaguely understood to be inner forces or pushes. When corrected so that they reflect Kant's view of agents as acting on maxims, the objections have to be revised considerably, and much of the motivation for the worries about the sort of agent he holds in esteem disappears.

6

Sympathy and Coldness in Kant's Ethics

◆◆◆

1   I argued in Chapter 5 that Kant does not place excessive value on acting from duty as a primary motive. This addresses one of the concerns about Kant's emphasis on acting from duty which persisted after Chapter 4 sifted through and evaluated objections to acting from duty. The other concern is that in valorizing acting from duty, Kant undervalues love, affection, and fellow feeling and, more generally, fails to recognize the moral importance of affect. Could Kant allow that someone lacking in fellow feeling and affection is morally deficient?

This question is more straightforward than those of Chapter 5 and easier to articulate without the freight of misleading terminology. Fortunately, therefore, this chapter does not have to be as complex. There are, however, some common misconceptions about Kant's views that need to be addressed. The misconceptions are (1) that Kant holds that inclinations (and everything else affective) are bad; and (2) that Kant holds that we are not responsible for our inclinations and emotions because (3) we are passive with respect to them. On Kant's view, one critic asserts, feelings, such as the feeling of sympathy, "move us to act without our rational assent or assessment."[1] The misconceptions need to be examined before I tackle the main question before us. I begin with (3).[2]

1. David Cartwright, "Kant's View of the Moral Significance of Kindhearted Emotions and the Moral Insignificance of Kant's View," *Journal of Value Inquiry* 21 (1987): 296.
2. In developing the criticism I use 'inclinations', 'emotions', and 'feelings' loosely. I introduce Kant's terminology in Sec. 3. Throughout the chapter I use 'affect' (or 'everything affective') as a very general term, encompassing inclinations, emotions, passions, feelings, etc.

2   The claim that we are, on Kant's view, passive with respect to our emotions and feelings is a common one. It is not entirely clear what it means. I take the idea to be that as agents, we are not in control of our feelings; our feelings and emotions simply happen to us, just as feelings of pain do. On this view, whether we act rightly will depend almost exclusively on the strength of our various competing motives: if an inclination that runs contrary to duty is very strong, and my motive of duty is not very strong, I will not act as duty requires in this situation. If the motive of duty is stronger than any opposing inclination (all opposing inclinations combined?), I will act as duty requires. (I will not try to sort out details such as that raised by the parenthetical query in the last sentence, since I think the entire picture is demonstrably false.)

Here is one statement of the view that we are passive with respect to our emotions: "Kant's attitude toward emotions and morality presupposes a psychology: Emotions are brute forces unconnected with higher mental functions. Pain is the obvious model. Pain is a brute force; it is beyond the will; it is, or at least typically is, independent of reason. . . . The closer the psychology of emotion fits the model of pain, the better prepared it is to play the role in moral life, or in our judgments of character, that a Kantian offers it."[3]

That Kant does *not* hold that we are passive with respect to our emotions and feelings is easy to establish. The *Anthropology* is full of suggestions of how we can shape our own affective responses; for example, frequent smiling, at least in children, helps to establish a disposition to joy, friendliness, and sociability (*A* 265). In the *Lectures on Ethics* Kant has this to say in favor of books "which serve no purpose beyond amusement, which entertain our imagination, and which may even treat

---

3. John Sabini and Maury Silver, "Emotions, Responsibility, and Character," in *Responsibility, Character, and the Emotions: New Essays in Moral Psychology*, ed. Ferdinand Schoeman (Cambridge: Cambridge University Press, 1987), p. 166. A similar but more subtle and more plausible view can be found in Julia Annas, "Personal Love and Kantian Ethics in *Effi Briest*," *Philosophy and Literature* 8 (1984): 15–31. Annas claims that on Kant's view, "*all* our particular attachments and commitments appear as mere inclinations with respect to which we are *passive*; they do not express anything significant about our moral personalities (there is no moral significance just in being a philanthropist rather than a profit-maker); and the choices between alternatives that they express and lead to are all morally indifferent" (p. 25). But in fact they do not appear as "mere inclinations"; they are, or express, ends that we have chosen. The choices reflect different maxims, and it is evident that the philanthropist has adopted the obligatory end of others' happiness while it is not apparent that the profit-maker has done so. I reply to her article in "Was Effi Briest a Victim of Kantian Morality?" *Philosophy and Literature* 12 (1988): 95–113.

of certain passions, such as love, at a degree of intensity which passes the recognized bounds of ordinary conduct": "they refine our sentiments" (*LE* 237). So, here is another way in which we can take an active role in shaping our sentiments. He also suggests that by being polite and courteous we can make ourselves more "gentle and refined" (*LE* 236). At *MM* 402 he claims that if we often help others, our beneficence will (at least if we succeed in realizing our beneficent intention) lead us to have more love for them. (Cf. *LE* 197.) In a passage from the *Doctrine of Virtue* to be examined later in this chapter, Kant says that we are to cultivate our sympathetic feelings, and he suggests that we can do so by, for example, seeking out "places where the poor who lack the most basic necessities are to be found" (*MM* 457).[4] This passage tells against (2) as well as against (3).

Kant's distinction between sensitivity and sentimentality is further evidence that in his view we play a significant role as agents in determining how we respond affectively. "Sensitivity is a *power* and *strength* by which we grant or refuse permission for the state of pleasure or displeasure to enter our mind, so that it implies a choice." By contrast, "sentimentality is a weakness by which we can be affected, even against our will, by sympathy for another's plight" (*A* 236). Clearly, then, we are not always passive with respect to our emotions and feelings: sensitivity does not involve such passivity.

Interestingly, although sentimentality does involve passivity, the passivity seems to be somewhat voluntary: it is a self-inflicted weakness. Kant remarks in speaking of sentimentality that "to share ineffectually in others' feelings, to *attune* our feelings sympathetically to theirs and so *let* ourselves be affected in a merely passive way, is silly and childish" (*A* 236, my emphasis). The sentimental person *is* passive with respect to his sympathetic feelings, but this is not due to the nature of sympathy or of emotions. Rather, the person attunes his feelings to those of others, and *lets* himself be affected in a merely passive way.

The passage on sensitivity and sentimentality is a clue to the underlying error in the view that Kant believes that we are passive with respect to our feelings. As we saw in the second interlude, central to Kant's theory of agency is this thesis: "an incentive can determine the will^w to an action *only so far as the individual has incorporated it into his maxim*" (*R* 24/ 19). In other words, a desire does not simply overcome me; if I act as the desire directs me, I do so because I decide to do so.

---

4. See also *CJ* 433–434.

This model, with its very strong notion of agency, is diametrically opposed to the picture drawn by Sabini and Silver, according to which emotions function, on Kant's view, much as pain does. It is a serious mistake to think that Kant's psychology of emotion even approximately fits the model of pain and that feelings such as sympathy "move us to act without our rational assent or assessment."[5] For the same reason, it is a mistake to think that the strength of a motive (relative to other motives)—the strength of its motivating force—decides how we act. *We* decide how we act. If Kant is to be faulted, it is for too robust a conception of agency, not for a view of agents as passive with respect to their feelings.

Similarly, it would be more plausible to criticize Kant for attributing to us too much responsibility for our feelings and emotions than to attribute to him the position that we are not responsible for them. His is not a picture of adults whose characters are essentially "set," who, if they are good, are good largely because they were trained as children to have the right desires, and if bad, are bad due to poor training.[6] We bear a great deal of responsibility for our characters, and for allowing ourselves to be moved by this or that feeling. We cannot beg off responsibility for our actions by citing a feeling that overcame us, or by pointing out that we were not properly trained as children to have the right desires and cannot help it if we are now assailed by untoward urges.

Now, although the views that I have been discussing are very far from Kant's view, there is a kernel of plausibility in the attribution of them to Kant. One might argue that although Kant thinks we are responsible for acting on a particular feeling and that we deceive ourselves if we think that we acted because we were overcome by a feeling, still he holds that we are not responsible for the feelings themselves. For this reason, there is, arguably, no room for moral criticism of someone for *having* a certain feeling, but only for acting on it.[7]

Whether Kant allows that moral criticism could be in order for merely having a feeling is not entirely clear, but there is certainly some indication that he does. Consider his remarks about arrogance: "*Arrogance*

---

5. Cartwright, "Kant's View," p. 296.

6. See *Anthropology* 294–295 and most of *Education* for a discussion of acquiring character.

7. Lawrence Blum puts forth roughly this argument in chap. 8 of his *Friendship, Altruism, and Morality* (London: Routledge and Kegan Paul, 1980). On the Kantian view, Blum claims, the "only relevance of our feelings to morality lies in whether we choose to act from them or not" (p. 170).

(*superbia* and, as this word expresses it, the inclination to be always *on top*) is a kind of *ambition* (*ambitio*) in which we demand that others think little of themselves in comparison with us. It is, therefore, a vice opposed to the respect that every man can lawfully claim" (*MM* 465). The vice does not seem to be one of doing something toward others—for example, actually conveying to them a demand that they think little of themselves—but rather of having a particular inclination (to be always on top) and a particular attitude toward others. Consider too his remarks about malice, which he lists as a vice of hatred for men (*MM* 458):

> It is indeed natural that, by the laws of imagination (namely, the law of contrast), we feel our own well-being and even our good conduct more strongly when the misfortune of others or their downfall in scandal is put next to our own condition, as a foil to show it in so much the brighter light. But to rejoice immediately in the existence of such *enormities* destroying what is best in the world as a whole, and so also to wish for them to happen, is secretly to hate men; and this is the direct opposite of love for our neighbor, which is incumbent on us as a duty. (*MM* 460)

But even if he does not recognize that moral criticism can be in order for merely having a feeling (whether or not the agent is held responsible for that feeling), it is undeniable that Kant's view is not that moral criticism could be in order only for acting on the objectionable feeling. First of all, Kant clearly does think that it can be morally objectionable to *harbor* certain feelings even if the agent does not take objectionable action accordingly. Similarly, it is morally objectionable to cultivate certain feelings, such as envy, or to fail to cultivate others, such as sympathetic feelings.[8] So it is wrong to suppose that on Kant's view only action on certain feelings is wrong, never anything that more directly concerns the feelings themselves. Third, Kant holds that people are responsible for feeling tempted, where this means not that we are responsible for having the desires that we have, but that we are responsible for regarding as a real option acting as the desires direct.[9] It is "man *himself* who puts these obstacles in the way of his maxims" (*MM* 394). The virtuous person feels little temptation to act wrongly, and to the extent that she does, she resists temptation easily. (As Kant often remarks,

---

8. See secs. 32–36 of *The Doctrine of Virtue* in *MM*.

9. See Henry Allison, *Kant's Theory of Freedom* (Cambridge: Cambridge University Press, 1990), pp. 163–164; and Karl Ameriks, "Kant on the Good Will," in *Grundlegung zur Metaphysik der Sitten*, ed. Otfried Höffe (Frankfurt: Vittorio Klostermann), pp. 59–62.

cheerfulness in doing what morality requires is a mark of virtue.)[10] A virtuous person may have a desire to do *x*, where *x* is wrong—her will, after all, is not "holy"—but she does not take her desire to be a reason for action and does not regard doing *x* as a genuine option.

In short, it may be that merely *having* the feeling is not something that Kant sees to be morally objectionable—or at least something for which the agent may legitimately be held responsible. But he does recognize responsibility for harboring, cultivating, or failing to cultivate certain desires or feelings and for taking the desires to be reasons to act accordingly.

I turn now to the other misconception—(1), in the second paragraph of this chapter—namely, that Kant holds that everything affective is bad.

3   Kant is widely read as believing that inclinations are, quite simply, bad. The *Groundwork* contains passages that support that reading:

> Inclinations themselves, as sources of needs, are so far from having an absolute value to make them desirable for their own sake that it must rather be the universal wish of every rational being to be wholly free from them. (*G* 428)

And if one has already come to that understandable reading, there are passages in the *Critique of Practical Reason* which seem to confirm it:

> Inclination, be it good-natured or otherwise, is blind and slavish; reason, when it is a question of morality, must not play the part of mere guardian of the inclinations, but, without regard to them, as pure practical reason it must care for its own interest to the exclusion of all else. (*PrR* 118)

Inclinations are repeatedly presented as annoying encumbrances and dangers.

> Sensuous contentment (improperly so called) which rests on the satisfaction of inclinations, however refined they may be, can never be adequate to that which is conceived under contentment. For inclinations vary; they grow with the indulgence we allow them, and they leave behind a greater void than the one we intended to fill. They are consequently always burdensome to a rational being, and, though he cannot put them aside, they nevertheless elicit from him the wish to be free of them. (*PrR* 118)

10. See *R* 24n/18n; *MM* 409 and 484–485; and *A* 235.

In later works, however, Kant states explicitly that inclinations are not generically bad. Differentiating his position from what he takes to be the Stoic view,[11] he states:

> Natural inclinations, *considered in themselves*, are *good*, that is, not a matter of reproach, and it is not only futile to want to extirpate them but to do so would also be harmful and blameworthy. Rather, let them be tamed and instead of clashing with one another they can be brought into harmony in a wholeness which is called happiness. (R 58/51)[12]

Evil, on Kant's view, resides not in untoward inclinations but in certain maxims, specifically, maxims that subordinate the moral law to something else. The "distinction between a good man and one who is evil cannot lie in the difference between the incentives which they adopt into their maxim (not in the content of the maxim), but rather must depend upon *subordination* (the form of the maxim), *i.e., which of the two incentives he makes the condition of the other*" (R 36/31). Inclinations, or more broadly, the "incentives" of one's "sensuous nature," are not evil; but it is evil to take them into one's maxim "*as in themselves wholly adequate* to the determination of the will^w", without troubling himself about the moral law" (R 36/31). It is not wrong to adopt them into one's maxim. It is wrong to subordinate acting morally to fulfilling one's inclinations.

There are passages in the *Anthropology* which, if read in isolation from the surrounding text, might seem to confirm the view that Kant thinks everything affective is bad. After all, Kant says that "passions are . . . without exception *evil*" (A 267). But passions are, in Kant's taxonomy, but one type of affect, so we cannot read off his view of affect in general from his remarks about passions. A detailed discussion in *Anthropology* distinguishes passions [*Leidenschaften*] from agitations [*Affekten*] and distinguishes both from inclinations [*Neigungen*].[13]

11. Michael J. Seidler argues that the Stoic view is in fact closer to Kant's view than to the view that Kant attributes to the Stoics. See Seidler, "Kant and the Stoics on the Emotional Life," *Philosophy Research Archives* 7, no. 4 (1981): 1–56, esp. 10–11.

12. See also Kant's "Speculative Beginning of Human History," where he writes in a lengthy footnote: "nature certainly has not placed instincts and abilities in living creatures so that they should fight and suppress them" (117/54–55).

13. Mary Gregor translates *Affekten* as *affects* in the *Anthropology* and in her 1991 translation of the *Tugendlehre*, though in her 1964 translation of the *Tugendlehre* she translated it as as *agitations*. I am using *agitations* because I want to be able to use the word *affect* broadly to refer to feelings, passions, inclinations, and agitations. In quoting from the *Anthropology* I substitute *agitation* for *Affekt*, where Gregor uses *affect*.

A passion is an inclination "that the subject's reason can subdue only with difficulty or not at all." By contrast, an agitation is a "feeling of pleasure or displeasure" in the agent's "present state that does not let him rise to *reflection*" (*A* 251).[14] Agitations impede reflection, but they can be subdued and tend to be short-lived. Passions, by contrast, resist taming by reason and can actually become more deeply rooted through reflection. His metaphors provide a more vivid picture.

> An agitation works like water breaking through a dam: a passion, like a stream that burrows ever deeper in its bed. An agitation works on our health like an apoplectic fit: a passion, like consumption or emaciation.... We should think of an agitation as a drunken fit that we sleep off: of a passion, as a madness that broods over an idea which settles in ever more deeply. (*A* 252–253)

A casual reading of his remarks on passions and agitations might leave one with the impression that anything affective is, in Kant's view, bad, though passions are worse than agitations. This is almost right with respect to passions and agitations. Both are generally depicted negatively, with passions posing a more serious threat to moral health. Kant does, however, have an occasional kind word for agitations. Laughing and weeping are agitations "by which nature promotes health in a mechanical way" (*A* 262). In "On Philosophers' Medicine of the Body" he writes that although they "agitate the body by a certain assault on it," agitations "can be healthful, provided they do not reach the point of enervating it." Joy and indignation are healthful, as is "surprise, a certain alternation of fear and hope such as people experience in games of chance."[15]

He is more firmly positive regarding inclinations (setting aside, for the

---

The distinction between passions and agitations also appears in *MM* (at, e.g., 407–408) and *CJ* (at, e.g., 272). See also Kant's "On Philosophers' Medicine of the Body," trans. Mary J. Gregor, in *Kant's Latin Writings*, ed. Lewis White Beck (New York: Peter Lang, 1986). For a discussion of the distinction in Kant's works and an attempt to trace it to the Stoics, see M. Seidler, "Kant and the Stoics."

14. An inclination is simply a habitual sensuous appetite, and an appetite is "the self-determination of a subject's power through the idea of some future thing as an effect of this power" (*A* 251). See also *MM* 407–408.

15. "On Philosophers' Medicine of the Body," pp. 228–229. This work was published in 1881 by Johannes Reicke, who found the manuscript among the papers of his father, Rudolf Reicke, archivist of Kant's *Nachlass*. Mary Gregor's English translation of the Latin manuscript, which appears to have been written in 1788 or possibly 1786, is published together with her helpful introduction in *Kant's Latin Writings*.

moment, the remarks cited above from the *Groundwork* and the *Critique of Practical Reason*). His positive statement is embedded in some harsh remarks concerning passions. After stating that "passions are . . . without exception, *evil*," Kant notes that others are of a different opinion: "Yet . . . it is said that nothing great has ever been accomplished in the world without intense passion, and that Providence itself has wisely implanted the passions in human nature as incentives" (A 267). To this he replies:

> We can indeed admit this of the various *inclinations* that, as natural animal needs, are indispensable to living nature (even man's nature). But Providence did not will that these inclinations might, indeed even should, become *passions*. (A 267)

The picture of affects that Kant presents in the *Anthropology* coheres with what he says about inclinations in the *Religion*. There is nothing objectionable about inclinations as such. Misconduct is due not to them but to our stance toward them: we act wrongly when we give their gratification priority over conforming our conduct to the moral law. (One way of doing this is to allow them to become passions, i.e., to allow them to so overwhelm us that *we* are under *their* control, rather than the other way around.) Kant makes a similar claim in the *Doctrine of Virtue*:

> Ethical gymnastics . . . consists only in combatting natural impulses sufficiently to be able to master them when a situation comes up in which they threaten morality; hence it makes one valiant and cheerful in the consciousness of one's restored freedom. (MM 485)

Kant's remarks on apathy [*Affektlosigkeit*] shed further light on his view. The many passages in his works which extol apathy might be taken as evidence that he thinks it best if we are devoid of feeling of any sort other than respect for the moral law. But in fact what he regards as desirable is *self-control*, and what he means by apathy is *not* a lack of feeling, but a lack of passion or (strong) agitation, that is, a lack of that which blinds us or prevents us from thinking clearly. He explicitly disavows the former meaning, remarking that the "word 'apathy' has fallen into disrepute, as it if meant lack of feeling and so subjective indifference with respect to objects of choice" (MM 408). He understands apathy as follows:

> Since virtue is based on inner freedom, it contains a positive command
> to a man, namely to bring all his capacities and inclinations under his
> (reason's) control and so to rule over himself, which goes beyond forbid-
> ding him to let himself be governed by his feelings and inclinations (the
> duty of *apathy*); for unless reason holds the reins of government in its own
> hands, man's feelings and inclinations play the master over him. (*MM* 408)

The duty of apathy is the duty to govern oneself and not to allow oneself
to be governed by one's feelings and inclinations.[16]

It is evident that Kant's position in his later ethical works—the *Religion*, the *Metaphysics of Morals*, and the *Anthropology*—is not that
inclinations are in themselves bad, but only that we must control them
rather than let them control us and must not ever subordinate duty to
inclination. How does this square with his remarks about inclination in
the *Groundwork* and the second *Critique*? The conflict is less deep than
might first appear. The more detailed discussion in the later works draws
distinctions not drawn earlier (distinctions between passions and emotional agitations, and between these and inclinations). But in all the
works his view is that we are to tame and control inclination and
emotion. We are to avoid indulging them, since "they grow with the
indulgence we allow them"; we must prevent them from ruling us or
compromising our moral commitments.

The only conflict approximating a contradiction arises from his claim
in *Groundwork* and *Critique of Practical Reason* that the inclinations
elicit from a rational being a wish to be rid of them. In the *Religion* he
says that it is futile and would be a matter of reproach to "want to
extirpate" them. The earlier remark should be understood as an over-
statement of the point that our inclinations—our desires, more generally—can be burdens to us, particularly in that they grow and multiply as
we indulge them. Not only do they become more numerous; they become
more demanding, sometimes becoming passions. It is very understandable, Kant thinks, that we might think that life would be easier without
them; indeed, we are all bound to feel this way at times.[17] Nonetheless,

16. As Mary Gregor points out in an endnote to her translation of the *Anthropology*,
Kant sometimes means by apathy something different yet, namely, "what Kant has earlier
called an 'even temper', a quality of temperament which, though not itself moral, can
facilitate the practice of morality" (*A* 206, n. 42). See *A* 235 and *A* 290 for a discussion of
apathy in this sense.

17. Kant's claim is, it must be admitted, a strange one. It is understandable that we
would want to be free of some of our inclinations—but all of them? It is hard to imagine
what it would mean to change from being as we now are into people who have absolutely

a wish to be free of them is futile and wrongheaded. Rather than cursing them, we should seek to bring them into harmony and tame them so that they will not become passions.

Given the projects of the second *Critique* and *Groundwork*, it is not surprising that Kant would in those works emphasize how unsuited inclinations (and everything affective) are to serving a foundational role in morality. In those works he is seeking to show that moral motivation does not require the aid of inclination and that the supreme principle of morality can and must have a purely nonempirical foundation. Since the *Doctrine of Virtue*, *Religion*, and *Anthropology* build on the earlier works and are not primarily concerned with foundations, he has no need to emphasize in those later works that inclinations are not suited to serve a foundational role in morality. There may be a further reason for Kant's negative remarks about affect in the *Groundwork* and the second *Critique*: his earlier endorsement of a version of moral sense theory. Given that endorsement, it would not be surprising to find him at pains to distance himself from it in the first ethical works he writes after changing his view, and perhaps this accounts for the hyperbole.[18]

When we take into account the difference in emphasis, the contrast between Kant's view of emotion in the *Groundwork* and the second *Critique* and the view presented in the three later ethical works turns out not to be as sharp as it might otherwise appear.[19] A close look at the former two works discloses that Kant's primary practical point about affect is the same as that expressed in the later works: we must control our inclinations, not let them control us, and we must allow them no hearing as challengers to duty. We must not seek a compromise between

no inclinations, and harder still to imagine someone wishing or longing to be devoid of inclinations.

18. Michael Seidler makes this point in "Kant and the Stoics," pp. 54–55. For Kant's earlier view, see Josef Schmucker, *Die Ursprünge der Ethik Kants* (Meisenheim am Glan: Anton Hain, 1961); Paul Schilpp, *Kant's Pre-Critical Ethics*, 2d ed. (Evanston: Northwestern University Press, 1960); Christine Korsgaard, "Kant," *Ethics in the History of Western Philosophy*, ed. Robert J. Cavalier, James Gouinlock, and James P. Sterba (New York: St. Martin's Press, 1989), pp. 201–243; Keith Ward, *The Development of Kant's View of Ethics* (Oxford: Basil Blackwell, 1972); as well as G. B. Kerferd and D. E. Walford, eds., *Kant: Selected Pre-Critical Writings and Correspondence with Beck* (Manchester: Manchester University Press, 1968).

19. We should note, too, that the *Groundwork* and the second *Critique* contain passages that portray affect in a more positive light than do the passages from those works quoted above. See, e.g., G 394 and PrR 85–86.

duty and what we want. When they come into conflict, we must always put duty first.

4   Kant's position is that although inclinations must be subordinate to duty, they are not in themselves bad. But the harder question is this: Can he attribute *positive value* to any inclinations? He does not hold, nor is he committed to holding, that they are bad; but can he grant that a desire to help someone can be good and that the lack of any desire to help another can be bad? It is not enough that he does not think that it is better to have no desire to help than to have a desire to help; surely it should be seen as better *to want to help*.

The worry can be broadened to cover more than inclinations. What many of Kant's readers find particularly disturbing about his view of character and moral motivation is that he seems to see no positive value in wanting to help or in feeling concerned, being distressed about another's suffering, and the like.

Broadened, the criticisms concern dispositions, attitudes, and affective responses. Affective responses are critical to what might be called 'expressive acts', that is, acts primarily intended to express something to another person. As Nancy Sherman observes, the point of helping in many cases "is to reassure another that we care—to show patience, loyalty, considerateness, empathy."[20] But of course we do not exhibit these qualities if we do not have them. (We may pretend to exhibit them, but that is another matter. That would be false reassurance, not genuine reassurance.)

Our affective responses are morally important. How I react to the news of a death of someone I know, or news of serious illness, matters, and not just because of the effect that my reaction might have on others. The same is true of my reaction to someone's very good news—receipt of a major award, the birth of a child, and the like. It says something about my character if my main reaction upon hearing that a colleague received a major award is to think that she did not deserve it, or if my first and persistent thought upon learning that a neighbor has a serious illness is that I too might be stricken by that illness or some equally grave illness (or that I am not likely to be stricken with the illness, since I do not smoke, and have a more wholesome diet than he does).

20. Nancy Sherman, "The Place of Emotions in Kantian Morality," in *Identity, Character, and Morality: Essays in Moral Psychology*, ed. Owen Flanagan and Amélie Oksenberg Rorty (Cambridge: MIT Press, 1990), pp. 150–151.

Can Kant recognize that the character of someone who has inappropriate or inadequate affective responses is flawed? Or that someone who helps others from duty, but never wants to, and has to push himself to help is morally deficient? Can he, to allude to the discussion in Chapter 4 of Stocker's example, recognize that something is amiss if someone helps from duty, but *begrudgingly*; or although not begrudgingly, *cheerlessly*?

This last question is easy to answer. He *does*, and so unless there is some reason to think that he is inconsistent in so doing, the answer is *yes*. At the end of *The Doctrine of Virtue* he devotes a section entitled "Ethical Ascetic" to repudiating excessive asceticism. "The rules for practicing virtue (*exercitiorum virtutis*) aim at a frame of mind that is *valiant* and *cheerful* in fulfilling its duties (*animus strenuus et hilaris*)" (*MM* 484).[21]

But cheerfulness here might only be cheerfulness in doing one's duty, cheerfulness that need not reflect a genuine concern for the person whom one aims to help. And so the harder question remains: Could Kant find there to be anything missing in someone who acts from duty—cheerfully, without resentment, and so on—but without inclination and, where another person is involved, without any real feeling for the person?

It is easy to marshal evidence for an affirmative answer. Kant indicates many fairly specific duties to cultivate attitudes and feelings in ourselves. In *MM* he mentions, among other duties, a duty to cultivate a conciliatory spirit, duties of gratitude, duties not to be envious and not to take malicious joy in others' misfortunes, and the duty of friendship, all of which require that we shape our characters accordingly.[22] And as noted

21. The passage continues: "What is not done with pleasure but merely as compulsory service has no inner worth for one who attends to his duty in this way and such service is not loved by him; instead, he shirks as much as possible occasions for practicing virtue" (*MM* 484). See too Kant's reply to Schiller's objection (*R* 24n/19n). Further evidence comes from Kant's discussion of gratitude. His insistence on the importance of helping others in such a way as not to make them feel obligated to one (*MM* 448–449) would urge against helping them begrudgingly (or at least, would mandate that one conceal one's begrudging attitude).

22. One might think that gratitude requires, on Kant's view, only certain external acts. But without making it clear exactly what gratitude does require, the following passage indicates that it requires something more. Gratitude requires that we not regard "a kindness received as a burden one would gladly be rid of . . . but . . . [take] the occasion for gratitude as a moral kindness, that is, as an opportunity given one to unite the virtue of gratitude with love of man, to combine the *cordiality* of a benevolent disposition with *sensitivity* to benevolence (attentiveness to the smallest degree of this disposition in one's thought of

earlier, we have a duty to cultivate the "compassionate natural (aesthetic [*ästhetische*]) feelings in us" (*MM* 457).[23]

4.1 Yet at times Kant seems to deny altogether the importance of such feelings as sympathetic sorrow or, worse yet, to assert that it is better *not* to have them. The most troublesome passage is this:[24]

> It was a sublime way of thinking that the Stoic ascribed to his wise man when he had him say, "I wish for a friend, not that he might help *me* in poverty, sickness, imprisonment, etc., but rather that I might stand by *him* and rescue a man." But the same wise man, when he could not rescue his friend, said to himself, "What is it to me?" In other words, he repudiated imparted suffering [*verwarf die Mitleidenschaft*]. (*MM* 457)[25]

---

duty), and so to cultivate one's love of man" (*MM* 456). On the duty of friendship, and indeed on the general topic of the present chapter, see Paul Guyer, *Kant and the Experience of Freedom: Essays on Aesthetics and Morality* (Cambridge: Cambridge University Press, 1993), chap. 10. Because it was published as I was completing my book, I was not able to utilize Guyer's discussion as fully as I would have liked.

23. The brackets are Gregor's. Another relevant passage is in *Education*, where he says that we must encourage youth to be cheerful, good-humored, and even-tempered, and to take "an interest in the progress of the world" (*E* 499/121).

24. Similar remarks occur at *LE* 199–200. Yet another worrisome passage is the following, from the *Lectures on Ethics*:

> A cold temperament is one which is unemotional and unmoved by love. A man whose spirit is never moved to impulses of kindness is said to be cold. Coldness is not necessarily a thing to be condemned. Poets, who boast an excess of warm feelings and affection, condemn it, but if a man of cold temperament is at the same time a man of principles and of good dispositions, he is at all times reliable. A cold-blooded but well-disposed guardian, advocate, or patriot, is a man of cool deliberation who will resolutely do his utmost for our good. Wickedness, if cold-blooded, is all the worse for it, but (although this may not sound well) cold-blooded goodness is better than a warmth of affection; because it is more reliable. (*LE* 198–199)

Coldness, Kant seems to be saying, is not a character deficiency. And that *is* worrisome.

In *Anthropology* he fills in the picture of the cold man in a way that makes it less disturbing. Under the heading "The Phlegmatic Temperament of the Cold-Blooded Man," he writes:

> Phlegma as *strength* . . . is the quality of not being moved easily or *rashly* but, if slowly, still *persistently*. The man with a good portion of phlegma in his constitution warms up slowly but retains his warmth longer. He is not easily angered, but reflects first whether he should get angry. The choleric man, for his own part, may well rage at not being able to draw such a stable man out of his *sangfroid*.
>
> The cold-blooded man has nothing to regret if nature gives him a quite ordinary portion of reason but also adds this phlegma, so that, without being spectacular, he still proceeds from principles and not from instinct. (*A* 290)

25. I have altered Gregor's translation, replacing a fragment with a part of her 1964

It is difficult not to read Kant as praising the wise man for repudiating compassion (imparted suffering). The wise man is very ready to help his friend but turns coldly away if it is not possible to help. Thus, it seems in this passage that Kant not only fails to place a proper value on compassion, but even regards the person who lacks feelings of compassion in a situation where he cannot help his friend as better, in that respect, than the person who in the same situation feels compassion.

Susan Mendus has tried to put a better face on this troubling passage. She writes, "This is hard doctrine, for it is surely the case that a sympathetic ear may often be of comfort. But in such a case I precisely *am* in a position to alter the situation of the man who suffers. If I really can do *nothing* to improve his situation, it seems much less harsh to suggest that I might well withdraw from the scene."[26] Perhaps Kant's way of putting it makes it sound worse than it really is. We picture someone whose friend is dying of an incurable disease: he turns away because he cannot cure his friend. But, Mendus reminds us, curing someone of a fatal illness is not the only way of helping him (even if it is what one would ideally do, were it only possible). One can sometimes help in small but significant ways by (for example) visiting one's friend, even if the friend is too ill to chat and only dimly knows that one is there. So Kant's remarks need not be read as saying that we should simply turn away if we cannot save him from his sad fate.

This is a helpful point, but it does not meet all reasonable concerns about the disturbing passage. First of all, Kant does not write, "But the same wise man, when he could not help his friend, said to himself, 'What is it to me?'." He says, "When he could not rescue [*retten*] his friend . . ." The suggestion seems to be not that if there is absolutely nothing we can do to make things better for someone, we might as well turn away and seek to shut ourselves off emotionally from his sorrows. Rather, it seems to be that if we cannot save our friend—rectify the problem—we might as well turn away. This might, however, be a misstatement on Kant's part. Indeed, in the next paragraph he does use the word 'help': "When another suffers and, although I cannot help him, I let myself be infected

---

translation. The first paragraph ends, "er verwarf die Mitleidenschaft"; she translates this as "he rejected compassion." The alteration helps to bring out the fact that what the wise man rejects is catching or being infected by another's pain. In my discussion I use both 'compassion' and 'imparted suffering'.

26. Susan Mendus, "The Practical and the Pathological," *Journal of Value Inquiry* 19 (1985): 241.

by his pain (through my imagination), then two of us suffer, though the evil really (in nature) affects only *one*."[27] Likewise, in a passage in the *Lectures on Ethics*, Kant asserts that someone who is indifferent to others' suffering just insofar as he cannot help is "practical"; "his heart is a kind heart."[28] Here again, what matters is that he can (or cannot) help the suffering person, not that he can (or cannot) rescue him from his problems. And in any case I see nothing in Kant's view that requires or even supports the assertion that the wise man turns away from his friend's suffering unless he can rectify the problem.

But even if we regard Kant's use of '*retten*' as an error and thus treat that part of the passage cited as a misstatement, there is another problem that Mendus's gloss does not address. Suppose the situation is one in which I cannot help. My friend is comatose, terminally ill, and virtually certain not to emerge from the coma. Of course in many such situations I can still help by showing concern and support to his relatives, and by clearly and sincerely expressing my desire to help in any way I can (providing transportation or lodging for relatives coming to see him, etc.). But imagine that here I cannot help even in those ways (not because of me, but because of the situation). Do I show a "sublime way of thinking" if to the fullest extent that I possibly can I "repudiate imparted suffering"? Is it *better* that I try hard (and largely succeed) in turning off my emotions?

There is much to be said against romantic notions that the more we weep and the more overcome by sadness we are in a situation such as that just described, the better our characters are. It is all too easy to content ourselves with and pride ourselves on feeling compassion. The merit,

27. Arguably the German, *abhelfen*, should not be translated as 'help'. The German reads, "Wenn ein anderer leidet und ich mich durch seinen Schmerz, dem ich doch nicht abhelfen kann, auch (vermittelst der Einbildungskraft) anstecken lasse. . . ." An alternative to "although I cannot help him" would be 'although I cannot alleviate his pain'. Alleviating his pain is more like helping him than rescuing him, though, since one can alleviate pain without rescuing the person from his problem. So the point remains that Kant does not consistently take the stand, in the passage in question, that if we cannot rescue our friend from his predicament, we might as well turn away.

28. The passage noted reads as follows: "Men believe that sympathy in another's misfortune and kindness of heart consist in wishes and feelings, but when a man is indifferent to the wretchedness of others just in so far as he can do nothing to change it, and troubles only where he can do some good and be of some help, such a man is practical; his heart is a kind heart, though he makes no show; he does not wear it on his sleeve, as do those who think that friendship consists in empty wishes, but his sympathy is practical because it is active" (*LE* 200).

Kant repeatedly emphasizes, lies in doing something to help, not in feeling sad for the suffering person.

> I see a man miserable and I feel for him; but it is useless to wish that he might be rid of his misery; I ought to try to rid him of it. (*LE* 199)

> Children . . . ought to be prevented from contracting the habit of a sentimental maudlin sympathy. . . . It is distinct from compassion, and it is an evil, consisting as it does merely in lamenting over a thing. It is a good thing to give children some pocket-money of their own, that they may help the needy; and in this way we should see if they are really compassionate or not. (*E* 487/97–98)[29]

There is much (though not quite as much) to be said for the idea that we should not wallow in sorrow and should at times push ourselves a bit to detach from an all-consuming sadness, grief, or anxiety about the well-being of a friend or our intense awareness of tragic loss. This is especially the case when our emotion impedes us from helping, as when our overwhelming sadness over the death of a friend's infant leads us to avoid her,[30] or when our grief prevents us from attending properly to our own children or meeting some other very important responsibility.[31] Kant speaks at one point of a "sympathetic grief that refuses to be consoled" (*CJ* 273). Just as one may nurse a wound, it is possible to "nurse" one's grief or sympathetic sadness. Sometimes it is important to "let go" of one's grief (though this is very different from "turning away" or "shutting it off").

But that is, I think, the very most that should be granted.[32] There is no nobility in shutting off—to the extent that we can—the flood of sadness

29. See also *PrR* 155; and Sec. 7 of this chapter.

30. No doubt the explanation of this all-too-common reaction is not merely that we are overwhelmed by sadness; often it is that we do not know what to say and we fear saying the wrong thing. (I thank Steve Johnson for pointing this out.) In addition we may want to avoid full recognition that the terrible thing really did happen. Perhaps we want to keep as far from such calamities as possible and avoid confronting the possibility that such things could befall us, too.

31. I qualified 'responsibility' because I do not think that we should detach ourselves from grief for just any responsibility, for example a responsibility to keep our appointments, grade papers promptly, etc. Even here, however, we need to check our grief enough to remember the appointments so that we can at least notify people that we cannot keep them.

32. It may be granting too much. See Blum's critical discussion in *Friendship, Altruism, and Morality*, pp. 152–157, of, as he puts it, the "Kantian thought" that " 'What really counts is what you do, not what you feel' " (p. 157).

upon learning that a colleague's spouse is terminally ill at the age of forty, or that an acquaintance has died in a car accident. And the case is all the clearer when it is a close friend. Nor is it even the case that shutting off one's emotions is morally indifferent. It is not just that it does not show a sublime way of thinking; there is something wrong if a person is never awash with emotion when for example, a friend or relative is killed or maimed. It seems clearly to be a problem for Kant's ethics if it cannot recognize this.

4.2   Kant is in less of a difficulty than the three preceding paragraphs suggest. First of all, *he does not say that the Sage shows a sublime way of thinking when he repudiates imparted suffering*. The sublimity attaches not to the repudiation of imparted suffering but to his wishing for a friend so that he might stand by him (and so on). ("It was a sublime way of thinking that the Stoic ascribed to his wise man when he had him say, 'I wish for a friend, not that he might help *me* in poverty . . ., but rather that I might stand by *him*. . . .' But the same wise man, when he could not rescue his friend, said to himself, 'What is it to me?'.")

Second, it is important to bear in mind that the aim of the discussion in which this passage occurs is to explain our duties of virtue *to others*. The aim is not to list the emotional responses that we are (or are not) to foster in ourselves. The duties of virtue to others include a duty to cultivate our sympathetic feelings, but do not include a duty to suffer with one's suffering friend. Kant is concerned to show the difference between the actual duty and the would-be duty, and to explain why the duties of virtue do not include the latter. The primary reason why there could not be a duty to suffer with one's suffering friend is that there cannot be a duty to increase the evil in the world, and yet, assuming that my suffering with him does not help him, all that it accomplishes is an increase in the suffering—and thus the evil—in the world.[33] "When another suffers and, although I cannot help him, I let myself be infected

---

33. The other reason Kant offers is somewhat obscure. It involves the suspicion that the sentiment involved is pity and that one who feels pity typically sees the person pitied as her inferior. Thus it is "an insulting kind of beneficence." See the full quotation below. Our beneficence should reflect respect for those we aid as *moral equals*. See also *MM* 473, where Kant contrasts the friend of humanity (*Freund der Menschen*) to the philanthropist (*Menschenfreund*). The former has, while the latter lacks, "thought and consideration for the *equality* among men" (*MM* 473). Walter Schaller offers a helpful discussion of Kant's misgivings about pity in his "Virtue and the Moral Law: An Analysis of Virtue and Moral Worth in Kant's Moral Philosophy," Ph.D. diss. (University of Wisconsin–Madison, 1984), pp. 151–158.

by his pain (through my imagination), then two of us suffer, though the evil really (in nature) affects only *one*. But there cannot possibly be a duty to increase the evil in the world, and so it cannot be a duty to do good from *sympathetic sadness*" (MM 457).[34]

4.3   But this will not satisfy critics, even those who grant the truth of all that I have said. In fact, it does not satisfy me. For although the point of the passage is to explain why there is no duty to suffer with one's suffering friend, Kant *does* seem to be endorsing the chilly, heartless behavior of the wise man. The passage does not commit Kant to saying that it is better to feel no grief in such circumstances, but it suggests that he does think that.

To better understand what Kant is endorsing, it may help to look at the text surrounding the problematic line and to focus our attention on an apparent tension in his view.[35] The problem is that his endorsement of the wise man's behavior is hard to square with his claim, just a few sentences after the passage about the Stoic and the Sage, that we have a duty to cultivate our sympathetic feelings. To see the puzzle more fully and to determine what Kant's view is, it will be helpful to have several paragraphs of text before us.

Sympathetic Feeling Is Generally a Duty

§ 34.

Sympathetic joy [*Mitfreude*] and *sadness* [Mitleid] (*sympathia moralis*) are sensible feelings of pleasure or pain (which are therefore to be called "aesthetic" [*ästhetisch*]) at another's state of joy or sorrow (shared feeling, sympathetic feeling [*Mitgefühl, teilnehmende Empfindung*].) Nature has already implanted in man susceptibility to these feelings. But to use this as

34. I substituted "and so it cannot be a duty to do good from *sympathetic sadness*" (preceded by a comma) for "and so to do good *from compassion.*" The German reads: "[Es kann aber unmöglich Pflicht sein, die Übel in der Welt zu vermehren,] mithin auch nicht, aus Mitleid wohl zu tun." (I include in brackets the words preceding the part in question.) The substitution replaces Gregor's 1991 translation with her 1964 translation.

35. Another approach would be to try to determine to which Stoic passages Kant is referring (if indeed he is referring to specific passages). If Kant's view can be assumed to be that of the Stoic he cites, the Stoic passages and the surrounding text would hopefully yield an answer to the question of just what Kant is endorsing. The problem with such an approach is that generally there is no reason to assume that we can read off the author's view from that put forth in a source that she or he cites approvingly. The problem is particularly clear when the author is Kant, since he often loosely borrows from texts, using them as a base on which to construct a rather different point. (Recall his imaginative retelling of the story of the Fall in *Religion* [cited above in Chap. 5, Sec. 4].) So there is no reason to assume that Kant's view is that of the Stoic he cites. I have in fact located some

a means to promoting active and rational benevolence is still a particular, though only a conditional, duty. It is called the duty of *humanity* (*humanitas*) because man is regarded here not merely as a rational being but also as an animal endowed with reason. Now humanity can be located either in the *capacity* and the *will* to *share in others' feelings* (*humanitas practica*) or merely in the *susceptibility*, given by nature itself, to feel joy and sadness in common with others (*humanitas aesthetica*). The first is *free*, and is therefore called *sympathetic* (*communio sentiendi liberalis*); it is based on practical reason. The second is *unfree* (*communio sentiendi illiberalis, servilis*); it can be called *communicable* (since it is like the susceptibility to warmth or contagious diseases), and also imparted suffering [*Mitleidenschaft*], since it spreads naturally among men living near one another. There is obligation only to the first. (*MM* 456–457)[36]

That nature implanted in humans a susceptibility to sympathetic feelings is stated earlier in the *Doctrine of Virtue* under the heading "Concepts of What Is Presupposed on the Part of Feeling [*Aesthetische Vorbegriffe*] by the Mind's Receptivity to Concepts of Duty as Such" (*MM* 399). These "moral endowments" are "such that anyone lacking them could have no duty to acquire them" and "they lie at the basis of morality, as *subjective* conditions of receptiveness to the concept of duty." The moral endowments are "*moral feeling, conscience, love* of one's neighbor, and *respect* for oneself (*self-esteem*)." I take it that *humanitas aesthetica* is a part of love of one's neighbor. (Whether it is identical to it or somewhat narrower is not entirely clear.)

To resume the lengthy quotation:

> It was a sublime way of thinking that the Stoic ascribed to his wise man when he had him say, "I wish for a friend, not that he might help *me* in poverty, sickness, imprisonment, etc., but rather that I might stand by *him* and rescue a man." But the same wise man, when he could not rescue his friend, said to himself, "What is it to me?" In other words, he repudiated imparted suffering.
>
> In fact, when another suffers and, although I cannot help him, I let myself be infected by his pain (through my imagination), then two of us

---

lines in Seneca that match quite well the first part of the troubling passage (" 'I wish for a friend . . .' ") but have not found a close match for the troubling part of the passage (" 'What is it to me?' "). See Sec. 7, below, for relevant passages in Seneca and for points of contrast, as well as points of contact, between Seneca's and Kant's views on sympathy.

36. I have translated *Mitleidenschaft* as 'imparted suffering' rather than as 'compassion'. See n. 25, above. I also note that except for 'ästhetisch', which Gregor inserted, all terms in square brackets are my insertions.

suffer, though the evil really (in nature) affects only *one*. But there cannot possibly be a duty to increase the evil in the world, and so it cannot be a duty to do good *from sympathetic sadness* [*Mitleid*]. This would also be an insulting kind of beneficence, since it expresses the kind of benevolence one has toward someone unworthy, called *pity* [*Barmherzigkeit*]; and this has no place in men's relations with one another, since they are not to make a display of their worthiness to be happy.

§ 35.

But while it is not in itself a duty to share the sufferings (as well as the joys) of others, it is a duty to sympathize actively in their fate; and to this end it is therefore an indirect duty to cultivate the compassionate natural (aesthetic [*ästhetische*]) feelings in us, and to make use of them as so many means to sympathy based on moral principles and the feeling appropriate to them. It is therefore a duty not to avoid the places where the poor who lack the most basic necessities are to be found but rather to seek them out, and not to shun sick-rooms or debtors' prisons and so forth in order to avoid the painful sympathetic feelings that one may not be able to resist. For this is still one of the impulses that nature has implanted in us to do what the representation of duty alone would not accomplish.[37]

The puzzle is this: Kant says that it is our duty "not to avoid the places where the poor who lack the most basic necessities are to be found but rather to seek them out" apparently in order to "cultivate the compassionate natural . . . feelings in us."[38] He seems to claim that we should seek out places or situations which will elicit or foster painful sympathetic feelings, and he unquestionably claims that we are not to avoid such situations. Yet surely one such situation is that of the wise man: a situation in which his friend suffers, and he can do nothing to help him. Why, then, should the wise man be applauded for turning coldly away? If it is good not to avoid sickrooms and the like, since sickrooms elicit

37. I have altered the translation in three places, the first simply repeating the alteration noted in n. 25 above, and the second repeating the alteration explained in n. 36, above. The third translates *dem schmerzhaften Mitgefühl, dessen* as "the painful sympathetic feelings that" rather than as Gregor does: "sharing painful feelings." Once again, except for 'ästhetische', which Gregor inserted, all terms in square brackets are my insertions.

38. I say "apparently" because although he clearly is saying that there is a duty to seek out such places and that there is a duty not to shun sickrooms and debtors' prisons in order to avoid painful sympathetic feelings, he does not explicitly say that we are to seek them out *in order to* cultivate sympathetic impulses. But that seems to be the implication.

sympathetic impulses that we should cultivate, it would also be good not to cut oneself off from the sadness that one feels for the friend whom one cannot help. If Kant holds that there is a duty not to avoid sickrooms, and the like, in order to spare oneself the painful feelings of sympathy which a visit might elicit, why should he hold—or does he?—that it is good to repudiate imparted suffering? Why doesn't he hold that we should not wallow in it and should not let it paralyze us, and more generally should try not to be entirely passive with respect to it, but that we should use it to improve our characters and conduct?

There is at least an apparent inconsistency here. On the one hand, Kant seems to applaud the wise man for turning away and saying, "What is it to me?", thus putting up a guard against sympathetic feelings that the situation would otherwise elicit. Yet at the same time he claims that we should not avoid and, moreover, should seek out situations that elicit painful sympathetic feelings. I say "*seems* to applaud" for Kant may be applauding him only for his unselfish reasons for wanting a friend, and may be merely expressing approval for the "What is it to me?". But substituting 'approve of' (or even 'condone') for 'applaud' would not remove the appearance of inconsistency. (The degree of approbation Kant has for the 'What is it to me' attitude is unclear, so I will leave open whether 'applause' or 'approval' is more apt.)

How else might we resolve the problem? One might suggest that Kant's view is that we should seek out situations that will elicit or foster sympathetic feelings only if we think it likely that we can be helpful in those situations. But the passage quoted at length makes it plain that this is not his view. Rather, the idea is that because we have a duty to sympathize actively in the fate of others, we have a duty to cultivate our natural (aesthetic) feelings of sympathetic joy and sadness; and to cultivate the latter we are to put ourselves in situations that will foster painful sympathetic feelings. This can be rendered consistent with his approval for the wise man's stance in the following way: although we are to seek out such situations in order to cultivate our sympathetic feelings, there is no reason why we should, for the rest of our lives, place ourselves in such situations frequently, or even why, whenever we find ourselves in such situations, we should allow the feelings to affect us as much as possible. Notice that what we have a duty to cultivate are our *aesthetic* sympathetic feelings. As I understand it, we are first to help them to become more intense; we then turn them into "practical" feelings. We cultivate them; we do not suppress them. We do not put up a guard against them;

we allow them "access" and do not try to avoid situations in which they are likely to be elicited. But we keep them under control, quelling them, if possible, when they do no good and perhaps do harm. What we want to avoid is being in a state of emotional agitation. Thus Kant writes: "That the sage must never be in a state of emotional agitation, not even in that of sympathetic sorrow over his best friend's misfortune . . . is a quite correct and sublime moral principle of the Stoic school" (A 253).

In short, the inconsistency disappears if we understand Kant's approval for the wise man's stance to be approval for being ready and able to "turn off" his sadness if his sadness does no good. This renders his remarks consistent with the duty to participate actively in the fate of others and, to this end, to cultivate our sympathetic feelings (and even to seek out situations that will elicit such feelings). For Kant can hold both that we have a duty to cultivate these feelings and that we should take care that they not overpower us. We should cultivate them but keep them in check. If this is the idea, there is no reason to think that he believes that people who never feel sympathetic sadness (or grief) are, *caeteris paribus*, better than people who do, something which he cannot hold consistently with believing that there is a duty to cultivate (painful as well as joyful) sympathetic feelings.

If I am right, there is no reason to attribute to Kant the view that a person who lacks feelings of compassion is morally better than someone who has them, or even that someone who lacks them in the circumstances described in the passage at *MM* 457 is morally better than someone who, in those circumstances, has them. His approbation of the wise man's behavior is approbation for the wise man's (admittedly extreme) *control* of his feelings. Similarly, the remarks about the wise man provide no basis, in the final analysis, for claiming that Kant denies the importance of feelings of compassion. (Still, there are grounds for dissatisfaction with Kant's position, as I will elaborate shortly.)

My reading renders compatible claims that certainly should—especially given that they occur on the same page of the text—be compatible. It also fits nicely with the distinction drawn just before the remark about the Stoic, the distinction between *humanitas practica* and *humanitas aesthetica*: the latter is located in the mere susceptibility to feel joy and sadness in common with others and is unfree, while the former is located in the capacity and the will to share in others' feelings. The difference is that the former involves us as agents, while the latter does not. Kant sees no value in being passively "infected" by another's sadness, but actively sharing in their feelings is another matter. This point corresponds to the distinction in *Anthropology*, noted earlier, between sensitivity and sentimentality: "sensitivity is a *power* and *strength* by which we grant or refuse permission for the state of pleasure or displeasure to enter our mind"; sentimentality is "a *weakness* by which we can be affected, even against our will, by sympathy for another's plight." To "share ineffectually in others' feelings, to attune our feelings sympathetically to theirs and so let ourselves be affected in a merely passive way, is silly and childish" (*A* 236). The emphasis throughout is on agency and, more specifically, Stoical self-control. "When someone deliberately ruminates on a sorrow, as something that will end only with his life, we say that he is *brooding over it* (a misfortune). —But we must not brood over anything: what we cannot change we must drive from our mind, since it would be absurd to want to undo what has happened" (*A* 236).

We are now in a position to summarize, albeit incompletely, Kant's views regarding the value of sympathetic impulses and our duties concerning them:

1. We have no duty to act from sympathetic sadness.
2. We have a duty to sympathize actively with the fate of others and, to that end, to cultivate our sympathetic impulses. This entails seeking out situations that will elicit such feelings.
3. We must not suppose, however, that having such feelings is a substitute for doing something to help the suffering person, or even that when we cannot do anything to improve his situation, we somehow do some good simply by suffering with him. Our sympathetic suffering does him no good. We must resist the temptation to revel in sadness for him, and, in particular, to suppose that we help him by feeling grief or sadness for him or that we are better people if we suffer with him.
4. In cultivating our sympathetic impulses, what we cultivate should not be overwhelming feelings (agitations or passions) which impair agency or a tendency to catch, mindlessly, others' feelings, but feelings that are under our control.

At the start of 4.1, it was observed that Kant seems at times to deny the importance of sympathetic feelings altogether or, worse yet, to assert that it is better not to have them. It is now clear that he does not hold that it is better not to have them. Nor does he deny their importance altogether, though it might plausibly be argued (as Sec. 6 will suggest) that he does not fully recognize their importance.

5 If this—(1) through (4)—is Kant's view, some questions remain. What is the nature of the duty to cultivate our sympathetic or compassionate feelings? Why are we to cultivate them? What role or importance do they have, on Kant's view? To answer these questions, we need to take a closer look at the passage quoted above from *MM* 457, specifically the final sentence: "For this is still one of the impulses that nature has implanted in us to do what the representation of duty alone would not accomplish."

We know this much: the role of the sympathetic impulses is to do what the representation of duty alone would not accomplish. But *what* is it that duty alone would not accomplish? (Also: Under what circumstances would it fail to accomplish it?) Some commentators have read Kant as saying that duty will not suffice to motivate us—some of us, in some circumstances—and so nature has wisely supplied us with sympathetic impulses to boost our motivation to do what is right. On this reading, the 'it' that duty would not accomplish is adequate motivation.[39]

This interpretation admits of more than one variation, but it is unnecessary to enumerate the possibilities. The interpretation itself, in all its variations, is at odds with Kant's stern stance in *Religion* against "impurity" and, more fundamentally, with his conception of freedom.

The conflict is the one noted in Section 10 of Chapter 5. One thing that Kant is quite clear about is that we can do what is morally required simply because it is morally required. We do not need the assistance of inclinations, and to seek to utilize them to help us to do our duty would be to cultivate an impure will (*R* 29–30/25).

To appreciate the conflict (and along with it, some attendant problems), consider how we might, on the interpretation under consideration, utilize the sympathetic impulses. Here is one possibility: suppose that we do not care enough about morality to do what it requires (if what it

39. Henry Allison and Henning Jensen interpret Kant in roughly this way, though Allison's is a complex version of this interpretation. See Allison, *Kant's Theory of Freedom*, pp. 166–167; and Jensen, "Kant on Overdetermination, Indirect Duties, and Moral Worth," *Proceedings: Sixth International Kant Congress*, edited by G. Funke and Th. M. Seebohm (Washington, D.C.: Center for Advanced Research in Phenomenology; University Press of America, 1989), 161–170. See also Paul Guyer, *Kant and the Experience of Freedom*, chap. 10. I discuss Allison's interpretation in my "Freedom, Frailty, and Impurity," *Inquiry* 36 (1993): 431–441, and Allison replies in the same issue.

requires is hard for us to do). The sympathetic impulses can help. They can help by making us care more about what morality asks. Problem: there is no reason to assume that the sympathetic impulses will be on the side of morality. They might pull in the direction of helping a friend to cheat. So, although they might aid us in acting morally, they could instead make it harder to comply with what morality asks of us in this instance, or weaken our concern to do what morality in this instance demands.

One might object that this describes an agent who is not very committed to doing what morality asks and propose that we consider an agent who is very committed. *This* agent's problem is that despite her serious commitment, sometimes what morality asks is just too hard. The sympathetic impulses can help: she can enlist them to make it easier for her to do what she sees to be morally required. Now the problem mentioned in the previous paragraph can be avoided: this agent, let us suppose, takes care to utilize her sympathetic impulses only to do what morality requires. But there are two problems with this solution. First, it violates Kant's theory of freedom to suppose that she really cannot do what morality asks without the help of sympathetic impulses; and second (and closely related to the first point), to suggest that she make use of her sympathetic impulses to do what she sees to be morally required is to advocate "impurity": it is to advocate that she seek out nonmoral reasons for doing what she sees to be morally required.

This would seem to be an excellent reason for rejecting any reading that says that we need the sympathetic impulses to aid in motivating us to do what is morally required of us. On the other hand, the reading seems to fit what Kant says in *MM* 457 all too well![40] So what are we to do?

The first thing is to notice that there is more than one way in which the sympathetic impulses might aid in motivating us to do our duty. One way that cannot be what Kant has in mind is this: the sympathetic impulses join forces with the motive of duty so that their combined strength is more able to combat competing forces than is the motive of duty alone. This cannot be Kant's view since this is the wrong picture of human motivation, a picture that sees agents as passive subjects, batted about by

---

40. It also fits well with some of Kant's earlier works. See his *Observations on the Feeling of the Beautiful and the Sublime* 217/60–61, and *Praktische Philosophie Powalski* 227. See also a late work (1794): "The End of All Things" 338.

competing impulses. If there *is* some way that duty can use the help of sympathetic impulses, it is not by acquiring added "motive force" so that the combined force is greater than that of the (combined) opposing inclinations.[41]

How else might the sympathetic impulses help to motivate us? The answer will be obvious once we pay attention to the sort of duty that they are to help us to fulfill: *imperfect* duties (and, more specifically, the duty of love to others). Kant never suggests that our sympathetic impulses are to aid us with regard to perfect duties. They are, rather, to help us to do things that it is generally impossible, because of the nature of imperfect duties, to do from duty alone (for reasons elaborated in Chap. 5). I cannot from duty do my elderly and ailing neighbor's laundry, since it is not my duty to do her laundry (though doing her laundry falls under the heading of an imperfect duty). The role of the sympathetic feelings now clearly emerges: our sympathetic feelings help to prompt us to perform specific acts of helping others. They help to direct our interest and our attention to the needs of particular others and to ways we might help. One might plausibly add (although the text neither supports nor conflicts with this) that they provide us with a sensitivity that we would not otherwise have and that is needed for us to notice where help is needed.

This reading squares both with the text and with Kant's theory of freedom and agency. Our sympathetic impulses do indeed accomplish something that the representation of duty alone would not accomplish, but their role is not to "join forces" with another motive—duty—to "push" the agent to do what duty alone would not accomplish. Thus, Kant's assertion that we need these impulses is not in conflict with his position that we can do what is morally required of us from duty alone and should not seek out other reasons to do what is morally required. For this position applies to perfect duties, not, generally, to imperfect duties. With respect to imperfect duties, sympathetic impulses have an important role to play. They help us to have more than a merely notional sense that we ought to help others, and they draw our attention to human need and to ways in which we might help.

6 In the last two sections I offered an interpretation of *MM* 457 which renders Kant's recognition of a duty to cultivate sympathetic

---

41. I discuss this in my "Freedom, Frailty, and Impurity." See Henry Allison's reply in the same issue.

impulses consistent with his remarks about the wise man. It avoids attributing to him the view that it is better not to feel grief or sympathetic sadness, and it attributes to him a somewhat positive view of such feelings. But only somewhat positive, and herein lies the problem. The value that Kant attributes to sympathetic impulses does not capture their full value.

Two corrections to Kant's view are in order. First, the person who does not grieve for his dying friend seems to us to lack something, to be morally worse than the person who does—even supposing that the latter, like the former, has sympathetic feelings on those occasions where it is possible to do something to help, and even supposing that the grief needs to be moderated. Better to feel grief and need to moderate it than to feel no grief at all. Second, notice that I use the term 'moderate' here. Yet the picture Kant presents in his description of the wise man is not of someone who 'moderates' emotion, but of one who either does not have it or turns it off. Why should the idea be to turn it off—supposing that your grief is not helping, and threatens to harm—rather than merely moderate it? Why should the idea be to say 'What is it to me?' rather than try to take hold of yourself (so as to be able to carry on at least in a minimal fashion, buying groceries for you and your dependents, meeting your classes, or at least phoning to say that you cannot, remaining available to those who are dependent on you, or at least explaining to them why you cannot be available) and not be paralyzed by your emotion? Rather than reject or repudiate the emotion, as if a worthier person would not feel it at all, surely the idea should be simply to temper or moderate it.

These, I think, are the chief problems that remain. But it is important not to misconstrue or exaggerate the difficulty here. Without suggesting that the problems are trivial, I note a consideration that shows them to be less serious than they might seem.

That dreadful "What's it to me?" in the passage about the Stoic and the wise man might lead some to attribute the following view to Kant: although it may sometimes be appropriate to feel intense sadness over one's *own* calamities, it is not appropriate with respect to one's friend's calamities. "What's it to me?" sounds rather like "Hey, this is his problem, not mine; I'll worry about my own problems." Kant's view may thus seem to be that my friend's problems are his, not mine, and *therefore* are not anything that I should let myself weep over. But the relevant fact for Kant is not that these are our friend's woes rather than our woes, but rather that *there is nothing that we can do about the problem*. He affirms (with some qualifications, as noted below) the Stoic view that what we cannot change we should not allow to trouble us. "The wretched man is he who thinks himself so" (*LE* 146).[42]

I emphasize this because part of what is troubling about that 'What's it to me?' is that it seems to suggest a view according to which it is appropriate to see others' troubles as *their* troubles, and to sharply distinguish between my woes and theirs, and between my well-being and theirs. Kant may thus seem to be endorsing an attitude of indifference toward others' woes and, more generally, a very individualistic, self-centered attitude. That this is far from the truth is clear not only from the points just made about the unfortunate remark but, more important, from our duty to promote others' happiness. This is not a duty simply to do good deeds from time to time; it is a duty to "make others' ends my own (provided only that these are not immoral)" (*MM* 450).[43] It is "a universal duty of people, just because they are to be considered fellow humans, that is, rational beings with needs, united by nature in one dwelling place so that they can help one another" (*MM* 453).[44] Kant affirms what he calls "the principle of sympathy" (as "expressed by Terence's honest Chremes"): "'I am a man; whatever befalls man concerns me too'" (*MM* 460).

Nonetheless, the problems remain, even if they are not quite as serious as is often supposed. It may help to understand Kant's tough stand if we view it in relation to the Stoic position.

7   The passage that has been the focus of much of this chapter seems clearly to refer to a specific Stoic text, though Kant does not cite the text or name the author. Which Stoic does Kant have in mind when he says, "It was a sublime way of thinking that the Stoic ascribed to his wise man when he had him say . . ."? I believe it is Seneca.[45] In Epistle IX, "On Philosophy and Friendship," Seneca takes issue with Epicurus:

42. See also *CJ* 178n.

43. I omitted Kant's underlining of the word 'ends'.

44. I have altered Gregor's translation, translating *Menschen* as 'people' rather than as 'men' and *Mitmenschen* as 'fellow humans' rather than as 'fellow men'. As I mentioned in my "Abbreviations, Sources, and Translations," *Menschen*, unlike 'men', is gender-neutral. In many passages there is nonetheless reason to believe that Kant had only men in mind when he used *Menschen*, but I see no reason for thinking that is the case in this passage.

45. The similarity between *MM* 457 and Seneca's Epistle IX is itself very strong evidence. In addition, we have it from Kant's biographer, R. B. Jachmann, that Kant studied Seneca with great interest. Reinhold B. Jachmann, "Immanuel Kant geschildert in Briefen an einen Freund," in *Wer War Kant? Drei zeitgenössische Biographien von Borowski, Jachmann, und Wasianski*, ed. Siegfried Drescher (Pfüllingen, 1974).

The wise man . . . , self-sufficient though he be, nevertheless desires friends. . . . Not, however, for the purpose mentioned by Epicurus in the letter quoted above: "That there may be someone to sit by him when he is ill, to help him when he is in prison or in want"; but that he may have someone by whose sick-bed he himself may sit, someone a prisoner in hostile hands whom he himself may set free.[46]

Unfortunately, there is to my knowledge nothing that as closely resembles the rest of the passage at *MM* 457. But Seneca's remarks on pity in *De Clementia* are strongly suggestive:

All else which I would have those who feel pity do, he [the wise man] will do gladly and with a lofty spirit; he will bring relief to another's tears, but will not add his own; to the shipwrecked man he will give a hand, to the exile shelter, to the needy alms; he will not do as most of those who wish to be thought pitiful do—fling insultingly their alms, and scorn those whom they help, and shrink from contact with them—but he will give as a man to his fellow-man out of the common store; . . . he will release the gladiator from his training, he will bury the carcass even of a criminal, but he will do these things with unruffled mind, and a countenance under control. The wise man, therefore, will not pity, but will succour, will benefit.[47]

Pity is akin to wretchedness. . . . One knows that his eyes are weak if they too are suffused at the sight of another's blear eyes, just as always to laugh when other people laugh is . . . not merriment, but a disease, and for one to stretch his jaws too when everybody else yawns is a disease. Pity is a weakness of the mind that is over-much perturbed by suffering.[48]

The similarity between Kant and Seneca on pity is striking. Both suspect that the person who pities regards himself as superior to the person he pities. They contrast the person who feels pity to the person who helps "his fellow-man out of the common store," as Seneca puts it. (Cf. *MM* 473.) Both find something self-indulgent and self-serving in intense sadness for another. Seneca: "Do you wish to know the reason for lamentations and excessive weeping? It is because we seek the proofs of our bereavement in our tears, and do not give way to sorrow, but

46. Seneca, Epistle IX, "On Philosophy and Friendship," in his *Epistulae Morales*, vol. 1, trans. Richard M. Gummere (London: William Heinemann and Harvard University Press, 1970), p. 47.

47. Seneca, *De Clementia* II.vi.2–3. In Seneca, *Moral Essays*, vol. 1, trans. John W. Basore (London: William Heinemann; Loeb Classical Library, 1928), pp. 441–443.

48. Ibid., II.vi.4, p. 443.

merely parade it. . . . There is an element of self-seeking even in our sorrow" (Epistle LXIII, p. 431). Without pointedly suggesting that the sorrow is feigned, Kant suspects that many people content themselves with feeling sad for another. Priding themselves on their noble and intense feelings, they do nothing to help. (See the quotes in Sec. 4.1, above, from *LE* and *E*.)

But beyond these similarities lie some sharp differences regarding the value of affect.[49] The points of convergence and divergence emerge more clearly if we situate Seneca's view in relation to Aristotle's.

In sharp contrast to Aristotle, Seneca emphasizes that emotion is not required for virtuous conduct. The virtuous person does not need the emotion of pity to move him to help another.[50] The virtuous person who lacks pity will take action to help, no less than the person who feels pity. But, we may ask, will he do so grudgingly? No, according to Seneca; he will help "with a lofty spirit." Kant partly agrees and partly disagrees. True, one can act from duty alone; emotion is not required to do what morality demands. Still, our sympathetic impulses are there for a reason. Not only is our predisposition to them a prerequisite for being affected by concepts of duty; cultivation of them is obligatory since sympathetic impulses, properly cultivated, are crucial aids for fulfilling our duties of virtue.

Unlike Seneca, Kant sees value in our sympathetic impulses. He departs from Seneca in believing that we should cultivate them; moreover, he departs from Seneca in that he distinguishes *humanitas practica* from what they agree is *not* admirable and asserts that there is an obligation to *humanitas practica*. Sharing in others' feelings is not something to be eschewed, on Kant's view, but passively allowing oneself to "catch," willy-nilly, all the emotions and moods of one's companion's, is. (In this he is surely right. Why passively allow oneself to catch a companion's depression, rancor, or envy?)

Kant's distinction (and the parallel distinction between the practical and the pathological) allows him to agree with Seneca and other Stoics

---

49 As well as other differences, some of which are elaborated in Michael J. Seidler, "Kant and the Stoics on Suicide," *Journal of the History of Ideas* 44 (1983): 429–453. Moreover, we know from Kant's various critical remarks concerning Stoicism that he by no means buys into it. See, e.g., *PrR* 126–127 and *Lectures on Philosophical Theology* 103.

50. Seneca makes a similar point in *De Ira* regarding anger. For an excellent discussion of the Stoics on emotion and their disagreement with Aristotle, see Julia Annas's *The Morality of Happiness* (New York: Oxford University Press, 1993).

up to a point, while holding that affect does not only take the form in which, they agree, it is *not* admirable. To the extent that they spread like yawns, to the extent that we let them wash over us and make no attempt ever to check or moderate them, emotions and feelings are nothing to admire or be proud of. (Kant and the Stoics liken them, thus understood, to diseases; moods would seem to be a more apt comparison.) But that is not the only form that many emotions and feelings take, as Kant sees it; certainly it is not the only form that feelings of compassion take. (Recall Kant's distinction between passions and other affects, and his claim in *Religion* that the Stoics "mistook their enemy: for he is not to be sought in the merely undisciplined natural inclinations" [R 57/50].)

A wise man, on Seneca's view, is inaccessible to sadness. "Nothing ... so much befits a man as superiority of mind; but the mind cannot at the same time be superior and sad. Sorrow blunts its powers, dissipates and hampers them; this will not happen to a wise man ...; he will maintain always the same calm, unshaken appearance, and he could not do this if he were accessible to sadness."[51] Kant denies this, holding instead that the wise man is accessible to sadness but turns it off under certain conditions.[52]

The chief similarities between Kant and the Stoics are the emphasis placed on helping rather than on feeling sad for the person in need and the value placed on self-control. But the second similarity is somewhat superficial, for they understand self-control differently. While the Stoics favor extirpation of most affects, Kant favors cultivation and taming.[53] (Recall R 58/51, quoted above in Sec. 3.) This is a very substantial disagreement. Kant favors cultivation and taming partly because he thinks it is impossible to extirpate them, but not only for this reason.

51. *De Clementia* II.v.4–5, p. 441.

52. The suggestion at *MM* 457 is that these conditions include any time when the sadness is unhelpful because the agent can do nothing to help the person in need. However, the *Lectures on Ethics* indicate circumstances where, even if one cannot help, emotion akin to sorrow is decidedly appropriate: "With regard to all the ills in the world man ought to show himself steady, resolute and calm of mind; but not so in regard to wickedness; only a profligate mind and an infamous character can remain calm and composed in the face of wickedness, for such an attitude merely intensifies the evil; wicked acts ought rather to be accompanied by a consciousness of spiritual pain" (*LE* 144–145).

53. The Stoics favored extirpation of most but not all emotional states; those to be extirpated are the *pathé*. The virtuous person will have the emotional states called *eupatheiai*; these consist of joy, caution, and wishing. For a detailed discussion, see Annas, *The Morality of Happiness* and chap. 5 of her *Hellenistic Philosophy of Mind* (Berkeley: University of California Press, 1992).

Properly cultivated, some affects are crucial for virtuous conduct (and, less significantly, some agitations are, in moderation, important for our health). Interestingly, Kant is in this respect closer to Aristotle than to the Stoics (though of course affect plays a much larger role in Aristotle's picture of virtue than in Kant's).[54]

It is illuminating to read Kant on affect and its role in virtuous conduct as charting his own view by reference to other dominant views, principally, the romanticism of his time and Stoicism. While he indicates his differences from the Stoics, he still seems to take a Stoic approach to the value of affect as his starting point. Perhaps this is one reason why his stand on affect is as stern as it is. Despite his differences with them, he repeatedly cites Stoicism approvingly (often, as in *MM* 457, without naming a particular Stoic). Part of the point is to repudiate in no uncertain terms the tendency in his time to celebrate intense feeling for its own sake, not only when it did no good, but even when it did harm. In his zeal to distance himself from romanticism, he aligns himself with the Stoics more than he should and more than his theory would seem to mandate, differing from them on some points, yet retaining too restrictive a view of the value of affect.[55]

54. The differences between Aristotle and Kant are often exaggerated, and the fact that Aristotle, like Kant, thought that emotion should be carefully modulated and controlled is sometimes neglected. Recall, for example, that in discussing mildness, the mean concerned with anger, Aristotle says that "being a mild person means being undisturbed, not led by feeling, but irritated at whatever reason prescribes and for the length of time it prescribes." *Nicomachean Ethics* 1125b 33–35, trans. Terence Irwin (Hackett, 1985), p. 105.

55. I was aided in writing this last section by some work in progress that Nancy Sherman shared with me: a discussion of the Stoics in her book manuscript, tentatively titled *Making a Necessity of Virtue: Aristotelian and Kantian Virtue*.

Conclusion

In Part I of this work I challenged the claim that a theory that is unable to recognize a category of supererogatory acts is necessarily defective. It is important to contemporary ethics, as well as to a fair appraisal of Kant's ethics, to see that there is more than one way for a moral theory to avoid demanding that one do as much, morally, at all times as one possibly can.

Contrasting Kant's approach to the supererogationist approach throws into relief disagreements in ethics which, because they have no names, are rarely discussed directly. These include disagreements concerning the nature of duty, the relationship between freedom and moral constraint, the nature of moral excellence—whether there is a morally best type of character or, instead, a variety of very good character types that it is futile to try to rank—whether we have a duty to improve our characters, and related matters. One's assessment of the Kantian approach to what are standardly classified as supererogatory acts will depend on one's views about these matters. In any case there is no warrant for assuming that a theory with a very broad conception of duty, too broad to allow room for the supererogatory, is therefore defective. One must ask first whether it can avoid the twin perils of demanding too much, on the one hand, and, on the other, offering too little by putting forth nothing but a list of what Urmson calls "basic duties." Kant's ethics steers clear of both since it neither demands that one do as much good as one possibly can at all times nor limits morality to minimal duties.

In Part II, I sought first to defend acting from duty against objections to the effect that to act from duty is to act only minimally morally, and that acting from duty tends to alienate one from others or to express alienation from, or lack of affection for, others. I granted that acting from duty can indeed be construed in a way that warrants these objections and that a moral theory that places great value on performing actions from duty alone gives rise to such worries. Kant's ethics is usually regarded as precisely such a theory. Against this I argued that the value that he places on acting from duty attaches primarily to duty operating as a "secondary motive"—to one's conduct being governed by a commitment to doing what one morally ought to do—and not to individual actions being done from, or prompted by, duty.

The final chapter examined Kant's ethics where it is, I think, vulnerable to criticism: its treatment of affect. Even here, however, the weaknesses tend to be exaggerated and the subtlety of Kant's position overlooked. The problem is not that he supposes that we cannot be responsible for our emotions, or that it is morally irrelevant whether we feel compassion or scorn; neither is his view.[1] The problem, rather, is that he locates the value of compassion or sympathetic suffering primarily in its tendency to help us to act morally and seems to hold that if the feeling is painful and does no good, we do well to turn it off, insofar as that is possible. Although this certainly seems to me to accord too little value to sentiments, it is difficult to judge how serious a criticism this is. As some of my students observed when we discussed this issue in class, our view that one ought to feel sympathetic sadness and ought not try to turn it off if it does no good is a reflection of current cultural (and philosophical) fashion. There is a sort of cultural bias in the claim that Kant's theory is flawed because it does not accord to such sentiments the value that we believe them to have. I take this point seriously, more seriously than I take many claims of cultural bias. As a point of contrast: our judgment that Kant's theory is flawed insofar as it fails to regard women as full-fledged moral agents does not, it seems to me, reflect a cultural bias.[2] In so regarding women we clearly have made progress. But in our judgment that it is

1. Nor is it the case that, for Kant, love and friendship "lie outside of morality." Martha Nussbaum claims that they do in chap. 1 of her *Love's Knowledge: Essays on Philosophy and Literature* (New York: Oxford University Press, 1990), p. 50

2. It should be borne in mind that it may be appropriate to criticize a theory for its view of (e.g.) women even if it is not appropriate to regard the author of the theory as blameworthy. One needn't hold that Kant should have known better; whether or not he should have is a separate issue. For an interesting discussion of responsibility for morally outrageous views, see Michelle Moody-Adams, "Culture, Responsibility, and Affected Ignorance," *Ethics* 104 (1994): 291–309.

better not to turn off sympathetic sadness (though it is good to moderate it) have we "advanced" beyond those who in another era denied this or felt unsure about the matter or simply did not think the matter an important one? About that I am far less certain, and thus my criticism of Kant on this score is somewhat tentative.

Not long after drafting the above paragraph I received a letter (dated May 9, 1994) which leaves me yet more tentative in my criticism of Kant. Commenting on my Chapter 6, Susan Mendus indicates that she does not altogether agree with my claim that there is something wrong if a person is never awash with emotion and with my assessment that Kant allies himself too closely to the Stoics. "In Britain (home of the "stiff upper lip"!) it is very important not to be awash with emotion, and people are often spoken of approvingly if, in times of bereavement, for example, they 'keep control'. Equally, it is thought to be weak and wrong to 'give way'—however desperate the situation." I am not sure just how close this is to Kant's view, though certainly it is closer than the view I endorsed in my criticism of Kant. One might endorse the "British" view while holding that it is better to feel grief and need to moderate it than to feel no sadness at all over the loss of a loved one, and that moderating one's emotions is more appropriate (and not merely more attainable) than turning them off. So there might still be room within the "British" view for criticism of Kant's position. But in any case, Mendus's remarks are a reminder of the need to be cautious before criticizing Kant's ethics for taking a different stand on the value of sympathetic suffering from the one that we (whoever "we" are) take.

Selected Bibliography

◈◈◈

Adams, R. M. "Saints." *Journal of Philosophy* 81 (1984): 392–401.

Allison, Henry. "Justification and Freedom in the *Critique of Practical Reason.*" In *Kant's Transcendental Deductions*, edited by Eckart Förster, pp. 114–130. Stanford: Stanford University Press, 1989.

——. "Kant on Freedom: A Reply to my Critics." *Inquiry* 36 (1993): 443–464.

——. *Kant's Theory of Freedom.* Cambridge: Cambridge University Press, 1990.

——. "Morality and Freedom: Kant's Reciprocity Thesis." *Philosophical Review* 95 (July 1986): 393–425.

Ameriks, Karl. "The Hegelian Critique of Kantian Morality." In *New Essays on Kant*, edited by Bernard den Ouden and Marcia Moen, pp. 179–212. New York: Peter Lang, 1987.

——. "Kant on the Good Will." In *"Grundlegung zur Metaphysik der Sitten": Ein Kooperativer Kommentar*, edited by Otfried Höffe, pp. 45–65. Frankfurt: Vittorio Klostermann, 1989.

Anderson-Gold, Sharon. "Kant's Ethical Commonwealth: The Highest Good as a Social Goal." *International Philosophical Quarterly* 26 (March 1986): 23–32.

——. "Kant's Rejection of Devilishness: The Limits of Human Volition." *Idealistic Studies* 14 (1984): 35–48.

Annas, Julia. "Ancient Ethics and Modern Morality." In *Philosophical Perspectives* 6, edited by James E. Tomberlin, pp. 119–136. Atascadero, California: Ridgeview, 1992.

——. *Hellenistic Philosophy of Mind.* Berkeley: University of California Press, 1991.

——. *The Morality of Happiness.* London: Oxford University Press, 1993.

——. "Personal Love and Kantian Ethics in *Effi Briest.*" *Philosophy and Literature* 8 (1984): 15–31. Reprinted in *Friendship: A Philosophical Reader*, edited by Neera Kapur Badhwar. Ithaca: Cornell University Press, 1993.

Anscombe, Elizabeth. "Modern Moral Philosophy." *Philosophy* 33 (1958): 1–19. Reprinted in her *Ethics, Religion, and Politics*. Minneapolis: University of Minnesota Press, 1981.

Arendt, Hannah. *Eichmann in Jerusalem: A Report on the Banality of Evil.* Rev. and enl. ed. New York: Penguin, 1994.

Aristotle. *Nicomachean Ethics.* Translated by Terence Irwin. Indianapolis: Hackett, 1985.

Atwell, John E. *Ends and Principles in Kant's Moral Thought.* Dordrecht: Nijhoff, 1986.

Auxter, Thomas. *Kant's Moral Teleology.* Macon, Ga.: Mercer University Press, 1982.

Badhwar, Neera K. "Friendship, Justice, and Supererogation." *American Philosophical Quarterly* 22 (1985): 123–132.

——, ed. *Friendship: A Philosophical Reader.* Ithaca: Cornell University Press, 1993.

Baier, Annette. "The Need for More than Justice." In *Science, Morality, and Feminist Theory,* edited by Marsha Hanen and Kai Nielsen, pp. 41–56. Calgary: University of Calgary Press, 1987.

——. "Trust and Anti-Trust." *Ethics* 96 (1986): 231–260.

Baker, Judith. "Do One's Motives Have to Be Pure?" In *Philosophical Grounds of Rationality,* edited by Richard Grandy and Richard Warner, pp. 457–473. London: Oxford University Press, 1986.

Baron, Marcia. "The Alleged Moral Repugnance of Acting from Duty." *Journal of Philosophy* 81 (1984): 197–220.

——. "The Ethics of Duty/Ethics of Virtue Debate and Its Relevance to Educational Theory." *Educational Theory* 35 (1985): 135–149.

——. "Freedom, Frailty, and Impurity." *Inquiry* 36 (1993): 431–441.

——. "Impartiality and Friendship." *Ethics* 101 (1991): 836–857.

——. "Kantian Ethics and Supererogation." *Journal of Philosophy* 84 (1987): 237–262.

——. "Morality as a Back-Up System: Hume's View?" *Hume Studies* 14 (1988): 25–52.

——. "Patriotism and 'Liberal' Morality." In *Mind, Value, and Culture: Essays in Honor of E. M. Adams,* edited by David Weissbord, 269–300. Atascadero, Calif.: Ridgeview, 1989.

——. "Remorse and Agent-Regret." *Midwest Studies in Philosophy* 13 (1988): 259–281.

——. "Was Effi Briest a Victim of Kantian Morality?" *Philosophy and Literature* 12 (1988): 95–113. Reprinted in *Friendship: A Philosophical Reader,* edited by Neera K. Badhwar. Ithaca: Cornell University Press, 1993.

Beck, Lewis White. *A Commentary on Kant's "Critique of Practical Reason."* Chicago: University of Chicago Press, 1960.

——. "Sir David Ross on Duty and Purpose in Kant." *Philosophy and Phenomenological Research* 16 (1955): 98–107.

Becker, Lawrence C. "The Neglect of Virtue." *Ethics* 85 (1975): 110–122.

——. *Reciprocity.* New York: Routledge and Kegan Paul, 1986.

Bennett, Jonathan. "The Conscience of Huckleberry Finn." *Philosophy* 69 (1974): 123–134.

Benson, Paul. "Moral Worth." *Philosophical Studies* 51 (1987): 365–382.

Blum, Lawrence. "Compassion." In *Explaining Emotions,* edited by Amélie

Oksenberg Rorty, pp. 507–518. Berkeley: University of California Press, 1980.

——. *Friendship, Altruism, and Morality*. Boston: Routledge and Kegan Paul, 1980.

——. "Iris Murdoch and the Domain of the Moral." *Philosophical Studies* 50 (1986): 343–367.

——. "Particularity and Responsiveness." In *The Emergence of Morality in Young Children*, edited by Jerome Kagan and Sharon Lamb, 306–337. Chicago: University of Chicago Press, 1987.

Brink, David. "Utilitarian Morality and the Personal Point of View." *Journal of Philosophy* 83 (1986): 417–438.

Buchanan, Allen. "Categorical Imperatives and Moral Principles." *Philosophical Studies* 31 (1977): 249–260.

Burchill, Lorenne M. "In Defense of Saints and Heroes." *Philosophy* 40 (1965): 152–157.

Calhoun, Cheshire. "Justice, Care, Gender Bias." *Journal of Philosophy* 85 (1988): 451–463.

Campbell, John. "Kantian Conceptions of Moral Goodness." *Canadian Journal of Philosophy* 13 (1983): 527–550.

Card, Claudia. "On Mercy." *Philosophical Review* 81 (1972): 182–207.

Care, Norman. "Career Choices." *Ethics* 94 (1984): 283–302. Reprinted in Care, *Sharing Fate*. Philadelphia: Temple University Press, 1987.

Cartwright, David. "Kant's View of the Moral Significance of Kindhearted Emotions and the Moral Insignificance of Kant's View." *Journal of Value Inquiry* 21 (1987): 291–304.

Chisholm, Roderick. "Supererogation and Offense: A Conceptual Scheme for Ethics." *Ratio* 5 (1963): 1–14.

Chopra, Yogendra. "Professor Urmson on Saints and Heroes." *Philosophy* 38 (1963): 160–166.

Clark, Michael. "The Meritorious and the Mandatory." *Proceedings of the Aristotelian Society*, n.s., 79 (1978/79): 23–33.

Code, Lorraine. *What Can She Know? Feminist Theory and the Construction of Knowledge*. Ithaca: Cornell University Press, 1991.

Cole, Eve Browning, and Susan Coultrap-McQuin, eds. *Explorations in Feminist Ethics*. Bloomington: Indiana University Press, 1992.

Conly, Sarah. "Flourishing and the Failure of the Ethics of Virtue." *Midwest Studies in Philosophy* 13 (1988): 83–96.

——. "The Objectivity of Morals and the Subjectivity of Agents." *American Philosophical Quarterly* 22 (1985): 275–286.

——. "Utilitarianism and Integrity." *Monist* 66 (1983): 298–311.

Davidson, Arnold. "Is Rawls a Kantian?" *Pacific Philosophical Quarterly* 66 (1985): 48–77.

Dillon, Robin S. "Respect and Care: Toward Moral Integration." *Canadian Journal of Philosophy* 22 (1992): 105–132.

Driver, Julia. "The Virtues of Ignorance." *Journal of Philosophy* 86 (1989): 373–384.

Duff, Anthony. "Desire, Duty, and Moral Absolutes." *Philosophy* 55 (1980): 223–238.

Eisenberg, Paul. "Basic Ethical Categories of Kant's *Tugendlehre*." *American Philo-*

sophical Quarterly 3 (1966): 255–269.

Engstrom, Stephen. "Conditioned Autonomy." *Philosophy and Phenomenological Research* 48 (1988): 435–453.

——. "Herman on Mutual Aid." *Ethics* 96 (1986): 346–349.

Epictetus. *Handbook.* Translated by Nicholas P. White. Indianapolis: Hackett, 1983.

Esheté, Andreas. "Character, Virtue, and Freedom." *Philosophy* 57 (1982): 495–513.

Falk, W. D. *Ought, Reasons, and Morality.* Ithaca: Cornell University Press, 1986.

Feinberg, Joel. *Doing and Deserving: Essays in the Theory of Responsibility.* Princeton: Princeton University Press, 1970.

——, ed. *Moral Concepts.* London: Oxford University Press, 1969.

Fishkin, James S. *The Limits of Obligation.* New Haven: Yale University Press, 1982.

Flanagan, Owen. "Admirable Immorality and Admirable Imperfection." *Journal of Philosophy* 83 (1986): 41–60.

Flanagan, Owen, and Amélie Oksenberg Rorty, eds. *Identity, Character, and Morality: Essays in Moral Psychology.* Cambridge: MIT Press, 1990.

Fleming, Arthur. "Reviving the Virtues." *Ethics* 40 (July 1980): 587–595.

Fontane, Theodor. *Effi Briest.* Translated by Douglas Parme. London: Penguin Classics, 1967.

Foot, Philippa. *Virtues and Vices and Other Essays in Moral Philosophy.* New York: Basil Blackwell, 1978.

Frankena, William K. "Beneficence/Benevolence." *Social Philosophy and Policy* 4 (1987): 1–20.

——. "Beneficence in an Ethics of Virtue." In *Beneficence and Health Care,* edited by Earl E. Shelp, 63–81. Dordrecht: D. Reidel Publishing, 1982.

——. "Moral Decency." Unpublished manuscript.

——. "Prichard and the Ethics of Virtue: Notes on a Footnote." *Monist* 54 (January 1970): 1–17.

——. *Three Historical Philosophies of Education: Aristotle, Kant, Dewey.* Glenview, Ill.: Scott, Foresman, 1965.

Fried, Charles. *An Anatomy of Values.* Cambridge: Cambridge University Press, 1980.

Friedman, Marilyn. *What Are Friends For? Feminist Perspectives on Personal Relationships and Moral Theory.* Ithaca: Cornell University Press, 1993.

Galvin, Richard. "Does Kant's Psychology of Morality Need Basic Revision?" *Mind* 100 (April 1991): 221–236.

Gilligan, Carol. *In a Different Voice: Psychological Theory and Women's Development.* Cambridge: Harvard University Press, 1982.

Graham, George, and Hugh LaFollette, eds. *Person to Person.* Philadelphia: Temple University Press, 1989.

Grandy, Richard, and Richard Warner, eds. *Philosophical Grounds of Rationality.* London: Oxford University Press, 1986.

Gregor, Mary. *Laws of Freedom: A Study of Kant's Method of Applying the Categorical Imperative in the "Metaphysik der Sitten".* Oxford: Basil Blackwell, 1963.

——. Translator's introduction to "On Philosophers' Medicine of the Body," by Immanuel Kant. In *Kant's Latin Writings,* edited by Lewis White Beck, pp. 217–227. New York: Peter Lang, 1986.

——. Translator's introduction to *The Metaphysics of Morals*, by Immanuel Kant. Cambridge: Cambridge University Press, 1991.

Grimshaw, Jean. *Philosophy and Feminist Thinking*. Minneapolis: University of Minnesota Press, 1986.

Guyer, Paul. *Kant and the Experience of Freedom: Essays on Aesthetics and Morality*. Cambridge: Cambridge University Press, 1993.

Hallie, Philip. *Lest Innocent Blood Be Shed*. New York: Harper Torchbooks, 1985.

Hampshire, Stuart. *Public and Private Morality*. Cambridge: Cambridge University Press, 1978.

Hardwig, John. "In Search of an Ethics of Personal Relationships." In *Person to Person*, edited by George Graham and Hugh LaFollette, pp. 63–81. Philadelphia: Temple University Press, 1989.

Henson, Richard. "What Kant Might Have Said: Moral Worth and the Overdetermination of Dutiful Action." *Philosophical Review* 88 (1979): 39–54.

Herman, Barbara. "Integrity and Impartiality." *Monist* 66 (1983): 233–250.

——. "On the Value of Acting from the Motive of Duty." *Philosophical Review* 66 (1981): 359–382.

——. *The Practice of Moral Judgment*. Cambridge: Harvard University Press, 1993.

Heyd, David. *Supererogation: Its Status in Ethical Theory*. Cambridge: Cambridge University Press, 1982.

Hill, Thomas E. Jr. *Autonomy and Self-Respect*. Cambridge: Cambridge University Press, 1991.

——. *Dignity and Practical Reason in Kant's Moral Theory*. Ithaca: Cornell University Press, 1992.

Hinman, Lawrence M. "On the Purity of Our Moral Motives: A Critique of Kant's Account of the Emotions and Acting for the Sake of Duty." *Monist* 66 (1983): 251–267.

Höffe, Otfried, ed. *"Grundlegung zur Metaphysik der Sitten": Ein Kooperativer Kommentar*. Frankfurt: Vittorio Klostermann, 1989.

Hume, David. *Enquiries concerning the Human Understanding and concerning the Principles of Morals*. Edited by L. A. Selby-Bigge. 3d ed. revised by P. H. Nidditch. Oxford: Clarendon Press, 1975.

——. *A Treatise of Human Nature*. Edited by L. A. Selby-Bigge. 2d edition with text revised and variant readings by P. H. Nidditch. Oxford: Clarendon Press, 1978.

Hunt, Lester H. "Generosity." *American Philosophical Quarterly* 12 (1975): 235–244.

Jachmann, Reinhold B. "Immanuel Kant geschildert in Briefen an einen Freund." In *Wer War Kant? Drei zeitgenössische Biographien von Borowski, Jachmann, und Wasianski*, edited by Siegfried Drescher. Pfüllingen, 1974.

Jensen, Henning. "Kant and Moral Integrity." *Philosophical Studies* 57 (1989): 193–205.

——. "Kant on Overdetermination, Indirect Duties, and Moral Worth." In *Proceedings: Sixth International Kant Congress*, edited by G. Funke and Th. M. Seebohm, 161–170. Washington, D.C.: Center for Advanced Research in Phenomenology: University Press of America, 1989.

Kalin, Jesse. "Lies, Secrets, and Love: The Inadequacy of Contemporary Moral Philosophy." *Journal of Value Inquiry* 10 (1976): 253–265.

Kekes, John. "Moral Sensitivity." *Philosophy* 59 (1984): 3–21.

Kerferd, G. B., and Walford, D. E., eds. *Kant: Selected Pre-Critical Writings and Correspondence with Beck.* Manchester: Manchester University Press, 1968.

Kersting, Wolfgang. "Das Starke Gesetz der Schuldigkeit und das Schwächere der Gütigkeit." *Studia Leibnitiana* 14 (1982): 184–220.

Kim, Scott. "Morality, Identity, and Happiness: An Essay on the Kantian Moral Life." Ph.D. diss., University of Chicago, 1993.

Kittay, Eve, and Diane Meyers, eds. *Women and Moral Theory.* Totowa, N.J.: Rowman and Littlefield, 1987.

Kleinig, John. "Mercy and Justice." *Philosophy* 44 (1969): 341–342.

Korsgaard, Christine. "From Duty and for the Sake of the Noble: Kant and Aristotle on Morally Good Action." In *Aristotle, Kant and the Stoics: Rethinking Happiness and Duty*, edited by Jennifer Whiting and Stephen Engstrom. Cambridge: Cambridge University Press, forthcoming.

——. "Kant." In *Ethics in the History of Philosophy*, edited by Robert J. Cavalier, James Gouinlock, and James P. Sterba, pp. 201–243. New York: St. Martin's Press, 1989.

——. "Kant's Analysis of Obligation: The Argument of *Foundations I.*" *Monist* 72 (1989): 311–340.

——. "Kant's Formula of Humanity." *Kant-Studien* 77 (1986): 183–202.

——. "Kant's Formula of Universal Law." *Pacific Philosophical Quarterly* 66 (1985): 24–47.

——. "Morality as Freedom." In *Kant's Practical Philosophy Reconsidered: Papers Presented at the Seventh Jerusalem Philosophical Encounter*, edited by Yirmiahu Yovel, pp. 23–47. Dordrecht: Kluwer Academic, 1989.

——. "Two Distinctions in Goodness." *Philosophical Review* 92 (1983): 169–195.

Kruschwitz, Robert, and Robert Roberts, eds. *The Virtues: Contemporary Essays on Moral Character.* Belmont, Calif.: Wadsworth, 1987.

Kupperman, Joel. *Character.* New York: Oxford University Press, 1991.

——. "Character and Ethical Theory." *Midwest Studies in Philosophy* 13 (1988): 115–125.

Langton, Rae. "Duty and Desolation." *Philosophy* 67 (1992): 481–505.

Louden, Robert. "Can We Be Too Moral?" *Ethics* 98 (1988): 361–378.

——. "Kant's Virtue Ethics." *Philosophy* 61 (1986): 473–489.

——. *Morality and Moral Theory: A Reappraisal and Reaffirmation.* New York: Oxford University Press, 1992.

MacIntyre, Alasdair. *After Virtue*, 2d ed. Notre Dame: University of Notre Dame Press, 1984.

——. "Is Patriotism a Virtue?" Lawrence: University of Kansas Philosophy Department, 1984.

——. *A Short History of Ethics.* New York: MacMillan, 1966.

——. *Whose Justice? Which Rationality?* Notre Dame: University of Notre Dame Press, 1988.

McCarty, Richard. "The Limits of Kantian Duty, and Beyond." *American Philosophi-*

cal Quarterly 26 (1989): 43–52.

McDowell, John. "Virtue and Reason." *Monist* 62 (1979): 331–350.

McFall, Lynne. "Integrity." *Ethics* 98 (October 1987): 5–20.

McGoldrick, Patricia. "Saints and Heroes: A Plea for the Supererogatory." *Philosophy* 59 (1984): 523–528.

Mellema, Gregory. *Beyond the Call of Duty: Supererogation, Obligation, and Offence*. Albany: State University of New York Press, 1991.

Mendus, Susan. "The Practical and the Pathological." *Journal of Value Inquiry* 19 (1985): 235–243.

Mill, John Stuart. *Utilitarianism*. Indianapolis: Hackett, 1979.

Miller, Arthur. *The Crucible*. New York: Viking Press, 1953.

Montague, Phillip. "Acts, Agents, and Supererogation." *American Philosophical Quarterly* 26 (1989): 101–111.

Moody-Adams, Michelle. "Culture, Responsibility, and Affected Ignorance." *Ethics* 104 (1994): 291–309.

Moravcsik, J. M. E. "On What We Aim At and How We Live." In *The Greeks and the Good Life*, edited by David Depew, pp. 198–235. Indianapolis: Hackett, 1981.

Mulholland, Leslie A. *Kant's System of Rights*. New York: Columbia University Press, 1990.

Nathanson, Stephen. "In Defense of 'Moderate Patriotism'." *Ethics* 99 (1989): 535–552.

New, Christopher. "Saints, Heroes, and Utilitarians." *Philosophy* 49 (1974): 179–189.

Nisan, Mordecai. "Moral Balance: A Model of How People Arrive at Moral Decisions." In *The Moral Domain*, edited by Thomas E. Wren, pp. 283–314. Cambridge: MIT Press, 1990.

Noddings, Nel. *Caring: A Feminine Approach to Ethics and Moral Education*. Berkeley: University of California Press, 1984.

Nowell Smith, P. H. *Ethics*. London: Penguin Books, 1954.

Nussbaum, Martha. *The Fragility of Goodness*. Cambridge: Cambridge University Press, 1986.

———. *Love's Knowledge: Essays on Philosophy and Literature*. New York: Oxford University Press, 1990.

———. "The Stoics on the Extirpation of the Passions." *Apeiron* 20 (1987): 129–178.

O'Connor, Daniel. "Good and Evil Disposition." *Kant-Studien* 76 (1985): 288–302.

O'Neill, Onora. *Acting on Principle: An Essay on Kantian Ethics*. New York: Columbia University Press, 1975. O'Neill published this work under the name *Nell*.

———. *Constructions of Reason: Explorations of Kant's Practical Philosophy*. Cambridge: Cambridge University Press, 1989.

———. *Faces of Hunger: An Essay on Poverty, Development, and Justice*. London: George Allen and Unwin, 1986.

———. "Kant's Ethics and Kantian Ethics." Paper presented to the North American Kant Society at the Central Division meetings of the American Philosophical Association, Chicago, April 1991.

Oakley, Justin. *Morality and the Emotions*. London: Routledge, 1992.

Oldenquist, Andrew. "Loyalties." *Journal of Philosophy* 79 (1982): 173–193.

O'Shaughnessy, R. J. "Forgiveness." *Philosophy* 42 (1967): 336–352.

Palmer, P. F. "Indulgences." In *New Catholic Encyclopedia*. Vol. 7 (1967): 482–484.

Paton, H. J. *The Categorical Imperative: A Study in Kant's Moral Philosophy.* London: Hutchinson's University Library, 1947. Reprinted Philadelphia: University of Pennsylvania Press, 1971.

——. "Kant on Friendship." *Proceedings of the British Academy* 42 (1956): 45–66.

Pincoffs, Edmund L. *Quandaries and Virtues: Against Reductivism in Ethics.* Lawrence: University of Kansas Press, 1986.

Piper, Adrian. "Moral Theory and Moral Alienation." *Journal of Philosophy* 84 (1987): 102–118.

——. "Two Conceptions of the Self." *Philosophical Studies* 48 (1985): 173–197. Reprinted in *Philosopher's Annual* 8 (1985).

Potter, Nelson. "The Argument of Kant's *Grundlegung*, Chapter 1." *Canadian Journal of Philosophy*. Supp. vol. 1 (1974): 73–91.

——. "Kant on Ends That Are at the Same Time Duties." *Pacific Philosophical Quarterly* 66 (1985): 78–92.

Priest, Stephen, ed. *Hegel's Critique of Kant*. Oxford: Oxford University Press, 1987.

Pritchard, Michael. "Self-Regard and the Supererogatory." In *Respect For Persons*, edited by O. H. Green, 139–151. New Orleans: Tulane University Press, 1983.

Putnam, Ruth Anna. "Reciprocity and Virtue Ethics." *Ethics* 98 (January 1988): 379–389.

Pybus, Elizabeth M. "A Plea for the Supererogatory: A Reply." *Philosophy* 61 (1986): 526–531.

——. "Saints and Heroes." *Philosophy* 57 (1982): 193–199.

Railton, Peter. "Alienation, Consequentialism, and the Demands of Morality." *Philosophy and Public Affairs* 13 (1984): 134–171.

Rawls, John. "Themes in Kant's Moral Philosophy." In *Kant's Transcendental Deductions*, edited by Eckart Förster, pp. 81–113. Stanford: Stanford University Press, 1989.

Reath, Andrews. "The Categorical Imperative and Kant's Conception of Practical Rationality." *Monist* 72 (1989): 384–410.

——. "Hedonism, Heteronomy, and Kant's Principle of Happiness." *Pacific Philosophical Quarterly* 70 (1989): 42–72.

——. "Kant's Theory of Moral Sensibility: Respect for the Moral Law and the Influence of Inclination." *Kant-Studien* 80 (1989): 284–302.

Reich, Klaus. "Kant and Greek Ethics." Parts I and II. Trans. W. H. Walsh. *Mind* 48 (1939): 338–354, 446–463.

Rorty, Amélie. *Mind in Action: Essays in the Philosophy of Mind*. Boston: Beacon Press, 1988.

Rumsey, Jean. "Agency, Human Nature, and Character in Kantian Theory." *Journal of Value Inquiry* 24 (1990): 109–121.

——. "The Development of Character in Kantian Moral Theory." *Journal of the History of Philosophy* 27 (1989): 247–265.

Sabini, John, and Maury Silver. "Emotions, Responsibility, and Character." In *Responsibility, Character, and the Emotions*, edited by Ferdinand Schoeman, 165–175. Cambridge: Cambridge University Press, 1987.

Schaller, Walter. "Kant on Virtue and Moral Worth." *Southern Journal of Philosophy* 25 (1987): 559–573.
——. "Kant's Architectonic of Duties." *Philosophy and Phenomenological Research* (1987): 299–314.
——. "The Relation of Moral Worth to the Good Will in Kant's Ethics." *Journal of Philosophical Research* 17 (1992): 351–382.
——. "Should Kantians Care about Moral Worth?" *Dialogue* 32 (1993): 25–40.
——. "Virtue and the Moral Law: An Analysis of Virtue and Moral Worth in Kant's Moral Philosophy." Ph.D. diss., University of Wisconsin–Madison, 1984.
Scheffler, Samuel. *The Rejection of Consequentialism.* Oxford: Clarendon Press, 1982.
Schilpp, Paul. *Kant's Pre-Critical Ethics.* 2d ed. Evanston, Ill.: Northwestern University Press, 1960.
Schmucker, Josef. *Die Ursprünge der Ethik Kants.* Meisenheim am Glan: Anton Hain, 1961.
Schneewind, Jerome. "The Misfortunes of Virtue." *Ethics* 101 (October 1990): 42–63.
——. "Pufendorf's Place in the History of Ethics." *Synthese* 73 (1987): 122–155.
——, ed. *Moral Philosophy from Montaigne to Kant: An Anthology.* 2 vols. Cambridge: Cambridge University Press, 1990.
Schoeman, Ferdinand, ed. *Responsibility, Character, and the Emotions: New Essays in Moral Psychology.* New York: Cambridge University Press, 1989.
Schott, Robin. *Cognition and Eros: A Critique of the Kantian Paradigm.* Boston: Beacon Press, 1988.
——. "Kant's Treatment of Sensibility." In *New Essays on Kant,* edited by Bernard den Ouden and Marcia Moen, 213–226. New York: Peter Lang, 1987.
Schumaker, Millard. *Supererogation: An Analysis and Bibliography.* Edmonton: St. Stephen's College, 1977.
Seanor, Douglas, and Nicholas Fotion. *Hare and Critics: Essays on "Moral Thinking."* Oxford: Clarendon Press, 1983.
Sedgwick, Sally. "Can Kant's Ethics Survive the Feminist Critique?" *Pacific Philosophical Quarterly* 71 (1990): 60–79.
——. "On Lying and the Role of Content in Kant's Ethics." *Kant-Studien* 82 (1991): 42–62.
——. "On the Relation of Pure Reason to Content: A Reply to Hegel's Critique of Formalism in Kant's Ethics." *Philosophy and Phenomenological Research* 49 (1988): 59–80.
Seidler, Michael. "Kant and the Stoics on Suicide." *Journal of the History of Ideas* 94 (1983): 429–453.
——. "Kant and the Stoics on the Emotional Life." *Philosophy Research Archives* 7/4 (1981): 1–56.
Seidler, Victor J. *Kant, Respect, and Injustice.* London: Routledge and Kegan Paul, 1986.
Seneca. *De Clementia.* In Seneca, *Moral Essays,* translated by John W. Basore. London: William Heinemann; Loeb Classical Library, 1928.
——. *De Ira.* In Seneca, *Moral Essays,* translated by John W. Basore. London: William Heinemann; Loeb Classical Library, 1928.

———. *Epistulae Morales*. Translated by Richard M. Gummere. London: William Heinemann, 1970.

Sherman, Nancy. "Common Sense and Uncommon Virtue." *Midwest Studies in Philosophy* 13 (1988): 97–114.

———. *The Fabric of Character: Aristotle's Theory of Virtue*. Oxford: Oxford University Press, 1989.

———. "The Place of Emotions in Kantian Morality." In *Identity, Character, and Morality*, edited by Owen Flanagan and Amélie Oksenberg Rorty, pp. 149–170. Cambridge: MIT Press, 1990.

Simmons, Keith. "Kant on Moral Worth." *History of Philosophy Quarterly* 6 (1989): 85–100.

Singer, Peter. "Famine, Affluence, and Morality." In *Ethics and Public Policy*, edited by Tom L. Beauchamp and Terry P. Pinkard, pp. 191–205. Englewood Cliffs, N.J.: Prentice-Hall, 1983.

Slote, Michael. *From Morality to Virtue*. New York: Oxford University Press, 1992.

———. *Goods and Virtues*. New York: Oxford University Press, 1983.

Smart, Alwynne. "Mercy." *Philosophy* 48 (1968): 345–359.

Smith, Holly M. "Varieties of Moral Worth and Moral Credit." *Ethics* 101 (1991): 279–303.

Sorell, Tom. "Kant's Good Will and Our Good Nature: Second Thoughts about Henson and Herman." *Kant-Studien* 78 (1987): 87–101.

Stevens, Rex P. *Kant on Moral Practice*. Macon, Ga.: Mercer University Press, 1981.

Stocker, Michael. "Friendship and Duty: Some Difficult Relations." In *Identity, Character, and Morality*, edited by Owen Flanagan and Amélie Oksenberg Rorty, pp. 219–233. Cambridge: MIT Press, 1990.

———. "The Schizophrenia of Modern Ethical Theories." *Journal of Philosophy* 68 (1976): 453–466.

———. "Supererogation and Duties." In *Studies in Moral Philosophy*, edited by Nicholas Rescher. *American Philosophical Quarterly* Monograph Series (1968).

———. "Values and Purposes: The Limits of Teleology and the Ends of Friendship." *Journal of Philosophy* 78 (1981): 747–765.

Strawson, P. F. "Freedom and Resentment." In his *Studies in the Philosophy of Thought and Action*, pp. 71–96. London: Oxford University Press, 1968.

Sullivan, Roger J. *Immanuel Kant's Moral Theory*. Cambridge: Cambridge University Press, 1989.

Taylor, Charles. "Responsibility for Self." In *The Identities of Persons*, edited by Amélie Oksenberg Rorty, pp. 281–299. Berkeley: University of California Press, 1976.

Timmons, Mark. "Kant on the Possibility of Moral Motivation." *Southern Journal of Philosophy* 23 (1985): 377–398.

Trianosky, Gregory. "Supererogation, Wrongdoing, and Vice: The Autonomy of an Ethics of Virtue." *Journal of Philosophy* 83 (1986): 26–40.

Twambley, P. "Mercy and Forgiveness." *Analysis* 36 (1976): 84–90.

Urmson, J. O. "Hare on Intuitive Moral Thinking." In *Hare and Critics: Essays on "Moral Thinking,"* edited by Douglas Seanor and Nicholas Fotion, pp. 161–169. Oxford: Clarendon Press, 1983.

———. "Saints and Heroes." In *Moral Concepts*, edited by Joel Feinberg, pp. 60–73.

London: Oxford University Press, 1969.

Van der Linden, Harry. *Kantian Ethics and Socialism*. Indianapolis: Hackett, 1988.

Walker, Margaret Urban. "What Does the Different Voice Say?: Gilligan's Women and Moral Philosophy." *The Journal of Value Inquiry* 23 (1989): 123–134.

Wallace, James D. *Moral Relevance and Moral Conflict*. Ithaca: Cornell University Press, 1988.

———. *Virtues and Vices*. Ithaca: Cornell University Press, 1978.

Wallace, Kathleen. "Reconstructing Judgment: Emotion and Moral Judgment." *Hypatia* 8 (1993): 61–83.

Ward, Keith. *The Development of Kant's View of Ethics*. Oxford: Basil Blackwell, 1972.

Watson, Gary. "Free Agency." *Journal of Philosophy* 72 (1975): 205–220. Reprinted in Watson, ed., *Free Will*. London: Oxford University Press, 1982.

Whiting, Jennifer, and Stephen Engstrom, eds. *Aristotle, Kant, and the Stoics: Rethinking Happiness and Duty*. Cambridge: Cambridge University Press, forthcoming.

Wick, Warner. "Kant's Moral Philosophy." Introduction to *Ethical Philosophy: The Complete Texts of "Grounding of the Metaphysics of Morals" and "Metaphysical Elements of Virtue,"* [by Immanuel Kant]. Translated by James W. Ellington. Indianapolis: Hackett, 1983.

Wilcox, William. "Egoists, Consequentialists, and Their Friends." *Philosophy and Public Affairs* 16 (1987): 73–84.

Williams, Bernard. *Ethics and the Limits of Philosophy*. Cambridge: Harvard University Press, 1985.

———. *Moral Luck: Philosophical Papers 1973–1980*. Cambridge: Cambridge University Press, 1981.

———. *Problems of the Self*. Cambridge: Cambridge University Press, 1973.

Winch, Peter. "Moral Integrity." *Ethics and Action*. London: Routledge and Kegan Paul, 1982.

Wolf, Susan. "Above and Below the Line of Duty." *Philosophical Topics* 14 (1986): 131–148.

———. "The Failure of Autonomy." Ph.D. diss., Princeton University, 1978.

———. "Morality and Partiality." *Philosophical Perspectives* 6 (1992): 243–259.

———. "Moral Saints." *Journal of Philosophy* 79 (1982): 419–439.

Wood, Allen W. *Kant's Moral Religion*. Ithaca: Cornell University Press, 1970.

———. "Unsociable Sociability: The Anthropological Basis of Kantian Ethics." *Philosophical Topics* 19 (1991).

"Work on Virtue." Special issue. *Philosophia* 20 (1990).

Wren, Thomas E., ed. *The Moral Domain: Essays in the Ongoing Discussion between Philosophy and the Social Sciences*. Cambridge: MIT Press, 1990.

Yovel, Yirmiahu. *Kant and the Philosophy of History*. Princeton: Princeton University Press, 1980.

———, ed. *Kant's Practical Philosophy Reconsidered: Papers Presented at the Seventh Jerusalem Philosophical Encounter*. Dordrecht: Kluwer, 1989.

Zweig, Arnulf, ed. and trans. *Kant: Philosophical Correspondence, 1755–99*. Chicago: University of Chicago Press, 1967.

Index